Perspectives on Data Science for Software Engineering

Perspectives on Data Science for Software Engineering

Edited by

Tim Menzies

Laurie Williams

Thomas Zimmermann

AMSTERDAM • BOSTON • HEIDELBERG • LONDON
NEW YORK • OXFORD • PARIS • SAN DIEGO
SAN FRANCISCO • SINGAPORE • SYDNEY • TOKYO

Morgan Kaufmann is an imprint of Elsevier

Morgan Kaufmann is an imprint of Elsevier
50 Hampshire Street, 5th Floor, Cambridge, MA 02139, USA

Library of Congress Cataloging-in-Publication Data
A catalog record for this book is available from the Library of Congress

British Library Cataloguing-in-Publication Data
A catalogue record for this book is available from the British Library

ISBN: 978-0-12-804206-9

For information on all Morgan Kaufmann publications
visit our website at https://www.elsevier.com/

Working together to grow libraries in developing countries

www.elsevier.com • www.bookaid.org

Publisher: Todd Green
Editorial Project Manager: Lindsay Lawrence
Production Project Manager: Mohana Natarajan
Cover Designer: Mark Rogers

Typeset by SPi Global, India

Contents

INTRODUCTION

The Perils of Energy Mining: Measure a Bunch, Compare Just Once 97
A. Hindle

Identifying Fault-prone Files in Large Industrial Software Systems 103
E. Weyuker and T. Ostrand

A Tailored Suit: The Big Opportunity in Personalizing Issue Tracking 107
O. Baysal

TECHNIQUES

One Size Does Not Fit All 347
T. Zimmermann

While Models are Good, Simple Explanations are Better 349
Venkatesh-Prasad Ranganath

The White-Shirt Effect: Learning from Failed Expectations 353
L. Prechelt

Simpler Questions Can Lead to Better Insights 359
B. Turhan and K. Kuutti

Contributors

Bram Adams
Polytechnique Montréal, Canada

A. Bacchelli
Delft University of Technology, Delft, The Netherlands

T. Barik
North Carolina State University

E.T. Barr
University College London, London, United Kingdom

O. Baysal
Carleton University, Ottawa, ON, Canada

A. Bener
Ryerson University, Toronto ON, Canada

G.R. Bergersen
University of Oslo, Norway

C. Bird
Microsoft Research, Redmond, WA, United States

D. Budgen
Durham University, Durham, United Kingdom

B. Caglayan
Lero, University of Limerick, Ireland

T. Carnahan
Microsoft, Redmond, WA, United States

J. Czerwonka
Principal Architect Microsoft Corp., Redmond, WA, United States

P. Devanbu
UC Davis, Davis, CA, United States

M. Di Penta
University of Sannio, Benevento, Italy

S. Diehl
University of Trier, Trier, Germany

T. Dybå
SINTEF ICT, Trondheim, Norway

T. Fritz
University of Zurich, Zurich, CHE

M.W. Godfrey
University of Waterloo, Waterloo, ON, Canada

G. Gousios
Radboud University Nijmegen, Nijmegen, The Netherlands

P. Guo
University of Rochester, Rochester, NY, United States

K. Herzig
Software Development Engineer, Microsoft Corporation, Redmond, United States

A. Hindle
University of Alberta, Edmonton, AB, Canada

R. Holmes
University of British Columbia, Vancouver, Canada

Zhitao Hou
Microsoft Research, Beijing, China

J. Huang
Brown University, Providence, RI, United States

Andrew J. Ko
University of Washington, Seattle, WA, United States

N. Juristo
Universidad Politécnica de Madrid, Madrid, Spain

S. Just
Researcher, Software Engineering Chair & Center for IT-Security, Privacy and Accountability, Saarland University, Germany

M. Kim
University of California, Los Angeles

E. Kocaguneli
Microsoft, Seattle, WA, United States

K. Kuutti
University of Oulu, Oulu, Finland

Qingwei Lin
Microsoft Research, Beijing, China

Jian-Guang Lou
Microsoft Research, Beijing, China

N. Medvidovic
University of Southern California, Los Angeles, CA, United States

A. Meneely
Rochester Institute of Technology, Rochester, NY, United States

T. Menzies
North Carolina State University, Raleigh, NC, United States

L.L. Minku
University of Leicester, Leicester, United Kingdom

A. Mockus
The University Of Tennessee, Knoxville, TN, United States

J. Münch
Reutlingen University, Reutlingen, Germany; University of Helsinki, Helsinki, Finland; Herman Hollerith Center, Böblingen, Germany

G.C. Murphy
University of British Columbia, Vancouver, BC, Canada

B. Murphy
Microsoft Research, Cambridge, United Kingdom

E. Murphy-Hill
North Carolina State University

M. Nagappan
Rochester Institute of Technology, Rochester, NY, United States

M. Nayebi
University of Calgary, Calgary, AB, Canada

M. Oivo
University of Oulu, Oulu, Finland

A. Orso
Georgia Institute of Technology, Atlanta, GA, United States

T. Ostrand
Mälerdalen University, Västerås, Sweden

F. Peters
Lero - The Irish Software Research Centre, University of Limerick, Limerick, Ireland

D. Posnett
University of California, Davis, CA, United States

L. Prechelt
Freie Universität Berlin, Berlin, Germany

Venkatesh-Prasad Ranganath
Kansas State University, Manhattan, KS, United States

B. Ray
University of Virginia, Charlottesville, VA, United States

R. Robbes
University of Chile, Santiago, Chile

P. Rotella
Cisco Systems, Inc., Raleigh, NC, United States

G. Ruhe
University of Calgary, Calgary, AB, Canada

P. Runeson
Lund University, Lund, Sweden

B. Russo
Software Engineering Research Group, Faculty of Computer Science, Free
University of Bozen-Bolzano, Italy

M. Shepperd
Brunel University London, Uxbridge, United Kingdom

E. Shihab
Concordia University, Montreal, QC, Canada

D.I.K. Sjøberg
University of Oslo; SINTEF ICT, Trondheim, Norway

D. Spinellis
Athens University of Economics and Business, Athens, Greece

M.-A. Storey
University of Victoria, Victoria, BC, Canada

C. Theisen
North Carolina State University, Raleigh, NC, United States

A. Tosun
Istanbul Technical University, Maslak Istanbul, Turkey

B. Turhan
University of Oulu, Oulu, Finland

H. Valdivia-Garcia
Rochester Institute of Technology, Rochester, NY, United States

S. Vegas
Universidad Politécnica de Madrid, Madrid, Spain

S. Wagner
University of Stuttgart, Stuttgart, Germany

E. Weyuker
Mälerdalen University, Västerås, Sweden

J. Whitehead
University of California, Santa Cruz, CA, United States

L. Williams
North Carolina State University, Raleigh, NC, United States

Tao Xie
University of Illinois at Urbana-Champaign, Urbana, IL, United States

A. Zeller
Saarland University, Saarbrücken, Germany

Dongmei Zhang
Microsoft Research, Beijing, China

Hongyu Zhang
Microsoft Research, Beijing, China

Haidong Zhang
Microsoft Research, Beijing, China

T. Zimmermann
Microsoft Research, Redmond, WA, United States

Acknowledgments

A project this size is completed only with the dedicated help of many people. Accordingly, the editors of this book gratefully acknowledge the extensive and professional work of our authors and the Morgan Kaufmann editorial team. Also, special thanks to the staff and organizers of Schloss Dagstuhl (https://www.dagstuhl.de/ueber-dagstuhl/, where computer scientists meet) who hosted the original meeting that was the genesis of this book.

Introduction

Perspectives on data science for software engineering

T. Menzies*, L. Williams*, T. Zimmermann[†]
North Carolina State University, Raleigh, NC, United States[*]
Microsoft Research, Redmond, WA, United States[†]

CHAPTER OUTLINE

WHY THIS BOOK?

Historically, this book began as a week-long workshop in Dagstuhl, Germany [1]. The goal of that meeting was to document the wide range of work on software analytics.

That meeting had the following premise: *So little time, so much data.*

That is, given recent increases in how much data we can collect, and given a shortage in skilled analysts that can assess that data [2], there now exists more data than people to study it. Consequently, the analysis of real-world data (using semi-automatic or fully automatic methods) is an exploding field, to say this least.

This issue is made more pressing by two factors:

- *Many useful methods*: Decades of research in artificial intelligence, social science methods, visualizations, statistics, etc. has generated a large number of powerful methods for learning from data.
- *Much support for those methods*: Many of those methods are explored in standard textbooks and education programs. Those methods are also supported in toolkits that are widely available (sometimes, even via free downloads). Further, given the "Big Data" revolution, it is now possible to acquire the hardware necessary, even for the longest runs of these tools. So now the issue becomes not "how to *get* these tools" but, instead, how to "use" these tools.

If general analytics is an active field, software analytics is doubly so. Consider what we know about software projects:

- source code;
- emails about that code;
- check-ins;
- work items;
- bug reports;
- test suites;
- test executions;
- and even some background information on the developers.

All that information is recorded in software repositories, such as CVS, Subversion, GIT, GITHUB, and Bugzilla. Found in these repositories are telemetry data, run-time traces, and log files reflecting how customers experience software, application and feature usage, records of performance and reliability, and more.

Never before have we had so much information about the details on how people collaborate to

- use someone else's insights and software tools;
- generate and distribute new insights and software tools;
- maintain and update existing insights and software tools.

FIG. 1

The participants of the Dagstuhl Seminar 14261 on "Software Development Analytics" (June 22-27, 2014)

Here, by "tools" we mean everything from the four lines of SQL that are triggered when someone surfs to a web page, to scripts that might be only dozens to hundreds of lines of code, or to much larger open source and proprietary systems. Also, our use of "tools" includes building new tools as well as ongoing maintenance work, as well as combinations of hardware and software systems.

Accordingly, for your consideration, this book explores the process for analyzing data from software development applications to generate insights. The chapters here were written by participants at the Dagstuhl workshop (Fig. 1), plus numerous other experts in the field on industrial and academic data mining. Our goal is to summarize and distribute their experience and combined wisdom and understanding about the data analysis process.

ABOUT THIS BOOK

Each chapter is aimed at a generalized audience with some technical interest in software engineering (SE). Hence, the chapters are very short and to the point. Also, the chapter authors have taken care to avoid excessive and confusing techno-speak.

As to insights themselves, they are in two categories:

- *Lessons specific to software engineering*: Some chapters offer valuable comments on issues that are specific to data science for software engineering. For example, see Geunther Ruhe's excellent chapter on decision support for software engineering.
- *General lessons about data analytics*: Other chapters are more general. These comment on issues relating to drawing conclusions from real-world data. The case study material for these chapters comes from the domain of software engineering problems. That said, this material has much to offer data scientists working in many other domains.

Our insights take many forms:

- Some introductory material to set the scene;
- Success stories and application case studies;
- Techniques;
- Words of wisdom;
- Tips for success, traps for the unwary, as well as the steps required to avoid those traps.

That said, all our insights have one thing in common: *we wish we had known them years ago*! If we had, then that would have saved us and our clients so much time and money.

THE FUTURE

While these chapters were written by experts, they are hardly complete. Data science methods for SE are continually changing, so we view this book as a "first edition" that will need significant and regular updates. To that end, we have created a news group for posting new insights. Feel free to make any comment at all there.

- To browse the messages in that group, go to https://groups.google.com/forum/#! forum/perspectivesds4se
- To post to that group, send an email to perspectivesds4se@googlegroups.com
- To unsubscribe from that group, send an email to perspectivesds4se+ unsubscribe@googlegroups.com

Note that if you want to be considered for any future update of this book:

- Make the subject line an eye-catching "mantra"; ie, a slogan reflecting a best practice for data science for SE.
- The post should read something like the chapters of this book. That is, it should be:
  - Short, and to the point.
  - Make little or no use of jargon, formulas, diagrams, or references.
  - Be approachable by a broad audience and have a clear take-away message.

Share and enjoy!

REFERENCES

[1] Software development analytics (Dagstuhl Seminar 14261) Gall H, Menzies T, Williams L, Zimmermann T. Dagstuhl Rep J 2014;4(6):64–83, http://drops.dagstuhl.de/opus/volltexte/2014/4763/.
[2] Big data: The next frontier for competition. McKinsey & Company. http://www.mckinsey.com/features/big_data.

Software analytics and its application in practice

Dongmei Zhang*, Tao Xie[†]

Microsoft Research, Beijing, China* University of Illinois at Urbana-Champaign, Urbana, IL, United States[†]

Various types of data naturally exist in the software development process, such as source code, bug reports, check-in histories, and test cases. As software services and mobile applications are widely available in the Internet era, a huge amount of program runtime data, eg, traces, system events, and performance counters, as well as users' usage data, eg, usage logs, user surveys, online forum posts, blogs, and tweets, can be readily collected.

Considering the increasing abundance and importance of data in the software domain, *software analytics* [1,2] is to utilize data-driven approaches to enable software practitioners to perform data exploration and analysis in order to obtain insightful and actionable information for completing various tasks around software systems, software users, and the software development process.

Software analytics has broad applications in real practice. For example, using a mechanism similar to Windows error reporting [3], event tracing for Windows traces can be collected to achieve Windows performance debugging [4]. Given limited time and resources, a major challenge is to identify and prioritize the performance issues using millions of callstack traces. Another example is data-driven quality management for online services [5]. When a live-site issue occurs, a major challenge is to help service-operation personnel utilize the humongous number of service logs and performance counters to quickly diagnose the issue and restore the service.

In this chapter, we discuss software analytics from six perspectives. We also share our experiences on putting software analytics into practice.

SIX PERSPECTIVES OF SOFTWARE ANALYTICS

The six perspectives of software analytics include research topics, target audience input, output, technology pillars, and connections to practice. While the first four perspectives are easily accessible from the definition of software analytics, the last two need some elaboration.

As stated in the definition, software analytics focuses on software systems, software users, and the software development process. From the research point of view, these focuses constitute three *research topics*—software quality, user experience, and development productivity. As illustrated in the aforementioned examples, the variety of data *input* to software analytics is huge. Regarding the insightful and actionable *output*, it often requires well-designed and complex analytics techniques to create such output. It should be noted that the *target audience* of software analytics spans across a broad range of software practitioners, including developers, testers, program managers, product managers, operation engineers, usability engineers, UX designers, customer-support engineers, management personnel, etc.

Technology Pillars. In general, primary technologies employed by software analytics include large-scale computing (to handle large-scale datasets), analysis algorithms in machine learning, data mining and pattern recognition, etc. (to analyze data), and information visualization (to help with analyzing data and presenting insights). While the software domain is called the "vertical area" on which software analytics focuses, these three technology areas are called the horizontal research areas. Quite often, in the vertical area, there are challenges that cannot be readily addressed using the existing technologies in one or more of the horizontal areas. Such challenges can open up new research opportunities in the corresponding horizontal areas.

Connection-to-Practice. Software analytics is naturally tied with practice, with four *real* elements.

Real data. The data sources under study in software analytics come from real-world settings, including both industrial proprietary settings and open-source settings. For example, open-source communities provide a huge data vault of source code, bug history, and check-in information, etc.; and better yet, the vault is active and evolving, which makes the data sources fresh and live.

Real problems. There are various types of questions to be answered in practice using the rich software artifacts. For example, when a service system is down, how can service engineers quickly diagnose the problem and restore the service [5]? How to increase the monthly active users and daily active users based on the usage data?

Real users. The aforementioned target audience is the consumers of software analytics results, techniques, and tools. They are also a source of feedback for continuously improving and motivating software analytics research.

Real tools. Software artifacts are constantly changing. Getting actionable insights from such dynamic data sources is critical to completing many software-related tasks. To accomplish this, software analytics tools are often deployed as part of software systems, enabling rich, reliable, and timely analyses requested by software practitioners.

EXPERIENCES IN PUTTING SOFTWARE ANALYTICS INTO PRACTICE

The connection-to-practice nature opens up great opportunities for software analytics to make an impact with a focus on the *real* settings. Furthermore, there is huge potential for the impact to be broad and deep because software analytics spreads across the areas of system quality, user experience, development productivity, etc.

Despite these opportunities, there are still significant challenges when putting software analytics technologies into real use. For example, how to ensure the output of the analysis results is insightful and actionable? How do we know whether practitioners are concerned about the questions answered with the data? How do we evaluate our analysis techniques in real-world settings? Next we share some of our learnings from working on various software analytics projects [2,4–6].

Identifying essential problems. Various types of data are incredibly rich in the software domain, and the scale of data is significantly large. It is often not difficult to grab some datasets, apply certain data analysis techniques, and obtain some observations. However, these observations, even with good evaluation results from the data-analysis perspective, may not be useful for accomplishing the target task of practitioners. It is important to first identify essential problems for accomplishing the target task in practice, and then obtain the right data sets suitable to help solve the problems. These essential problems are those that can be solved by substantially improving the overall effectiveness of tackling the task, such as improving software quality, user experience, and practitioner productivity.

Usable system built early to collect feedback. It is an iterative process to create software analytics solutions to solve essential problems in practice. Therefore, it is much more effective to build a usable system early on in order to start the feedback loop with the software practitioners. The feedback is often valuable for formulating research problems and researching appropriate analysis algorithms. In addition, software analytics projects can benefit from early feedback in terms of building trust between researchers and practitioners, as well as enabling the evaluation of the results in real-world settings.

Using domain semantics for proper data preparation. Software artifacts often carry semantics specific to the software domain; therefore, they cannot be simply treated as generic data such as text and sequences. For example, callstacks are sequences with program execution logic, and bug reports contain relational data and free text describing software defects, etc. Understanding the semantics of software artifacts is a prerequisite for analyzing the data later on. In the case of StackMine [4], there was a deep learning curve for us to understand the performance traces before we could conduct any analysis.

In practice, understanding data is three-fold: data interpretation, data selection, and data filtering. To conduct data interpretation, researchers need to understand basic definitions of domain-specific terminologies and concepts. To conduct data selection, researchers need to understand the connections between the data and the problem being solved. To conduct data filtering, researchers need to understand defects and limitations of existing data to avoid incorrect inference. *Scalable and customizable solutions.* Due to the scale of data in real-world settings, scalable analytic solutions are often required to solve essential problems in practice. In fact, scalability may directly impact the underlying analysis algorithms for problem solving. Customization is another common requirement for incorporating domain knowledge due to the variations in software and services. The effectiveness of solution customization in analytics tasks can be summarized as (1) filtering noisy and irrelevant data, (2) specifying between data points their intrinsic relationships that cannot be derived from the data itself, (3) providing empirical and heuristic guidance to make the algorithms robust against biased data. The procedure of solution customization can be typically conducted in an iterative fashion via close collaboration between software analytics researchers and practitioners.

Evaluation criteria tied with real tasks in practice. Because of the natural connection with practice, software analytics projects should be (at least partly) evaluated using the real tasks that they are targeted to help with. Common evaluation criteria of data analysis, such as precision and recall, can be used to measure intermediate results. However, they are often not the only set of evaluation criteria when real tasks are involved. For example, in the StackMine project [4], we use the coverage of detected performance bottlenecks to evaluate our analysis results; such coverage is directly related to the analysis task of Windows analysts. When conducting an evaluation in practice with practitioners involved, researchers need to be aware of and cautious about the evaluation cost and benefits incurred for practitioners.

REFERENCES

[1] Zhang D, Dang Y, Lou J-G, Han S, Zhang H, Xie T. Software analytics as a learning case in practice: approaches and experiences. In: International workshop on machine learning technologies in software engineering (MALETS 2011); 2011. p. 55–8.

[2] Zhang D, Han S, Dang Y, Lou J-G, Zhang H, Xie T. Software analytics in practice. IEEE Software 2013;30(5):30–7. [Special issue on the many faces of software analytics].

[3] Glerum K, Kinshumann K, Greenberg S, Aul G, Orgovan V, Nichols G, Grant D, Loihle G, Hunt G. Debugging in the (very) large: ten years of implementation and experience. In: Proceedings of the ACM SIGOPS 22nd symposium on operating systems principles, SOSP 2009; 2009. p. 103–16.

[4] Han S, Dang Y, Ge S, Zhang D, Xie T. Performance debugging in the large via mining millions of stack traces. In: Proceedings of the 34th international conference on software engineering, ICSE 2012; 2012. p. 145–55.

[5] Lou J-G, Lin Q, Ding R, Fu Q, Zhang D, Xie T. Software analytics for incident management of online services: an experience report. In: Proceedings of 28th IEEE/ACM

international conference on automated software engineering, ASE 2013; 2013. p. 475–85. [Experience papers].

[6] Dang Y, Zhang D, Ge S, Chu C, Qiu Y, Xie Tao. XIAO: tuning code clones at hands of engineers in practice. In: Proceedings of the 28th annual computer security applications conference, ACSAC 2012; 2012. p. 369–78.

References

Seven principles of inductive software engineering: What we do is different

T. Menzies

North Carolina State University, Raleigh, NC, United States

CHAPTER OUTLINE

Different and Important 13
Principle #1: Humans Before Algorithms 13
Principle #2: Plan for Scale 14
Principle #3: Get Early Feedback 15
Principle #4: Be Open Minded 15
Principle #5: Be Smart with Your Learning 15
Principle #6: Live with the Data You Have 16
Principle #7: Develop a Broad Skill Set That Uses a Big Toolkit 17
References 17

DIFFERENT AND IMPORTANT

Inductive software engineering is the branch of software engineering focusing on the delivery of data-mining based software applications. Within those data mines, the core problem is *induction*, which is the extraction of small patterns from larger data sets. Inductive engineers spend much effort trying to understand business goals in order to inductively generate the models that matter the most.

Previously, with Christian Bird, Thomas Zimmermann, Wolfram Schulte, and Ekrem Kocaganeli, we wrote an *Inductive Engineering Manifesto* [1] that offered some details on this new kind of engineering. The whole manifesto is a little long, so here I offer a quick summary. Following are seven key principles which, if ignored, can make it harder to deploy analytics in the real world. For more details (and more principles), refer to the original document [1].

PRINCIPLE #1: HUMANS BEFORE ALGORITHMS

Mining algorithms are only good if humans find their use in real-world applications. This means that humans need to:

- understand the results
- understand that those results add value to their work.

Accordingly, it is strongly recommend that once the algorithms generate some model, then the inductive engineer *talks to humans* about those results. In the case of software analytics, these humans are the subject matter experts or business problem owners that are asking you to improve the ways they are generating software.

In our experience, such discussions lead to a second, third, fourth, etc., round of learning. To assess if you are talking in "the right way" to your humans, check the following:

- Do they bring their senior management to the meetings? If yes, great!
- Do they keep interrupting (you or each other) and debating your results? If yes, then stay quiet (and take lots of notes!)
- Do they indicate they understand your explanation of the results? For example, can they correctly extend your results to list desirable and undesirable implications of your results?
- Do your results touch on issues that concern them? This is *easy* to check... just count how many times they glance up from their notes, looking startled or alarmed.
- Do they offer more data sources for analysis? If yes, they like what you are doing and want you to do it more.
- Do they invite you to their workspace and ask you to teach them how to do XYZ? If yes, this is a real win.

PRINCIPLE #2: PLAN FOR SCALE

Data mining methods are usually repeated multiple times in order to:

- answer new questions, inspired by the current results;
- enhance data mining method or fix some bugs; and
- deploy the results, or the analysis methods, to different user groups.

So that means that, if it works, you will be asked to do it again (and again and again). To put that another way, *thou shalt not click*. That is, if all your analysis requires lots of pointing-and-clicking in a pretty GUI environment, then you are definitely *not* planning for scale.

Another issues is that as you scale up, your methods will need to scale up as well. For example, in our *Manifesto* document, we discussed the CRANE project at Microsoft that deployed data mining methods to the code base of Microsoft Windows. This was a *very large* project, so the way it started was *not* the way it ended:

- Initially, a single inductive engineer did some rapid prototyping for a few weeks, to explore a range of hypotheses and gain business interest (and get human feedback on the early results).

- Next, the inductive engineering team spent a few months conducting many experiments to find stable models (and to narrow in on the most important business goals).
- In the final stage, which took a year, the inductive engineers integrated the models into a deployment framework that was suitable for a target user base.

Note that the team size doubled at each stage—so anyone funding this work needs to know that increasingly useful conclusions can be increasingly expensive.

PRINCIPLE #3: GET EARLY FEEDBACK

This is mentioned previously, but it is worth repeating. Before conducting very elaborate studies (that take a long time to reach a conclusion), try applying very simple tools to gain rapid early feedback.

So, simplicity first! Get feedback early and often! For example, there are many linear time discretizers for learning what are good divisions of continuous attributes (eg, the Fayyad-Irani discretizer [2]). These methods can also report when breaking up an attribute is *not* useful since that attribute is not very informative. Using tools like these, it is possible to discover what attributes can be safely ignored (hint: usually, it's more than half).

PRINCIPLE #4: BE OPEN MINDED

The goal of inductive engineering for SE is to find better ideas than what was available when you started. So if you leave a data mining project with the same beliefs as when you started, you really wasted a lot of time and effort. Hence, some mantras to chant while data mining are:

- Avoid a fixed hypothesis. Be respectful but doubtful of all human-suggested domain hypotheses. Certainly, explore the issues that they raise, but also take the time to look further afield.
- Avoid a fixed approach for data mining (eg, just using decision trees all the time), particularly for data that has not been mined before.
- The most important initial results are the ones that radically and dramatically improve the goals of the project. So seek important results.

PRINCIPLE #5: BE SMART WITH YOUR LEARNING

Let's face it, any inductive agents (human or otherwise) have biases that can confuse the learning process. So don't torture the data to meet preconceptions (that is, it is ok to go "fishing" to look for new insights).

It also true that any inductive agent (and this includes you) can make mistakes. If organizations are going to use your results to change policy, the important outcomes are riding on your conclusions. This means you need to check and validate your results:

- Ask other people to do code reviews of your scripts.
- Check the conclusion stability against different sample policies. For example:
  - Policy1: divide data into (say) ten 90% samples (built at random). How much do your conclusions change across those samples?
  - Policy2: sort data by collection date (if available). Learn from the far past, the nearer past, then the most recent data. Does time change your results? Is time *still* changing your results? It is important to check.
  - Policy3,4,5, etc.: Are there any other natural divisions of your data (eg, east coast versus west coast, men versus women, etc.)? Do they affect your conclusions?
- When reporting multiple runs of a learner, don't just report mean results—also report the wriggle around the mean.
- In fact, do not report mean results at all since outliers can distort those mean values. Instead, try to report median and IQR results (the inter-quartile range is the difference between the 75th and 25th percentile).

PRINCIPLE #6: LIVE WITH THE DATA YOU HAVE

In practice, it is a rare analytics project that can dictate how data is collected in industrial contexts. Usually, inductive engineers have to cope with whatever data is available (rather than demand more data collected under more ideal conditions). This means that often you have to go mining with the data you have (and not the data you hope to have at some later date). So it's important to spend some time on data quality operators. For example:

- Use *feature selection* to remove spurious attributes. There are many ways to perform such feature selection, including the Fayyad-Irani method discussed herein. For a discussion of other feature selection methods, see [3].
- Use *row selection* to remove outliers and group-related rows into sets of clusters. For a discussion on row selection methods, see [4].

One benefit of replacing rows with clusters is that any signal that is spread out amongst the rows can be "amplified" in the clusters. If we cluster, then learn one model per cluster, then the resulting predictions have better median values and smaller variances [5].

In any case, we've often found row and feature selection discards to be up to 80% to 90% of the data, without damaging our ability to learn from the data. This means that ensuring quality of *all* the data can sometimes be less important that being able to extract quality data from large examples.

PRINCIPLE #7: DEVELOP A BROAD SKILL SET THAT USES A BIG TOOLKIT

The reason organizations need to hire inductive engineers is that they come equipped with a very broad range of tools. This is important since many problems need specialized methods to find good solutions.

So, to become an inductive engineer, look for the "big ecology" toolkits where lots of developers are constantly trying out new ideas. Languages like Python, Scala (and lately, Julia) have extensive online forums where developers share their data mining tips. Toolkits like R, MATLAB, and WEKA are continually being updated with new tools.

What a great time to be an inductive engineer! So much to learn, so much to try. Would you want to have it any other way?

REFERENCES

[1] Menzies T, Bird C, Zimmermann T, Schulte W, Kocaganeli E. The inductive software engineering manifesto: principles for industrial data mining. In: Proceedings of the international workshop on machine learning technologies in software engineering (MALETS '11). New York. NY, USA: ACM; 2011. p. 19–26. http://dx.doi.org/10.1145/2070821.2070824.

[2] Fayyad UM, Irani KB. On the handling of continuous-valued attributes in decision tree generation. Mach Learn 1992;8(1):87–102. http://dx.doi.org/10.1023/A:1022638503176.

[3] Hall MA, Holmes G. Benchmarking attribute selection techniques for discrete class data mining. IEEE Trans Knowl Data Eng 2003;15(6):1437–47. http://dx.doi.org/10.1109/TKDE.2003.1245283.

[4] Olvera-López JA, Carrasco-Ochoa JA, Martínez-Trinidad JF, Kittler J. A review of instance selection methods. Artif Intell Rev 2010;34(2):133–43. http://dx.doi.org/10.1007/s10462-010-9165-y.

[5] Menzies T, Butcher A, Cok D, Marcus A, Layman L, Shull F, Turhan B, Zimmermann T. Local versus global lessons for defect prediction and effort estimation. IEEE Trans Softw Eng 2013;39(6):822–34. http://dx.doi.org/10.1109/TSE.2012.83.

The need for data analysis patterns (in software engineering)

B. Russo

Software Engineering Research Group, Faculty of Computer Science,
Free University of Bozen-Bolzano, Italy

CHAPTER OUTLINE

THE REMEDY METAPHOR

When you call a doctor, you would expect that she would be prepared with a set of remedies for your disease. You would not be pleased to see her digging into a huge amount of clinical data while she makes a diagnosis and searches for a solution for your problem, neither would you expect her to propose a cure based on your case alone. The remedies she proposes are solutions to recurring problems that medical researchers identify by analyzing data of patients with similar symptoms and medical histories. Remedies are coded in a language that a doctor understands (eg, they tell when and how to treat a patient) and lead to meaningful conclusions for patients with the same disease (eg, they tell the probability that the disease will be defeated and eventually with which consequences). Once found, such solutions can be applied over and over again. With the repeated use of a solution, medical researchers can indeed gain knowledge on successes and failures of a remedy and provide meaningful conclusions to future patients thereafter.

The remedy metaphor helps describe how data analysis patterns are used in empirical sciences. First, a pattern is a coded solution of a recurring problem. When a problem occurs several times, we accumulate knowledge on the problem and its solutions. With this knowledge, we are able to code a solution in some sort of modeling language that increases its expressivity and capability of re-use. Second, a pattern is equipped with a sort of measure of success of the solution it represents. The solution and the measure result from the analysis of historical data and provide actionable insight for future cases.

Does it make sense to speak about patterns in modern software engineering? The answer can only be yes. Patterns are a form of re-use and re-use is one of the key principles in modern software engineering. Why is this? Re-use is an instrument to increase the economy of development and prevent human errors in software development processes. In their milestone book, Gamma et al. [1] introduced (design) patterns as a way "to reuse the experience instead of rediscovering it." Thus, patterns as a form of re-use help build software engineering knowledge from experience.

Does it make sense to speak about patterns of data analysis in modern software engineering? Definitely yes. Data analysis patterns are "remedies" for recurring data analysis problems that have arisen during the conception, development, and use of the software technology. They are codified solutions that lead to meaningful conclusions for software engineering stakeholders and can be reused for comparable data. In other words, a data analysis pattern is a sort of model expressed in a language that logically describes a solution to a recurring data analysis problem in software engineering. They can possibly be automated. As such, data analysis patterns help "rise from the drudgery of random action into the sphere of intentional design," [4].

Why aren't they already diffusely used? The majority of us have the ingrained belief that methods and results from individual software analysis pertain to the empirical context from which data has been collected. Thus, in almost every new study, we re-invent the data analysis wheel. It is as if we devised a new medical protocol for any new patient. Why is this? One of the reasons is related to software engineering data and the role it has taken over the years.

SOFTWARE ENGINEERING DATA

A large part of modern software engineering research builds new knowledge by analyzing data of different types. To study distributed development processes, we analyze textual interactions among developers of open source communities and use social networks, complex systems, or graph theories. If we instead want to predict if a new technology will take off in the IT market, we collect economic data and use the Roger's theory of diffusion of innovation. To understand the quality of modern software products, we mine code data and their evolution from previous versions. Sometimes, we also need to combine data of a different nature collected from different sources and analyzed with various statistical methods.

Thus, data types can be very different. For example, data can be structured or unstructured (ie, lines of code or free text in review comments and segments of videos), discrete or continuous (ie, number of bugs in software or response time of web services), qualitative or quantitative (ie, complexity of a software task and Cyclomatic code complexity), and subjective or objective (ie, ease of use of a technology or number of back links to web sites). In addition, with the Open Source Software (OSS) phenomenon, cloud computing, and the Big Data era, data has become more distributed, big, and accessible; but also noisy, redundant, and incomplete. As such, researchers must have a good command of analysis instruments and a feel for the kinds of problems and data they apply to.

NEEDS OF DATA ANALYSIS PATTERNS

The need for instruments like data analysis patterns becomes more apparent when we want to introduce novices to the research field. In these circumstances, we encounter the following issues.

Studies do not report entirely or sufficiently about their data analysis protocols. This implies that analyses are biased or not verifiable. Consequently, secondary studies like mapping studies and systematic literature reviews that are mandated to synthesize published research lose their power. Data analysis patterns provide software engineers with a verifiable protocol to compare, unify, and extract knowledge from existing studies.

Methods and data are not commonly shared. It is customary to develop ad-hoc scripts and keep them private or use tools as black-box statistical machines. In either case, we cannot access the statistical algorithm, verify, and re-use it. Data analysis patterns are packaged to be easily inspected, automated, and shared.

Tool-driven research has some known risks. Anyone can easily download statistical tools from the Internet and perform sophisticated statistical analyses. The Turin award Butler Lampson [2] warns not to abuse of statistical tools: "For one unfamiliar with the niceties of statistical analysis it is difficult to view with any feeling other than awe the elaborate edifice which the authors have erected to protect their data from the cutting winds of statistical insignificance." A catalog of data analysis patterns helps guide researchers in the selection of appropriate analysis instruments.

Analysis can be easily biased by the human factor. Reviewing papers on machine learning for defect prediction, Shepperd et al. [3] analyzed more than 600 samples from the highest quality studies on defect prediction to determine what factors influence predictive performance and find that "it matters more who does the work than what is done." This incredible result urges the use of data analysis patterns to make a solution independent from the researchers who conceived it.

BUILDING REMEDIES FOR DATA ANALYSIS IN SOFTWARE ENGINEERING RESEARCH

As in any research field, needs trigger opportunities and challenge researchers. Today, we are called to synthesize our methods of analysis [4], and examples of design patterns are already available [5]. We need more, though. The scikit-learn initiative [http://scikit-learn.org/stable/index.html] can help software engineers in case they need to solve problems with data mining, ie, the computational process of discovering patterns in data sets. The project provides online access to a wide range of state-of-the-art tools for data analysis as codified solutions. Each solution comes with a short rationale of use, a handful of algorithms implementing it, and a set of application examples. Fig. 1 illustrates how we can find the right estimator for a machine learning problem.

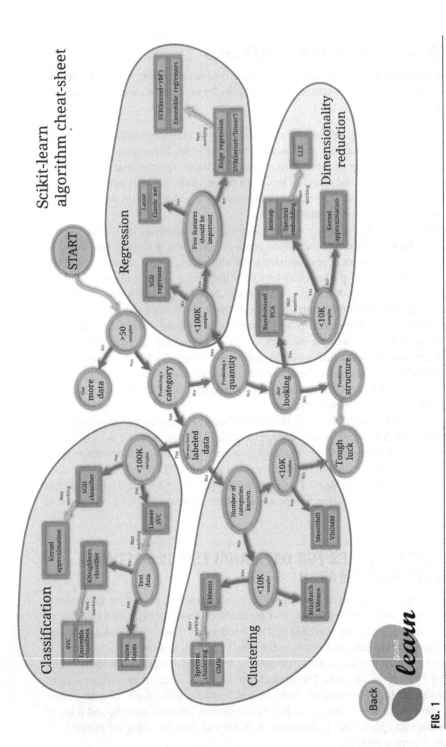

FIG. 1

Flowchart displaying different estimators and analysis path for a machine learning problem.

Source: http://scikit-learn.org/stable/tutorial/machine_learning_map/index.html

How can we import these, or similar tools, in the software engineering context? We need first to identify the requirements for a data analysis pattern in software engineering.

In our opinion, a data analysis pattern shall be:

- A solution to a recurrent a software engineering problem
- Re-usable in different software engineering contexts
- Automatable (eg, by coding algorithms of data analysis in some programming language)
- Actionable (eg, the scikit-learn tools)
- Successful to a certain degree (eg, by representing state-of-the-art data analysis in software engineering)

Then the key steps to construct such a pattern will include, but not be restricted to:

- Mining literature to extract candidate solutions
- Identifying a common language to express a solution in a form that software engineers can easily understand and re-use. For instance, we can think of an annotated Unified Modeling Language (UML) or algorithm notation expressing the logic of the analysis
- Defining a measure of success for a solution
- Validating the candidate solutions by replications and community surveys to achieve consensus in the research community.

Reflecting on the current situation, we also see the need to codify anti-patterns, ie, what not to do in data analysis. Given the amount of evidence in our field, this must be a much easier task!

REFERENCES

[1] Gamma E, Helm R, Johnson R, Vlissides J. Design patterns: elements of reusable object-oriented software. Boston, MA: Addison-Wesley Longman Publishing Company; 1995.
[2] Lampson BW. A critique of an exploratory investigation of programmer performance under on-line and off-line conditions. IEEE Trans Hum Factors Electron 1967;HFE-8 (1):48–51.
[3] Shepperd M, Bowes D, Hall T. Researcher bias: the use of machine learning in software defect prediction. IEEE Trans Softw Eng 2014;40(6):603–16.
[4] Johnson P, Ekstedt M, Jacobson I. Where's the theory for software engineering? IEEE Softw 2012;29(5):94–5.
[5] Russo B. Parametric classification over multiple samples. In: Proceedings of 2013 1st international workshop on data analysis patterns in software engineering (DAPSE), May 21, 2013, San Francisco, CA, USA, IEEE, 23–5; 2013.
[6] Bird C, Menzies T, Zimmermann T. First international workshop on data analysis patterns in software engineering (DAPSE 2013). In: Proceedings of the 2013 international conference on software engineering (ICSE 2013). Piscataway, NJ, USA: IEEE Press; 2013. p. 1517–8. DAPSE2013.

From software data to software theory: The path less traveled

J. Whitehead

University of California, Santa Cruz, CA, United States

CHAPTER OUTLINE

Software engineering is a pragmatic discipline. From the very beginning, the mindset of the software engineering research community has been focused on solving problems faced by practicing software engineers [1], and hence, much of software engineering work is motivated by pragmatic outcomes. To this day, software engineering research results typically require at least a semi-plausible scenario by which they can be used by practicing software engineers to assist in their development of software. Consistent with the broader software engineering community, Software Analytics also has a pragmatic bent. While this has generated many useful results, it has come at the expense of considering more theoretical outcomes from this data.

This chapter argues in favor of greater theory formation in software engineering in general, and software analytics in particular. While repository mining has yielded useful tools and techniques for practicing developers, it has also highlighted fundamental theoretical questions that remain unanswered. Examples abound. Consider the fact that most frequency distributions observed in software projects follow a power law or log normal distribution, to the extent that it is unusual to find one that is not. Why is that? To date, we have only partial explanations [2].

PATHWAYS OF SOFTWARE REPOSITORY RESEARCH

In software repository analysis, researchers use or create tools to make a local copy of project data, and then compute software metrics or software relationship networks. Examples include calculating the size of every file in a project, or finding all of the inheritance relationships among classes. This ability to compute a wide range of metrics and relationships forms a powerful new scientific instrument, a kind of software mass spectrometer. It provides researchers powerful new ways of observing software, letting us "see" things that were previously hidden, or impractical to compute. In a very real sense, this software mass spectrometer changes our understanding of the world by making the previously invisible, visible, allowing us to ponder what it means.

The typical pathway for software repository research starts with an *observational* research phase. Just as a traditional mass spectrometer provides a frequency distribution of the atoms or molecules available in a physical sample, typical outputs of our software mass spectrometer are frequency distributions computed over observed software metrics and relationships. These distributions are the frontline outputs of software repository analysis, the primary observations that researchers use as initial building blocks in their work. For example, directly measuring file size across all files in a project yields a (power law) frequency distribution of file size.

The most common next phase is application of the observational knowledge toward the betterment of software engineers. This usually takes the form of information or visualizations that can support managerial decision making, or some tool that provides benefits for software engineers. We term these *pragmatic* outcomes, since the explicit goal is improving the direct practice of software engineering activities. A software team presented with a list of the 20 largest code files, ordered by change frequency, could use this list to refactor and break apart these large files, thereby creating smaller, easier to maintain files that are changed less often.

A less common path forward from the observational step is *theory formation*. Here the goal is to use the frequency distributions and relationship networks to support fundamental understandings of what software is, and to understand the phenomena which occur during the development of software over time, and their underlying causes. This work seeks scientific outcomes, pure advances in our understanding of software and its development, and is not concerned with whether these understandings have any immediate pragmatic application.

FROM OBSERVATION, TO THEORY, TO PRACTICE

Two examples highlight the benefits of forming theories about software repository data: software power laws and software entropy.

The software analytics community has observed power law distributions for many different measures of software systems, such as file size [3], change sizes [4], and number of subclasses [5]. Recent work by Zhongpeng Lin provides one explanation for why power laws are so prevalent [2] via the simulated evolution of a large software system. Two generative mechanisms are used. One mechanism, *preferential attachment*, results in simulated software changes being made to larger files more commonly than smaller ones—the software version of the rich getting richer. A *self-organized criticality* process determines the size of software commits. Outside of software, self-organized criticality can be seen in growing sand piles, which have avalanches of varying sizes as sand trickles down. This generative simulation is able to render power law distributions out of fine-grained code changes, suggesting preferential attachment and self-organized criticality are the underlying mechanisms causing the power law distributions in software systems.

This theoretical result highlights the pathway going directly from observation to theory, without an intervening practical result. Yet the results have profound practical implications. "Preferential attachment" means that a trend toward large software files is inevitable in software systems, unless large files are continually refactored. Self-organized criticality implies that large, systemwide changes, though infrequent, are inevitable. A significant external change (hardware, requirement, market, etc.) is not required to trigger large software changes.

In our second example, Abram Hindle and collaborators use the concept of entropy from information theory to explore the surprisingness of sequences of tokens appearing in source code [6]. In natural language, entropy can be viewed as a measure of how surprising a word is, in context with preceding words. If you see the word "phone", it is not surprising if the following word is "call" or "book", but very surprising if it is "slug". Hindle et al. had the insight that since software is programmed using languages, it must be possible to measure the entropy of software. They mined a large corpus of Java language software, and then measured its average entropy for sequences of two, three, four, etc., language tokens in a row (called n-grams). These software entropy values were then compared against entropy computed in an English language corpus, revealing that software is much more predictable (less surprising) than English ($\sim$2.5–3.5 bits for software n-grams of 3 tokens and greater, as compared with $\sim$7.5 bits for English for n-grams of the same length).

This deeply theoretical result provides a different way of thinking about software. Compared to the prevailing view of software as a complex clockwork, software entropy values reveal software as having a high degree of local regularity. If there is a sequence of 3 or more programming language tokens, the following token tends to draw from a very small set of possibilities, and is easy to predict. This supports a view of software as being deeply idiomatic, and locally predictable. A beautiful theoretical result.

However, the authors didn't stop there. In a science focused field, reporting a major theoretical result would be sufficient. Software engineering, with its pragmatic focus, expected more. In the same paper announcing the entropy calculation, they also explored just how well this approach could predict the next token, so as to support the construction of an improved suggestion engine for integrated development environments. They found that the improved token suggestions were substantially better than those found in native Eclipse. The paper thus provides a pragmatic, utilitarian application for the research that could plausibly aid real world software engineers in their daily work. In case that was not sufficient, the paper also contains an extensive future work section that details several additional plausible utilitarian applications of the work.

We hope this inspires practitioners of software analytics work to not just stop after achieving a pragmatic result, but also to understand this work in a broader context, and ask the deeper questions that yield deeper theoretical understandings.

Indeed, consideration of theory can prevent critical misunderstandings. A recent parody by Andreas Zeller and collaborators [7] shows the risk. After analyzing the source code from several releases of Eclipse, they find that the characters I, R, O, and P are highly correlated with software defects. Based on this, they create a keyboard with those characters removed, to eliminate these high-risk letters! While the flaws are obvious in this case, other problems with correlation and causation are more subtle. The implication? Software theory is important for everyone, academics and practitioners alike.

REFERENCES

[1] Naur P, Randell B, editors. Software engineering: report on a conference sponsored by the NATO Science Committee, Garmisch, Germany, October, 1968 (published January, 1969); 1968. Version accessed at http://www.scrummanager.net/files/nato1968e.pdf.

[2] Lin Z, Whitehead J. Why power laws? An explanation from fine-grained changes. In: Proceedings of 12th working conference on mining software repositories (MSR 2015), Florence, Italy, May 16–17; 2015.

[3] Herraiz DG, Hassan A. On the distribution of source code file sizes. In: International conference on software and data technologies. Seville, Spain: SciTe Press; 2011.

[4] Gorshenev A, Pis'mak Y. Punctuated equilibrium in software evolution. Phys Rev E 2004;70(6):067103.

[5] Turnu I, Concas G, Marchesi M, Pinna S, Tonelli R. A modified Yule process to model the evolution of some object-oriented system properties. Inform Sci 2011;181(4):883–902.

[6] Hindle A, Barr ET, Su Z, Gabel M, Devanbu P. On the naturalness of software. In: Proceedings of 2012 international conference on software engineering (ICSE 2012), Zurich, Switzerland, June 2–9; 2012.

[7] Zeller A, Zimmermann T, Bird C. Failure is a four-letter word: a parody in empirical research. In: Proceedings of the 7th international conference on predictive models in software engineering (Promise 2011); 2011.

Why theory matters

D.I.K. Sjøberg*[†], G.R. Bergersen*, T. Dybå[†]
University of Oslo, Norway SINTEF ICT, Trondheim, Norway[†]*

CHAPTER OUTLINE

INTRODUCTION

Data without theory is blind, but theory without data is mere intellectual play.
Paraphrased from Kant

It is relatively easy to generate and acquire much data from software engineering (SE) activities. The challenge is to obtain meaning from the data that represents something true, rather than spurious. To increase knowledge and insight, more theories should be built and used.

- Theories help predict what will happen in the future.
- Theories explain why things happen, that is, causes and effects as opposed to only identifying correlations.
- Theories help reduce the apparent complexity of the world.
- Theories summarize, condense and accumulate knowledge.

HOW TO USE THEORY

More than 10 years ago, we conducted an experiment on the effect of two different control styles in Java programs. The "centralized control style" was supposed to represent poor object-oriented programming. The alternative, the "delegated control style," was supposed to represent good object-oriented programming. Among the 156 consultants who participated, we found no difference between the control styles regarding the time spent on solving the given tasks, given that the solutions were correct.

Does this imply that type of control style does not matter? No, when digging into the data, we found that only the senior consultants performed consistently better on the "good" solution. For the junior consultants, the result was reversed; they consistently performed better on the "poor" solution.

So, we found the opposite effect of the control style depending on the category of consultants. That one style benefitted juniors and another one benefitted seniors, did that happen by coincidence in our experiment or did we encounter a more general phenomenon described in an existing theory? First, we searched through a literature review on the use of theories in SE experiments conducted by Hannay et al., but found no relevant theories. Then we searched in the scientific psychology literature and found Sweller's cognitive load theory (admittedly, after searching quite a long time). It states that the cognitive load of novices in learning processes may require other strategies than those that may benefit experts. One effect of the cognitive load theory is the "the expertise reversal effect," a term coined by Kalyuga et al. to denote the phenomenon that dictates that the best instructional technique may depend on the skills of the learner.

If we replace "instructional technique" with "control style" and consider senior consultants as experts and junior consultants as novices, the expertise reversal effect may also be applied to our case with control style.

HOW TO BUILD THEORY

To make SE a more mature, scientific discipline, we need theories that describe SE phenomena. Theory building may involve adapting an existing theory or developing a theory from scratch. Either case is certainly challenging, but one needs to be brave enough to start theorizing and then seek critique for the proposed theories. Through successive improvements made by the community, the theories will become better and better.

Even though it has hardly been discussed in the SE literature, could it be that the reversal effect that we found in the aforementioned experiment is a general phenomenon in SE? To start theorizing on this issue, let us propose a theory on the reversal effect of SE technology according to the elements recommended in Sjøberg et al.:

- Constructs (the basic concepts of the theory)
- Propositions (the interactions among the constructs)

- Explanations (the reasons for the claimed interactions)
- Scope (the circumstances under which the constructs, propositions, and explanations are valid)

Following is the theory on the reversal effect described according to this framework.

CONSTRUCTS

- Software development skill (the ability of a person to develop software)
- SE technology (method, technique, tool, language, etc. used to support software development)
- Performance (the quality gained and the time saved from using the technology)
- SE technology difficulty (how difficult it is to master the technology to exploit its potential; the more difficult the technology is, the better skills and/or more practice is needed to master it)
- Competing SE technologies (technologies that are supposed to support the same kind of SE activities)

PROPOSITIONS

- P1: Given that one masters two competing SE technologies, using the most difficult SE technology offers the highest development performance.
- P2: Given two competing SE technologies, T1 with little difficulty and T2 with great difficulty: T1 gives higher development performance than T2 for low-skilled developers; T2 gives higher development performance than T1 for high-skilled developers; see Fig. 1.

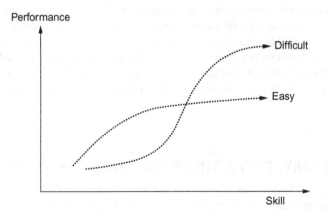

FIG. 1

A illustration of the propositions of the theory.

EXPLANATION

P1 may be explained by the general case that a more sophisticated technology may have many powerful features that lead to increased performance, but at the same time may be difficult to use. For example, a helicopter may transport more people and goods longer and faster, and across more diverse terrain than a bike, but a helicopter is also more difficult to use.

P2 may be explained by the general case that if you have not mastered the sophisticated technology, you will benefit more from using a less sophisticated technology. When asked to solve an unfamiliar problem, powerful features of the technology may require the understanding of certain abstractions. If one has no idea of what these abstractions represent, solving the problem becomes even harder. In those cases, one will benefit from stepping through the details that are available rather than dealing with abstractions that one does not understand. Think of a helicopter versus a bicycle if one does not know how to operate either. The pedals have a clear connection with the movement of the rear wheel. The operations of a helicopter are much more abstract and thus more difficult to operate without pre-established skills.

SCOPE

A theory should represent knowledge that is somewhat widely applicable, but still not trivial, or one that follows from a definition. For example, stating in a theory that "software development is a human activity" provides no new knowledge. In disciplines that involve human behavior, one would hardly find such universal theories as Einstein's general theory of relativity in physics. Given the many context factors that affect software development, it is a tough challenge to define an appropriate scope for an SE theory. In the case of the theory proposed here, we consider the scope to include only technologies that are either in use in industry or are likely to be useful on the basis of evidence from experiments in an artificial setting.

Kurt Lewin stated more than 60 years ago, "there is nothing so practical as a good theory." Particularly in an engineering discipline like SE, theory should have practical applications. For example, the theory proposed herein could be used in cost-benefit considerations: if an organization has low-skilled (or high-skilled) developers, an easy (or difficult) SE technology should be used. Of course, there are many trade-offs, but then one should consider whether it is sensible to let the high-skilled developers construct a system if only the low-skilled developers will perform maintenance in the future.

IN SUMMARY: FIND A THEORY OR BUILD ONE YOURSELF

So, the message here is that if you have obtained a set of data, you should interpret your data in the context of theory. If you do not find such a theory, use your data as a starting point for building theory yourself.

Note, paraphrasing Bunge, "premature theorizing is likely to be wrong—but not sterile—and that a long deferred beginning of theorizing is worse than any number of failures." Our proposed theory is obviously not generally valid. There are clearly cases where no reversal effect exists; that is, between two competing technologies, one of them may give better performance for all skill levels. A more refined theory may classify SE technologies into two more categories: easy to use technologies that give increased performance for all skill levels (this is a mega success) and more difficult to use technologies that give decreased performance for all skill levels (there are many examples of such failures).

Furthermore, a construct like efficiency or cost-benefit may be included in the theory. Two technologies may have similar efficiency if one of them is twice as difficult to learn as the other, one but also gives twice the performance. However, measuring difficulty and performance on a ratio scale may be difficult. Further theorizing and critiquing are therefore required.

It is the task of the research community to collect or produce more data that may strengthen, refine or refute a proposed theory. But first someone has to propose the initial theory. Why not you?

FURTHER READING

[1] Arisholm E, Sjøberg DIK. Evaluating the effect of a delegated versus centralized control style on the maintainability of object-oriented software. IEEE Trans Softw Eng 2004;30 (8):521–34.

[2] Hannay JE, Sjøberg DIK, Dybå T. A systematic review of theory use in software engineering experiments. IEEE Trans Softw Eng 2007;33(2):87–107.

[3] Kalyuga S, Ayres P, Chandler P, Sweller J. The expertise reversal effect. Educ Psychol 2003;38:23–31.

[4] Lewin K. The research center for group dynamics at Massachusetts Institute of Technology. Sociometry 1945;8:126–35.

[5] Sjøberg DIK, Dybå T, Anda BCD, Hannay JE. Building theories in software engineering. In: Shull F, Singer J, Sjøberg D, editors. Advanced topics in empirical software engineering. Berlin: Springer; 2008. p. 312–36.

[6] Sweller J. Cognitive load during problem solving: effects on learning. Cognit Sci 1988;12:257–85.

Success stories/
applications

Mining apps for anomalies

A. Zeller

Saarland University, Saarbrücken, Germany

CHAPTER OUTLINE

THE MILLION-DOLLAR QUESTION

So you have some program. It can be yours, or it can come from a third party. You want to use it. But before you do so, you may ask the million-dollar question: *does the program do what it is supposed to do*? And will it continue to do so in the future? To answer this question, we first need to know what it is the program should do, or, conversely, what it should not do. While it is easy to state a couple of desired and undesired properties, there is a huge gray area that is surprisingly hard to define.

Take a simple mobile game like Flappy Bird, for instance. Your aim is to move a little bird up and down such that it does not hit an obstacle. As a developer, you don't want the game to crash, that's for sure; so "no crashes" would definitely be on the list of undesired properties—together with "not spying," "not deleting all my files," and other generic properties we usually take for granted.

But suppose you want to teach a computer to *test* the game—to check whether the *desired* properties are all there. You'd have to specify the basic gameplay, let the computer control the bird, and check whether the game correctly ends if, and only if, the bird has crashed into an obstacle. How would you specify all this? And is it not as complex as writing the program in the first place?

We humans need no such detailed specification of how to play the game. That's because we humans base ourselves on our expectations, which in turn are based on *experience*—in this case, our experience with similar games: if you ever played a

Jump-And-Run game, you'll get the grasp of Flappy Bird. But not only will you be able to play the game, you will also be able to check it against its description. All this is based on your experience. The question is: can we teach a computer how to do this—*check a program against expectations*? To do this, we must find a way to have a computer learn such expectations, or in other words, to *learn what program behavior is normal in a given context*. And this is where app stores and app mining come into play.

APP MINING

The key idea of app mining is to *leverage the knowledge* encoded into the hundreds of thousands of apps available in app stores—specifically, to determine what would be normal (and thus expected) behavior, to detect what would be abnormal (possibly unexpected) behavior, and thus to guide programmers and users toward better security and usability.

From a researcher's perspective, app stores are just collections of programs—but here, an app is a bit more than just program code alone. Apps in app stores have three exciting features:

- First, apps come with all sorts of *metadata*, such as names, descriptions, categories, downloads, reviews, ratings, and user interfaces. All of these can be associated with program features, so you can, for instance, associate program behavior with descriptions. (You can also mine and associate *just* the metadata, finding that bad reviews correlate with low download numbers; in my opinion, though, this would be product mining, not app mining.)
- Second, apps are pretty much *uniform*, as they cater to one (mobile) platform only. They use the same binary format and the same libraries, which on top, use fairly recent designs. All this makes apps easy to analyze, execute, and test—and consequently, easy to compare.
- Third, apps are redundant. There are plenty of apps that all address similar problems—in similar or dissimilar ways. This is in sharp contrast to open source programs, where each solution would typically be implemented exactly once, and then reused. This redundancy in apps allows us to learn common patterns of how problems are addressed—and, in return, detect anomalies.

All of this offers plenty of research opportunities; all you need is the data and a means to dig through it. The data, though, is not that easy to get. You cannot simply download a huge app collection from some research server—that would be a huge copyright violation. Instead, you have to download your own collection from the app store of your choice, one app after another, together with the associated metadata.

Depending on your investigation, you may need several thousand apps. Since the offering in the app store does not necessarily match what's on user's devices, you should focus on frequently downloaded apps from all app categories, from gaming to productivity. As we usually assume the large majority of these apps to be benign, these apps and their metadata then form your source of knowledge—the very knowledge a computer can and should use as it comes to identifying "normal" behavior.

DETECTING ABNORMAL BEHAVIOR

One of the most important applications of app mining is to identify *malicious behavior*—that is, behavior that is directed against the user's interests. But how do we know what the user's interests are? And if we don't know, how can we tell whether some behavior is malicious or not? By mining a set of benign apps, we can at least tell whether some behavior is normal or abnormal. If it's normal, then it may well be expected and accepted; if it's abnormal, though, then it may require further scrutiny.

The problem with "normal" behavior is that it varies according to the app's purpose. If an app sends out text messages, for instance, that would normally be a sign of malicious behavior—unless it is a messaging application, where sending text messages is one of the advertised features. If an app continuously monitors your position, this might be malicious behavior—unless it is a tracking app that again advertises this as a feature. As a consequence, simply checking for a set of predefined "undesired" features is not enough—if the features are clearly advertised, then it is reasonable to assume the user tolerates, or even wants these features, because otherwise, she would not have chosen the app.

To determine what is normal, we thus must assess program behavior together with its *description*. If the behavior is advertised (or can be implied by the kind of application), then it's fine; if not, it may come as a surprise to the user, and thus should be flagged. This is the idea we followed in our first app mining work, the CHABADA tool.

CHABADA stands for "Checking App Behavior Against Descriptions of Apps"; it is a general tool to detect mismatches between the behavior of an app and its description. CHABADA works in two stages:

1. CHABADA starts with a (large) set of apps to be analyzed. It first applies tried-and-proven natural language processing techniques (stemming, LDA (Latent Dirichlet Analysis), topic analysis) to abstract the app descriptions into topics. It builds *clusters* of those apps whose topics have the most in common. Thus, all apps whose descriptions refer to messaging end up in a "Messaging" cluster. You may also get "Games" clusters, "Office" clusters, or "Travel" clusters, as well as a number of clusters featuring doubtful apps; all these will reproduce realities from the app store.

2. Within each cluster, CHABADA will now search for *outliers* regarding app behavior. As a proxy for behavior, CHABADA simply uses the set of API calls contained in each app; these are easy to extract using simple static analysis tools. To identify outliers, CHABADA uses tried-and-proven outlier analysis techniques, which provide a *ranking* of the apps in a cluster, depending on how far away their API usage is from the norm. Those apps that are ranked highest are the most likely outliers.

What do these rankings give you? We identified "Travel" applications that happily shared your device identifier and account information with the world (which is rare for "Travel" applications). Plenty of apps tracked all sorts of user information without mentioning this in their description. (We had a cluster named "Adware" which contained apps focusing on collecting data.) But outliers can also come to be because they are the one good app amongst several dubious ones. In our "Poker" cluster, only one app would not track user data—and would promptly be flagged as an outlier.

The real power of such approaches, however, comes when they are applied to detect *malicious* apps. Applied on a set of 22,500 apps, CHABADA can detect 74% of novel malware, with a false positive rate below 10%. Our recent MUDFLOW prototype, which learns normal *data flows* from apps, can even detect more than 90% of novel malware leaking sensitive data. Remember that these recognition rates come from learning *from benign samples only*. Thus, CHABADA and MUDFLOW can be applied to detect malware even if it is the very first of its kind—simply because it shows unusual behavior compared to the many benign apps found in app stores.

A TREASURE TROVE OF DATA …

At this point, API usage and static data barely scratch the surface of the many facets of behavior that can be extracted from apps. To whet your appetite, here's a number of ideas that app stores all make possible—and that all are based on the idea of mining *what is normal across apps*:

1. Future techniques will tie program analysis to *user interface analysis*, for instance, to detect whether the user agreed to specific terms and conditions before starting whatever questionable behavior. (And whether the terms and conditions were actually legible on the screen!)
2. Mining user interaction may reveal *behavior patterns* we could reuse in various contexts. For instance, we could learn from one app that to check out, one typically has to add items to a shopping cart first—and reapply this pattern when we want to automatically explore another shopping app.
3. Violating behavior patterns may also imply *usability issues*. If a button named "Login" does nothing, for instance, it would be very different from the other "Login" buttons used in other apps—and hopefully be flagged as an anomaly. (If it takes control over your device, this would hopefully be detected as an even larger anomaly!)
4. Given good test generators, one can systematically explore the dynamic behavior, and gain information on concrete text and resources accessed. For instance, an app that shows a map would typically send the location to a known maps service—but not necessarily to some obscure server we know nothing about.

The fun with apps is that they offer so many different data sources that can all be associated with each other—and there are so many instances of apps that one can indeed learn what makes for normal and expected behavior. And still, we are just at the beginning.

... BUT ALSO OBSTACLES

App mining is different. There's exciting data available, but there also is data that is normally *not* available, in particular compared to mining source code repositories. Here are a few *obstacles* that you may need to be aware of:

1. Getting apps is not hard, but not easy either. Besides the official stores, there is no publicly available repository of apps where you could simply download thousands of apps—simply because this would be a gross violation of copyright. Even researchers cannot share their app collections, for the exact same reason. You will have to download your own collection, and this takes time and effort. (Note that collections of *malicious* apps can be easily shared—but that's because it is unlikely that someone would enforce copyright.)

2. For apps, there's no easily accessible source code, version, or bug information. If you monitor a store for a sufficient time, you may be able to access and compare releases, but that's it. The vendors maintain their own code, version control, and bug databases, and they normally would not grant you access to these. And, the few apps that are available as open source would be neither popular nor representative. Fortunately, app byte code is not too hard to get through.

3. Metadata is only a very weak indicator of program quality. Lots of one-star reviews may refer to a recent price increase, which is independent of the app itself; or may come from fans collectively criticizing an app for political reasons; or be related to the app actually being nonfunctional. On the other hand, lots of reviews talking about crashes or malicious behavior might give clear signs.

4. Never underestimate developers. Vendors typically have a pretty clear picture of what their users do—by collecting and analyzing lots of usage and installation data, which you don't have access to. If you think you can mine metadata to predict release dates, reviews, or sentiments: talk to vendors first and check your proposal against the realities of app development.

In practice, overcoming these obstacles is not too hard: get or create a set of scripts that download a representative set of apps and their metadata; use a suitable tool chain for analyzing app code; and talk to app vendors and developers to understand their practice and identify their needs. Then get the data—and enjoy the ride!

EXECUTIVE SUMMARY

App mining leverages common knowledge in thousands of apps to automatically learn what is "normal" behavior—and in contrast, automatically identify "abnormal" behavior. This classification can guide programmers and users toward quality, productivity, and security. As an emerging field of research, app mining opens lots of opportunities for research that serves users, developers, and vendors alike. Enjoy app mining!

FURTHER READING

[1] Gorla A, Tavecchia I, Gross F, Zeller A. Checking app behavior against app descriptions. Proceedings of the international conference on software engineering, 2014.

[2] Kuznetsov K, Gorla A, Tavecchia I, Gross F, Zeller A. Mining Android apps for anomalies. In: Bird C, Menzies T, Zimmermann T, editors. Art and science of analyzing software data. Elsevier; 2015.

[3] Avdiienko V, Kuznetsov K, Gorla A, Zeller A, Arzt S, Rasthofer S, et al. Mining apps for abnormal usage of sensitive data. Proceedings of the international conference on software engineering, 2015.

[4] Saarland University app mining project page. https://www.st.cs.uni-saarland.de/appmining/.

Embrace dynamic artifacts

Venkatesh-Prasad Ranganath

Kansas State University, Manhattan, KS, United States

CHAPTER OUTLINE

CAN WE MINIMIZE THE USB DRIVER TEST SUITE?

When we talk about data science in the context of software engineering, we often only consider static artifacts that are independent of (or not generated by) the execution of software, eg, source code, version history, bug reports, mailing lists, developer network, and organization structure. We seldom consider dynamic artifacts that are dependent on (or generated by) the execution of software, eg, execution logs, crash/core dumps, call stacks, and traffic logs. Specifically, we seldom consider dynamic artifacts to enable the use of data science to improve software engineering tasks such as coding, testing, and debugging (in contrast to improving post-deployment activities such as monitoring for service degradation or security attacks).

I believe that we should, and we can, use dynamic artifacts with data science to improve software engineering tasks. Read on to see if you agree with me.

Here's an example from my personal experience when collaborating with the Windows USB driver team at Microsoft (after the development of Windows 8).

Before the USB device driver in Microsoft Windows is updated, the USB driver is tested by using it with USB devices that exercise its behavior. This form of testing is expensive, as the number of unique USB devices is huge and, consequently, the effort required to identify, procure, and use the devices to test the driver is prohibitive.

As in situations that involve a very large population, the Windows USB testing team uses a sample (test suite) of 1000+ USB devices to test the USB driver. To ensure the sample is diverse and representative of both the population and prevalent use of USB devices, the team uses expert knowledge to choose the sample. Even so, there can be redundancy in such a sample as many devices may exercise the same behavior of the USB driver, eg, devices may use the same ASIC (low-level circuitry) to implement the USB protocol, and such redundancy may elude even the experts. Consequently, this can lead to wasted time and effort, which could be better utilized to test behaviors not exercised by devices in the sample.

Further, testing using 1000+ devices takes a non-trivial amount of manual effort. So, any elimination of redundancy would help expedite test cycles.

The Windows USB testing team described the situation to my team and asked if we could help identify a subset of the test suite that would expose the same bugs that were exposed by the entire test suite. In other words, they wanted to *minimize their test suite, preferably without affecting its bug coverage.*

YES, LET'S OBSERVE INTERACTIONS

As a solution, we proposed a technique based on interactions (ie, service requests and responses) observed at runtime at the published interface of the USB driver when servicing devices. After all, the goal was to test how the driver behaves under different inputs. (The fact that we had recently used such interactions to test compatibility between USB drivers had no influence on this decision.)

So, we combined an existing logging filter driver with an existing device testing setup to log interactions at the interface of the USB driver when testing sample devices. Then, we *mined structural and temporal patterns* [1] from these runtime logs and used the *patterns as features* [2] to cluster the devices using hierarchical clustering. From this clustering, we randomly picked representative devices from each cluster and used only the representatives to test the USB driver. The choice of the number of clusters was based on halving the number of sample devices (test suite). To protect against omission errors within clusters, in each weekly test cycle, we picked different representatives from each cluster. (Further, we planned to test all sample devices during each monthly test cycle.) With this simple solution, the testing team was able to use only half the number of sample devices to achieve 75–80% of bug coverage.

WHY DID OUR SOLUTION WORK?

The solution worked as *interaction logs captured exactly what happened when devices interacted with the USB driver*, ie, the exact inputs/requests provided to the driver and the exact outputs/responses provided back by the driver. The exactness of the data automatically (and aggressively) eliminated numerous possibilities that would have been considered in alternative solutions, such as static analysis of the source code of device drivers. Further, since the logs did not contain extraneous information, we did not have to clean the data. (This may not be true in all cases involving dynamic artifacts.) Also, we reduced the cost of data collection by reusing existing infrastructure to collect logs. While we did not use the history of various data points in the logs, this information existed in the logs, and it could have been used to reconstruct the context and help understand how and why an interaction transpired.

STILL NOT CONVINCED? HERE'S MORE

In 2009, *DebugAdvisor* [3] effort proposed a recommendation system to help with debugging. The idea was, when bugs are assigned to a developer, provide the developer with pointers to institutional knowledge relevant to expedite bug fixing. In DebugAdvisor, dynamic artifacts such as stack traces, core dumps, and debugging logs complemented static artifacts such as bug repository and code/fix ownership to help identify similar bugs reported in the past. The system was successfully piloted within the Windows serviceability group with 75% of the recommendations proving to be useful.

In 2010, the *StackMine* [4] system mined execution traces from Microsoft Windows to aid with performance debugging. The idea relied on "correlating" patterns observed in call stacks from execution traces to identify potential performance hotspots. This system helped identify performance bugs in Windows Explorer UI that were hidden in Windows 7 and even in previous versions of Windows.

DYNAMIC ARTIFACTS ARE HERE TO STAY

An observation common to all of the preceding examples is that dynamic artifacts fueled the data analysis that resulted in effective solutions to software engineering problems. Almost always, dynamic artifacts contain information that is either absent in or impossible to extract from static artifacts. Further, dynamic data collection has become easy today, as most software systems are either equipped with or run on top of platforms equipped with the ability to collect dynamic data via telemetry (in the form of logs). Also, while the amount of dynamic data collected from a system can pose a challenge in terms of efficient processing, we can now overcome this challenge by relying on cheap and accessible cloud computing. So, it is time to consider *dynamic artifacts as data science worthy artifacts and use them whenever they are available; specifically, to enable and improve software engineering tasks.*

So, don't shy away from or throw away dynamic artifacts. Learn to embrace them!

ACKNOWLEDGMENTS

The USB test suite minimization effort was carried out at Microsoft by Naren Datha, Robbie Harris, Aravind Namasivayam, Venkatesh-Prasad Ranganath, and Pradip Vallathol.

REFERENCES

[1] Lo D, Ramalingam G, Ranganath V-P, Vaswani K. Mining quantified temporal rules: formalism, algorithms, and evaluation. Sci Comput Program 2012;77(6):743–59. http://www.sciencedirect.com/science/article/pii/S0167642310001875.

[2] Ranganath V-P, Thomas J. Structural and temporal patterns-based features. In: International workshop on data analysis patterns in software engineering (DAPSE); 2013. http://ieeexplore.ieee.org/xpl/articleDetails.jsp?arnumber=6603808.

[3] Ashok B, Joy J, Liang H, Rajamani S, Srinivasa G, Vangala V. Debug Advisor: a recommender system for debugging. In: Foundations of software engineering (ESEC/FSE); 2009. http://dl.acm.org/citation.cfm?doid=1595696.1595766.

[4] Han S, Dang Y, Ge S, Zhang D, Xie T. Performance debugging in the large via mining millions of stack traces. In: International conference on software engineering (ICSE); 2012. http://dl.acm.org/citation.cfm?id=2337241.

Mobile app store analytics

M. Nagappan*, E. Shihab[†]

Rochester Institute of Technology, Rochester, NY, United States[*] Concordia University, Montreal, QC, Canada[†]

CHAPTER OUTLINE

INTRODUCTION

Today, software engineering research focuses on traditional software systems like the Firefox web browser or Microsoft Windows, which take years to develop by teams of designers, developers, and debuggers. Software engineering is rapidly changing, though. Emerging domains, such as mobile devices, are growing rapidly and depend heavily on new software operating systems like Android and the applications that they run, commonly referred to as "apps." Over the past few years, we have seen a boom in the popularity of mobile devices and mobile apps that run on these devices. Thus, solving the challenges faced by stakeholders such as mobile app developers, users, and platform owners (such as Apple/BlackBerry/Google/Microsoft) could create quite an impact.

Mobile apps, unlike traditional software, are distributed by the developers directly to the end users via a centralized platform called the app store. Along with the executable mobile app, the app stores contain a large set of metadata about the app. For each app, any end user is able to look at the name and contact details of the developer, a description of the app, sample screenshots, a feature set of the app, the number of downloads, and the price for the app. Additionally, the app stores allow users to post reviews of the apps. This is very different from traditional software. Mobile app developers get continuous feedback from users that can be leveraged to help them. For example, as described herein, prior work leveraged user reviews to extract user-faced issues and new requirements.

UNDERSTANDING END USERS

One of the key characteristics of mobile app stores is the fact that they allow users to review their apps. Generally, these app reviews consist of two parts: an app star rating (of which an aggregate makes up the overall app-level rating) and a review or comment that is used to rationalize the star rating. Previous research has shown that users tend to write reviews when they are either extremely satisfied or extremely dissatisfied with a product [1]. The low star reviews have a greater impact on sales than high star reviews, since buyers are more likely to react to low ratings and complaints [2]. It has also been proven that such user reviews can have a high impact on download counts (ie, purchases) and are a key measure of the app's success.

Therefore, it is always in a developer's best interest to make sure app reviews are as good as possible. To ensure high app ratings, a number of studies leverage app review analytics to help developers understand their users. An example of such a study is one that uses app reviews to understand "why users give low ratings to apps?" [3]. In particular, the aim of the study was to examine the most frequent and the most negatively impacting types of complaints users have. Since the study's goal was to understand complaints, it focused only on one and two star reviews of 20 different iOS apps. A statistically significant sample (6390) of user reviews were manually examined and tagged. The tags were meant to summarize the type of complaint the user mentions (eg, a complaint about a functional error or a privacy issue with the app). Then, the tagged reviews were grouped, and different analytics were calculated to make some insightful recommendations to developers about negative app reviews.

Since the main goal is to identify the different types of user complaints so developers can avoid them, the study starts by determining the most frequent types of complaints. The study found that the majority of negative app reviews can be classified into 12 different categories, namely (ordered in descending order of frequency), functional error; feature request; app crashing; network problem; interface design; feature removal; hidden cost; compatibility; privacy and ethical; unresponsive app; uninteresting content; and resource heavy. In fact, the three most common complaints, ie, functional errors, feature requests, and app crashing accounted for more than 50% of the reported complaints. Examining these complaints can help developers identify existing problems, and give guidance on potentially new features for their app. In fact, follow-up work by Iacob et al. [4] showed that app reviews can be mined to successfully identify new app feature requests.

In addition to simply determining the most frequent complaints, the study also investigated the most negatively impacting types of complaints. To do so, the study calculated the ratio of 1–2 star ratings for each complaint. This ratio helped us identify the most negatively perceived complaints. The findings showed an interesting and complementary view to the findings about the most frequent complaints. The most negatively impacting complaints were related to privacy and ethical issues, hidden costs, and feature removals (ie, disliked features that are degrading the end-user experience). The three aforementioned complaints were not the most frequent; however, clearly, they are the most negatively perceived by app users. On the other hand, the most frequent complaints (eg, functional errors), tend to be not as impacting. The study is a clear example of how user app review analytics can be leveraged to help mobile app developers better understand their users. More about this study is available in the full article [3].

CONCLUSION

Researchers have begun to mine the data in mobile app stores to address relevant software engineering issues [5,6]. Additionally, several companies like App Annie (which recently bought another company—Distimo) and Appfigures have even built successful businesses selling intelligence gained from observing the evolution of several hundred thousand apps in the app stores. Some advancements made by mining app store data include: code reuse in mobile apps, monetizing apps through ads, testing mobile apps, addressing device fragmentation, resource usage and optimization, and teaching programming on mobile devices. Practitioners can therefore leverage the tools built and intelligence gained through app stores to help them deliver higher quality products to end users in a shorter time span.

REFERENCES

[1] Hu N, Pavlou PA, Zhang J. Can online reviews reveal a product's true quality? empirical findings and analytical modeling of online word-of-mouth communication. In: Proceedings of the 7th ACM conference on Electronic commerce, EC '06; 2006. p. 324–30.
[2] Chevalier JA, Mayzlin D. The effect of word of mouth on sales: online book reviews. J Marketing Res 2006;43(3):345–54.
[3] Khalid H, Shihab E, Nagappan M, Hassan A. What do mobile app users complain about? Software, IEEE 2015;32(3):70–7.
[4] Iacob C, Harrison R. Retrieving and analyzing mobile apps feature requests from online reviews. In: Proceedings of the 10th working conference on mining software repositories, MSR '13; 2013. p. 41–4.
[5] Sarro F. The UCLAppA repository: a repository of research articles on mobile software engineering and app store analysis. http://www0.cs.ucl.ac.uk/staff/F.Sarro/projects/UCLappA/UCLappArepository.html.
[6] Nagappan M, Shihab E. Future trends in software engineering research for mobile apps. In: Proceedings of the future of software engineering track at 23rd IEEE international conference on software analysis, evolution, and reengineering (SANER 2016), March 14–18, 2016, Osaka, Japan; 2016.

The naturalness of software[☆]

E.T. Barr*, P. Devanbu†

University College London, London, United Kingdom* UC Davis, Davis, CA, United States†

CHAPTER OUTLINE

INTRODUCTION

Of all that we humans do, it is our use of language that most sets us apart from animals. Honed by millions of years of cultural and biological evolution, language is a natural, ordinary, even instinctive part of everyday life [2]. However much we authors may labor to fashion lucid prose for this learned tome, we speak and write spontaneously and freely in daily life: most of what we say is simple, repetitive, and effortless. This quotidian aspect of natural, human linguistic behavior, together with large online corpora of utterances, modern computing resources, and statistical innovations, has triggered a revolution in natural language processing, whose fruits we enjoy every day in the form of speech recognition and automated language translation.

But then, there is this funny thing about programming: it is primarily (even if sometimes unintentionally) *an act of communication*, from one human to another. Knuth said as much, 30 years ago:

Let us change our traditional attitude to the construction of programs: Instead of imagining that our main task is to instruct a computer what to do, let us concentrate rather on explaining to human beings what we want a computer to do.

[3]

If one, then, were to view programming as a speech act, is it driven by the "language instinct"? Do we program as we speak? Is our code largely simple, repetitive, and predictable? Is code *natural*?

Surely, not all code is. Turn to any sample code in Knuth's own *Art of Computer Programming*, and see just how simple and repetitive it is! However, *that* code is carefully wrought by an expert hand to stand forth as an exemplar of the programmer's art. Assuredly, most workaday programmers do not have the time to craft such masterpieces.

So, then, how much software is *natural*, that is to say, simple, repetitive, and effortlessly written? If a lot of "quotidian" code is, indeed, simple, and repetitive, can we use statistical methods from natural language processing to assist programmers in developing better code, faster? Can statistical methods help understand and characterize programmer behavior? Can these methods be used to build models to help beginners avoid and correct common mistakes? Can algorithms automatically translate between Java and C#, as we do from English to French?

These questions are representative of an entirely new direction of research in software engineering: the study and exploitation of the naturalness of software, using large, online corpora of open-source and other code. To investigate this new area, we first used *n*-gram models [4]. These models assign a probability to the next token based on the previous $n - 1$ tokens. These models have a long history in natural language processing. Modern *n*-gram models have sophisticated ways of dealing with issues like data sparsity: ie, some words never occur during model training, but are then encountered in practice. We gathered a large corpus of source code in C and Java, trained a modern *n*-gram model over that corpus, and measured the predictive accuracy of these models using 10-fold cross-validation. A standard measure here is *cross-entropy*, which evaluates the "surprisingness" of the code; it is the average negative log of the probability assigned by the model to each token in a test corpus. Intuitively, it measures the average *information content* of each token in bits.

Typically, the cross-entropy of English falls between 7 and 8 bits using modern *n*-gram models over words. What about code? Its syntax is simpler than natural language, but contains more neologisms and sometimes defines terms quite far from their uses. To our surprise, we found that source code was not only repetitive and predictable, but much *more so* than natural language, coming in around 3–4 bits. We remind the reader that this measure is log-scaled, and thus, code is roughly 8–16 times *more predictable* than English! This encouraging finding led us to seek applications.

The first application we tried was improving integrated development environments (IDEs) like Eclipse[1] and IntelliJ Idea[2]. IDEs have long offered *code*

---

[1]http://eclipse.org.
[2]https://www.jetbrains.com/idea/.

suggestions and completions (S&C). Completions complete a token fragment; suggestions complete token sequences. IDEs use sophisticated engines that exploit non-local information, like token types and variable scope; in contrast, the *n*-gram models we used were purely local. Our daring idea was that we could, nonetheless, improve the Eclipse S&C engine. We succeeded, using a fairly simple regimen of blending its suggestions from higher-probability ones offered by the *n*-gram model. In retrospect, it is reasonable to expect that these two approaches complement each other: Eclipse suggests tokens that *are allowed to appear* in a given context; the *n*-gram model, by comparison, suggests tokens that have most frequently appeared in similar contexts. This paper was published in ICSE 2012 [5] and, to our knowledge, was the first to explicitly observe the "naturalness of software" and lay out a research vision of work that studied and exploited this phenomenon. We followed up this success by engineering a robust Eclipse plug-in that uses our locality-enhanced cache-based language model [6] to provide more accurate suggestions and completions to enhance developer productivity.

TRANSFORMING SOFTWARE PRACTICE

Beyond its successful application to S&C tasks, the naturalness of software promises to transform software practice through its application to seminal problems like porting, effective community formation, program analysis, and assistive technologies.

PORTING AND TRANSLATION

Automated translation is a success story of statistical natural language processing. These tools are based on models trained using *aligned corpora* where parallel texts in two different languages are available. Here, the question is whether we successfully train a translation engine to translate between, say Java and C#, using parallel implementations in the two languages? Nguyen et al. [7,8] built a lexical translation engine that translated between Java and C#. Its training corpora contained projects with parallel Java and C# implementations, with method-level alignments. Using aligned code, this project also demonstrated the efficacy of statistical methods in detecting Application Program Interface (API) mappings across different languages and platforms [7]. More recent work has moved beyond lexemes to learning phrase-based translation [9].

THE "NATURAL LINGUISTICS" OF CODE

Linguistics has, *inter alia*, two notable aspects: (1) the study of language itself and (2) the study of related subjects (eg, psychology, sociology, anthropology) as they are manifested in linguistic behavior. If we view programming as a form of human linguistic behavior, one could study how large corpora of programs are written and evaluate the different language features they use. Allamanis et al. showed that language models can distinguish project-specific linguistic phenomena, and leveraged this finding to develop a tool that learns and enforces coding standards [10]. This finding suggests that code manifests "linguistic culture." The National Science Foundation has recently funded the pursuit of the second line of work, *that is to say*, the social and human aspects of code linguistics. This work aims to identify whether project members have coding styles that "signal" to others that they are in-group rather than out-group, similar to the way in which speech patterns and behavior can indicate whether a person belongs to a group. Success here may, for instance, provide ways to establish development processes that are more welcoming to newcomers.

ANALYSIS AND TOOLS

The predictability of code suggests that semantic properties of code are also predictable. In the extended version of our ICSE 2012 paper [5], we hypothesized that:

Semantic properties (of code) are *usually* manifest in *superficial* ways that are computationally cheap to detect, particularly when compared to the cost (or even infeasibility) of determining these properties by sound (or complete) static analysis.

We described (Section VI.D) the possibility of estimating a statistical model over a corpus of code, well-annotated with static analysis facts; and then using this translation approach to provide maximum a-posteriori probability guesses as to likely semantic properties, given easily detected "surface" features. A recent paper realized this approach, using Conditional Random Fields, for the task of suggesting reasonable names and likely type annotations in Javascript programs [11].

ASSISTIVE TECHNOLOGIES

Assistive technologies enable users with motion impairments to use computers. They must extract useful signals from constrained movements (such as limited hand movements with just one or two degrees of freedom) or from noisy signals (eg, speech or jittery movements). The user's observed input can be considered a sample drawn from a distribution conditioned on the intended input, and the task of the assistive device is to identify the intended input. In such settings, a good predictive model is essential.

Dasher [12] replaces a keyboard, allowing the rapid input of English text using motion limited to two dimensions. The user chooses the next letter from a streaming menu of letters that fly at him/her, based on the previous five letters. Dasher works remarkably well, since the hexagram-based entropy of letters in English is quite low, on the order of a few bits. Unfortunately, the token (ie, word) entropy of English is too high to allow Dasher to stream words instead of letters. In code, however, the token entropy is low enough that it is possible to choose tokens. We built a Dasher for code prototype to demonstrate this approach, which you can view online[3].

---

[3]http://naturalness.cs.ucdavis.edu.

CONCLUSION

Software is a natural product of human effort, and shares many statistical properties with natural language. This phenomenon promises a wealth of applications, leveraging prior work on statistical methods in natural language; it also offers the promise of using new scientific methodologies to investigate the human and social aspects of software, drawn from approaches in cognitive and social linguistics.

REFERENCES

[1] Devanbu P. The naturalness of software, ICSE 2015 NIER Track.
[2] Pinker S. The language instinct: the new science of language and mind, vol. 7529. London: Penguin; 1994.
[3] Knuth DE. Literate programming. Comput J 1984;27(2):97–111.
[4] Sparck Jones K. Natural language processing: a historical review. In: Zampolli A, Calzolari N, Palmer M, editors. Current issues in computational linguistics: in honour of Don Walker. Amsterdam: Kluwer; 1994.
[5] Hindle A, Barr E, Gabel M, Su Z, Devanbu P. On the naturalness of software. http://macbeth.cs.ucdavis.edu/natural.pdf, 2012 [Extended version of the work published at the International conference on software engineering; 2012, Online; accessed 08-Feb-2015].
[6] Tu Z, Su Z, Devanbu P. On the localness of software. In: Proceedings of the joint meeting on foundations of software engineering. New York: ACM; 2014. p. 269–80.
[7] Nguyen AT, Nguyen HA, Nguyen TT, Nguyen TN. Statistical learning approach for mining API usage mappings for code migration. In: Proceedings of the conference on automated software engineering. New York: ACM; 2014. p. 457–68.
[8] Nguyen AT, Nguyen TT, Nguyen TN. Lexical statistical machine translation for language migration. In: Proceedings of the joint meeting on foundations of software engineering. New York: ACM; 2013. p. 651–4.
[9] Karaivanov S, Raychev V, Vechev M. Phrase-based statistical translation of programming languages. In: Proceedings of the 2014 ACM international symposium on new ideas, new paradigms, and reflections on programming & software. New York: ACM; 2014. p. 173–84.
[10] Allamanis M, Barr ET, Sutton C. Learning natural coding conventions. In: Proceedings of the joint meeting on foundations of software engineering; 2014.
[11] Raychev V, Vechev M, Krause A. Predicting program properties from "big code". In: Proceedings of the symposium on the principles of programming languages; 2015.
[12] Wills SA, MacKay DJ. Dasher-an efficient writing system for brain-computer interfaces? IEEE Trans Neural Syst Rehabil Eng 2006;14(2):244–6.

Advances in release readiness

P. Rotella

Cisco Systems, Inc., Raleigh, NC, United States

CHAPTER OUTLINE

A key question in the software development industry is "how do we know when a release is ready to ship to customers?" Is the release sufficiently reliable, or are there too many residual bugs remaining? These questions are difficult to answer with any certainty. To help ensure reliability, many development teams rely on traditional metrics, such as severity 1 and 2 backlog levels, test case execution percentages, and pass rates for function testing. Often, these types of metrics are aggregated into a "quality index" that uses weighted averages to gauge "release health" throughout the lifecycle, but are mainly focused during the function and system testing of the integration branch, the new release's total code base. These metrics and indices are considered useful, but usually there is not a known correlation between the key metrics/indices and the customer's reliability experience. In other words, we merely assume they are good indicators of release health—evidence is usually lacking that moving these metric/index "levers" by this much results in changes in the customer reliability experience by that much.

Why is it important, even critical, prior to releasing software to understand the quantitative relationship between key metrics and field performance? After all, customers do demand high feature velocity and realize that reliability often suffers as a result of high new feature counts, lower cycle times, and increasingly large and complex code bases. But both enterprise and service provider customers are also under heavy pressure to provide very high levels of software reliability and availability to their user base, and consequently are unwilling to implement new releases without quantifiable acceptance criteria for key metrics, in addition to thorough acceptance testing in their labs.

Probably the most effective way to ensure high reliability for customers is to practice rigorous "phase containment"—improving upstream design, code development, and testing practices. This is certainly true, but even where the bug injection rate is low, we still need to be fairly certain, during the testing cycle, what the field reliability is actually expected to be and that it will be sufficiently high. And we need to be able to convince customers that engineering's expectations are accurate and reliable.

PREDICTIVE TEST METRICS

At Cisco, we have investigated many test metric candidates in an effort to predict field experience for our wide range of software products. Ideally, we would prefer to find highly predictive metrics in each of the major testing "dimensions"— incoming, fixed, and backlog bugs. These dimensions characterize the testing process well, and are routinely used in our corporate environment, as well as in many others. (There are other important testing "dimensions," such as code coverage and key bug management, but studies of these are still in progress.)

To investigate the influences of these three major dimensions, our team gathered many metrics that are collected routinely during function and system testing on the main/integration branches of releases for a broad variety of major platforms. Our hope was to build a model, predictive of field reliability, that includes incoming, fix, and backlog variables. While we know that these dimensions are interdependent, they may turn out to be sufficiently orthogonal to not damage any resulting model because of high multicolinearity or other statistical difficulties.

The modeling work turned out to be quite successful: an incoming variable and a fix variable each correlated, in univariate linear regression models, with field reliability (the dependent variable) in the mid-80s% range, and in the multiple linear regression model that includes both independent variables, the correlation improved to the high-80s% level (since colinearity between the two is low).

The most highly predictive incoming bug variable is the cumulative count of incoming bugs discovered during the weeks of function and system testing. We have empirically determined that if 80% or more of the asymptote value of a Goel-Okumoto Shaped (GOS) cumulative incoming (S-shaped) growth curve is achieved during testing, the release is likely to be highly reliable in the field. In other words, if, with fairly constant test effort week to week, fewer and fewer bugs are found, at a certain point (i.e., 80% of the asymptote) in this weekly exponential decay, the release is likely to be in good shape. Here is a visual representation of this metric (Fig. 1).

The highly predictive bug fix variable is the decline of the weekly bug fix rate—if this rate declines to about 50% of the maximum observed weekly rate, the release is likely to be even more reliable than if only the incoming growth curve objective is met. This bug fix metric gauges late code churn, which many have found to be very damaging to code reliability. Bugs fixed late in the testing period are often found to

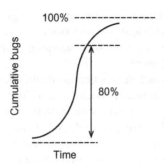

FIG. 1

Minimum cumulative incoming percentage needed to achieve best-in-class reliability

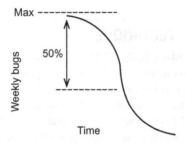

FIG. 2

Minimum weekly fix rate reduction needed to achieve best-in-class reliability

be inadequately tested, with a high percentage of the fixes causing collateral damage in the code. The following visual shows a weekly bug fixing profile, from the maximum weekly level to the end of testing. A reduction from the maximum of 50% or more is needed for high reliability (Fig. 2).

The modeled backlog metrics did not show strong predictive ability, largely because backlog reduction is already an important initiative, and under good control, for the company's major releases, and the releases of many other companies.

UNIVERSAL RELEASE CRITERIA MODEL

We call the overall model the "universal release criteria (URC)" model—"universal" only in the sense that we see strong correlations with customer experience for all the Cisco waterfall, hybrid waterfall/agile, and agile systems evaluated. These correlations are on the order of ~70% for the 195 releases on 77 different products evaluated so far. These releases/products constitute a broad range of operating systems, end user applications, collaboration tools, and other software products. As long as integration branch testing results in ~150 or more bugs, the accuracy of the field reliability predictions is sufficient, varying from ±9% at low cumulative growth levels to ±4% as the release nears the 80% incoming goal; the error bars are similar for the fix rate (late churn) metric.

Feature-level URC is used in practice to identify features that are underperforming either in the desired weekly decay of test finds or bug fixes. Problematic features are good candidates for exclusion from the release. Accurate tagging of bugs and query construction are essential, and if this is the case, we can track and assess the testing and bug fixing progress of features as small as three or four KLOC (thousands of lines of new+modified+ported source code). This surgical approach to ensure release readiness makes the URC technology more directly actionable, an attribute in high demand during the final stages of release preparation.

BEST ESTIMATION TECHNIQUE

We did not have, and could not find, a GOS routine that provides sufficient accuracy (<±15%) for calculations below ~60% of the software reliability growth curve's asymptote value. In order to provide test and bug fix teams with accurate weekly statuses during the first half or so of the test period, we developed a method that incorporates an improved slope-change detection algorithm that achieves an average of ~±7% measurement accuracy over the initial 60% of the growth curve. This novel approach has enabled us to give test and bug fix teams the ability to fairly accurately detect underachieving behavior early in the test cycle, giving them more time to implement remediation efforts. This technique is called the "best estimation technique," and is an example of how the need for close to real-time assessment of team behavior can be a practical outgrowth of the use of a well-known and powerful research method, the nonhomogeneous Poisson process (NHPP) growth modeling using the GOS method.

RESOURCE/SCHEDULE/CONTENT MODEL

The terms of the cumulative incoming growth and weekly fix rate model can be used to track weekly testing and bug fixing progress, often in time to detect underachievement and make some adjustments in resourcing, scheduling, or content. But at a minimum, we can use this reliability prediction model to help plan future releases. An extension of the URC calculation/reporting tool is a "what-if" release planning mechanism that is used to estimate additional test and/or bug fixing resources needed to achieve the URC metric goals. These estimates are based on the predecessor release's metrics performance. The test schedule time and content "dimensions" can likewise be adjusted, along with the resource dimensions, to optimize the release planning process. Our "resource/schedule/content (RSC)" model is the basis for a "what-if" capability in our release management toolset. This planning tool allows us to revise the test and bug fixing resources profile, the testing schedule, and the feature content to achieve improved URC metric results, based on URC metric values from underachieving predecessor releases. The RSC model can also be used in a "remediation" mode, where changes in resources, and/or schedule, and/or content can be adjusted during the test cycle. The resource/schedule/content planning questions exist, of course, in development and test environments that do not use the URC model ideas – therefore, we are developing a version of the RSC model that uses field bug levels of previous releases as a way to gauge how much additional resource, schedule, or content reduction is needed to achieve high reliability.

USING MODELS IN RELEASE MANAGEMENT

Release management staff, as well as the engineering groups, need to know, as soon as possible, if a release in testing is unlikely to meet customer reliability expectations. To provide this level of guidance, it is necessary to identify as accurately as possible the desired weekly incoming pattern as well as the desired weekly bug fix pattern. We routinely provide these weekly values by using the estimated new + modified + ported source code count for the upcoming release, multiplied by the historical defect density of the recent predecessor releases, to estimate the asymptote (i.e., the total bug content) of the new release. Fitting the growth curve to the test period and the fraction of the asymptote desired (80%), gives us a desired "target" curve for the cumulative incoming metric, and decomposing these values gives us the desired target curve for the weekly fix levels. Then, calculating the accuracy of the target curves, and the accuracies of the actual incoming growth and fix curves, enables us to construct error bars for all these curves, and in this way be quite sure if the teams are on track or underachieving each week during the test cycle.

For most teams, we goal these key metrics at aggressive levels in order to help them achieve best-in-class customer experience results (i.e., the software reliability experienced by the top 10% of the industry sector) for their customers in approximately three releases. For some teams, this timetable is too aggressive. To reach the goals, substantial changes need to be made, such as one or more of the following: adding resources, lengthening the test schedule, reducing the number of features, or substantially improving development and test practices. Some teams are not able to make substantial planning or process changes in three or four releases, particularly on short release-cycle projects. These teams are normally goaled less aggressively, but aggressively enough to ensure release-over-release improvement. Consistent release-over-release reliability improvement is the immediate goal, with best-in-class reliability as the longer-term objective. However, customer expectations are continually rising, even when best-in-class levels are reached, therefore release-over-release improvement continues to be critical.

RESEARCH TO IMPLEMENTATION: A DIFFICULT (BUT REWARDING) JOURNEY

Software engineering research, with a keen eye toward practical application, is essential in an organization that is striving to achieve best-in-class software reliability. But taking research from the proof of concept stage to the pilot stage to productional implementation is invariably a difficult task/journey. Organizations, and the individuals who comprise them, do not accept change readily. Therefore, new methods, even those based on solid software engineering concepts and experimental results, must be straightforward, intuitive, and adequately tooled. But if these goals are met, the rewards are large, including the increased work satisfaction of the engineers as best-in-class reliability becomes a reality.

How to tame your online services

Qingwei Lin, Jian-Guang Lou, Hongyu Zhang, Dongmei Zhang

Microsoft Research, Beijing, China

BACKGROUND

Online service systems, such as online banking systems and e-commerce systems, have become increasingly popular and important in our society. During the operation of an online service, a live-site service incident can happen: an unplanned interruption, outage, or degradation in the quality of the service. Such incidents can lead to huge economic loss or other serious consequences. For example, the estimated average cost of 1 h service downtime for Amazon.com is $180,000 [1].

Once a service incident occurs, the service provider should take actions immediately to diagnose the incident and restore the service as soon as possible. A typical procedure of incident management in practice (eg, at Microsoft and other service-provider companies) goes as follows. When the service monitoring system detects a service violation, the system automatically sends out an alert and makes a phone call to a group of on-call engineers to trigger an incident investigation. Given an incident, engineers need to understand what the problem is and how to resolve it. In ideal cases, engineers can identify the root cause of the incident and fix it quickly. However, in many cases, engineers are unable to identify or fix root causes within a short time, as it usually takes time to identify and fix the root causes, conduct regression testing, and re-deploy the new version to data centers. Thus, in order to recover the service as soon as possible, a common practice is to restore the service by identifying a temporary workaround solution (such as restarting a server component) to restore the service. Then, after service restoration, identifying and fixing the underlying root cause for the incident can be conducted via offline postmortem analysis. Incident management has become a critical task for online services. The goal is to minimize the service downtime and to ensure high quality of the provided services. In practice, incident management of an online service heavily depends on data collected at runtime of the service, such as service-level logs, performance counters, and machine/process/service-level events. Such monitoring data typically contains information that reflects the runtime state and behavior of the service. Based on the data collected, service incidents can be detected and mitigated in a timely way.

63

SERVICE ANALYSIS STUDIO

We formulated the problem of incident management for online services as a software analytics problem [2], which can be tackled with phases of task definition, data preparation, analytic-technology development, and deployment and feedback gathering. We carried out a 2-year research project, where we designed a set of incident management techniques based on the analysis of a huge amount of data collected at service runtime [3]. As a result of this project, we developed a tool called Service Analysis Studio (SAS), which targets real incident management scenarios of large-scale online services provided by Microsoft.

SAS includes a set of data-driven techniques for diagnosing service incidents. Each of these techniques targets a specific scenario and a certain type of data. Here we briefly introduce some of the major techniques SAS offers:

- *Identification of incident beacons from system metrics*: When engineers diagnose incidents of online services, they usually start by hunting for a small subset of system metrics that are symptoms of the incidents. We call such kinds of metrics "service-incident beacons." A service-incident beacon could provide useful information, helping engineers locate the cause of an incident. For example, when a resource-intensive SQL query blocks the execution of other queries accessing the same table, symptoms can be observed on monitoring data: the waiting time on the SQL-inducing lock becomes longer, and the event "SQL query time out failure" is triggered. Such metrics can be considered service-incident beacons. We developed data mining-based-techniques that helped engineers effectively and efficiently identify service-incident beacons from huge numbers of system metrics. The technical details can be found in [4,5].
- *Leveraging previous effort for recurrent incidents*: Engineers of an online service system may receive many similar incident reports. Therefore, leveraging the knowledge from past incidents can help improve the effectiveness and efficiency of incident management. The key here is to design a technique that automatically retrieves the past incidents similar to the new one, and then proposes a potential restoration action based on the past solutions. More details can be found in [6].
- *Mining suspicious execution patterns*: Transactional logs provide rich information for diagnosing service incidents. When scanning through the logs, engineers usually look for a set of log events that appear in the log sequences of failed requests, but not in the ones of the succeeded requests. Such a set of log events are named as suspicious execution patterns. A suspicious execution pattern could be an error message indicating a specific fault, or a combination of log events of several operations. For example, many normal execution paths look like (task start, user login, cookie validation success, access resource R, do the job, logout). In contrast, a failed execution path may look like (task start, user login, cookie not found, security token rebuild, access resource R error). The code branch reflected by (cookie not found, security token

rebuild, access resource R error) indicates a suspicious execution pattern. We proposed a mining-based technique to automatically identify suspicious execution patterns. The details of our technique can be found in [6].

SUCCESS STORY

We have successfully applied SAS to one of Microsoft's large-scale services (a geographically distributed, web-based service serving hundreds of millions of users). Similar to other online services, the Microsoft service is expected to provide high-quality service at all times. In the past, the service team faced great challenges in improving the effectiveness and efficiency of their incident management in order to provide high-quality service. SAS was first deployed to the datacenters of the service in June 2011. The engineers of the service team have been using SAS for incident management since then. The actual usage experience shows that SAS helps the engineers improve the effectiveness and efficiency of incident management. According to the usage data from a 6-month empirical study, about 91% of engineers used SAS to accomplish their incident management tasks and SAS was used to diagnose about 86% of service incidents. Now SAS has been successfully deployed to many Microsoft product datacenters and widely used by on-call engineers for incident management.

Our experience shows that incident management has become a critical task for a large-scale online service. Software analytics techniques can be successfully applied to ensure high quality and reliability of the service, utilizing the data collected at service runtime.

REFERENCES

[1] Patterson D. A simple way to estimate the cost of downtime. In: Proc. of LISA' 02; 2002. p. 185–8.
[2] Zhang D, Han S, Dang Y, Lou J, Zhang H, Xie T. Software analytics in practice. IEEE Softw 2013;30(5):30–7. (special issue on the many faces of software analytics).
[3] Lou J-G, Lin Q, Ding R, Fu Q, Zhang D, Xie T. Software analytics for incident management of online services: an experience report. In: Proceedings of the 28th IEEE/ACM international conference on automated software engineering (ASE 2013), Palo Alto, California; 2013.
[4] Lim M-H, Lou J-G, Zhang H, Fu Q, Teoh ABJ, Lin Q, et al. Identifying recurrent and unknown performance issues. In: Proceedings of IEEE international conference on data mining 2014 (ICDM 2014), Shenzhen, China; 2014.
[5] Fu Q, Lou J-G, Lin Q, Ding R, Zhang D, Ye Z, et al. Performance issue diagnosis for online service systems. In: Proceedings of 31st international symposium on reliable distributed systems (SRDS 2012); 2012.
[6] Ding R, Fu Q, Lou J-G, Lin Q, Zhang D, Shen J, et al. Healing online service systems via mining historical issue repositories. In: Proceedings of the 27th IEEE/ACM international conference on automated software engineering (ASE 2012), Essen, Germany; 2012.

Measuring individual productivity

T. Fritz
University of Zurich, Zurich, CHE

CHAPTER OUTLINE

In the last century, one company was said to have determined the price of a software product by the estimated number of lines of code written. In turn, the company also paid their software developers based on the number of lines of code produced per day. What happened next is that the company's developers started "gaming the system"—they suddenly wrote a lot more code, while the functionality captured in the code decreased. As one might imagine, adding more lines of code to a program without changing the behavior is easy. So incentivizing employees on a single outcome metric might just foster this behavior.

Overall, this example shows that it is not easy to find a good measure for a developer's success or productivity. In some domains, such as car manufacturing, specific measures on the quantity of the outcome, such as the number of cars produced in a day, have worked well to incentivize employees and to measure their success. In the software development domain, however, where the outcome and the overall process of developing software is less clearly defined and less tangible, such outcome measures are difficult to define. In particular, trying to reduce the complex activity of developing software into a single measure of one particular outcome of the development process is probably impossible.

NO SINGLE AND SIMPLE BEST METRIC FOR SUCCESS/ PRODUCTIVITY

In a study we conducted, we asked professional developers how they measure and assess their personal productivity [1]. The results show that software developers generally want a combination of measures to assess productivity, and these combinations varied significantly across developers. Even for the one metric that developers rated highest overall for assessing productivity—the number of work items (tasks, bugs) closed—developers stated that it heavily depends on the complexity and size of the task, so that further information is needed to interpret this metric.

These findings further indicate that there is no single and simple best measure for assessing a developer's productivity. Given the variety of artifacts produced during software development, such as code artifacts, test cases, bug reports, and documentation, it is also not surprising that just focusing on the code would does not adequately reflect the progress a developer makes in his/her work. As one example of the variety of artifacts generated by developers every day, are the around 10,000 Java source files, 26,000 Bugzilla bug reports and the 45,000 newsgroup entries that were created over one development cycle of Eclipse—an open source IDE [2]. While the code is being compiled and executed in the end, the other artifacts are just as important to the process to make sure the software product is developed the right way and works.

MEASURE THE PROCESS, NOT JUST THE OUTCOME

The variety in outcomes or artifacts generated in the process is just one important aspect for measuring a developer's work and productivity. A majority of the participants in our study also mentioned that they are particularly productive when they get into the "flow" without many context switches. So rather than just focusing on a measure of the outcomes of the development activity, such as the code artifacts, the process of developing the software is important as well. Software development is a complex process that is comprised of various activities and frequent interruptions and interactions with multiple stakeholders involved in the development process, such as fellow developers, requirements engineers, or even customers [3–5].

Measuring aspects of the process of developing software, such as flow or context switches, is difficult since their cost and impact on productivity vary and are difficult to determine. For example, take a developer who is testing a system and has to wait for a build or for the application to start up. Switching context in this situation to perform a shorter task and filling the time in between might actually increase his/ her productivity. On the other hand, take a developer who is programming and in the "flow." When the developer is interrupted by another developer and asked about last weekend's football scores, the forced context switch is expensive, decreases productivity, and can even result in more errors being made overall, as studies have shown [6]. So overall, while aspects of the process are important for measuring productivity, they are difficult to quantify and measure. Recently emerging biometric sensing technologies might provide new means to measure such aspects of individual productivity better, especially due to their pervasiveness and their decreasing invasiveness.

ALLOW FOR MEASURES TO EVOLVE

When it comes to a person's fitness and health, wearable fitness tracking devices, such as the Fitbit [7] or the Withings Pulse Band [8] have recently gained widespread adoption. Most of these devices employ a simple step count measure that has also been shown to be very successful in providing users valuable insights on their activity level and in promoting and improving health and fitness (eg, [9,10]). In an interview-based study with 30 participants who had used and adopted wearable activity tracking devices "in the wild" for between 3 and 54 months, we found that the step count provided long-term motivation for people to become and stay active. Yet, while for several participants, the devices helped foster engagement in fitness, the device, and in particular the step count measure, did not support their increasingly sophisticated fitness goals. As one example, the step count helped some participants to walk more and start running, but when they started adding new activities to further increase fitness, such as weight lifting or yoga, the devices failed to capture these [11].

Similarly, the activities and responsibilities of an individual developer evolve over time and thus the measures capturing his/her productivity have to evolve. For example, someone might start out as a developer in a team, and later on be promoted to manage teams. While in the first role, the number of bug fixes completed might be a reasonable proxy for their productivity, but as a manager, they will focus mostly on their team being productive and have little to no time to work on bug fixes themselves.

GOODHART'S LAW AND THE EFFECT OF MEASURING

Goodhart's law states that "When a measure becomes a target, it ceases to be a good measure." This effect happened in the first example presented in this chapter. As soon as the lines of code metric was used to measure a developer's productivity and affected the developer's salary, it ceased to be a good indicator, with developers gaming the system to benefit. Coming back to the fitness-tracking domain, we found from our interviews that the numerical feedback provided by the devices effected users' behavior in ways other than the intended fitness improvement. In many cases, the accountability and getting credit for activities became important, and even more important than the original goal, so that users adjusted their sports activities for better accountability, and became unhappy and annoyed when they forgot their devices despite being very active, or were merely "fishing for numbers" or gaming the system. One user, for example, stopped going backward on an elliptical machine since the device did not pick up on it.

The effect depends on how and what a measure is being used for, eg, is it just used for personal retrospection or is it used for adjusting someone's salary? In any case, one needs to assess the influence a certain measure might have on a developer's behavior and the risks it bears.

HOW TO MEASURE INDIVIDUAL PRODUCTIVITY?

Measuring productivity of individual developers is challenging given the complex and multifaceted nature of developing software. There is not a single and simple best measure that works for everyone. Rather, you will have to tailor the measurement to the specific situation and context you are looking at and the specific goal you have in mind with your measurement. For example, if you are conducting a research study on the productivity gain of a code navigation support tool, a measure such as the edit ratio [12], ie, the ratio between edit and select events, might be a good indicator. However, this neglects other aspects, such as interruptions that occur or the resumption lag, which might be important measures when looking at a more general developer productivity definition. Similarly, due to the collaborative nature of software development, it is not necessarily possible to isolate an individual's productivity from the team's productivity. Take, for example, the idea of reducing interruptions for an individual developer. While reducing interruptions for the single developer might very well increase her/his productivity, it could block other team members from working and decrease their productivity, as well as the team's overall.

One also has to assess who will or should have access to the measurement data and how might this affect the developer's behavior and thus the productivity measure in the end. If the developer knows that her/his boss will have access to certain parts of the data, it is likely that the developer will make sure that the data that the boss has access to fits the purpose rather than the reality; whereas, if the data is just for the developer or, for example, independent research that anonymizes data completely, it is more likely that the data will reflect reality. Finally, a very important point is the privacy of the collected data. Are you actually able to collect the data needed from the developers, are you allowed to analyze it and did you make sure that only the intended people have access to it? Since any productivity measure will most likely require fairly sensitive information that could be used for or against someone, you need to make sure to pay attention to privacy concerns, treat them carefully, and be transparent about who will have access to the data.

REFERENCES

[1] Meyer AN, Fritz T, Murphy GC, Zimmermann T. Software developers? Perceptions of productivity. In: Proc. of the ACM SIGSOFT 22nd international symposium on the foundations of software engineering 2014 (FSE'14); 2014.

[2] http://www.eclipse.org/eclipse/development/eclipse_3_0_stats.html.

[3] Müller S, Fritz T. Stakeholders' information needs for artifacts and their dependencies in a real world context. In: Proc. of the IEEE international conference on software maintenance 2013 (ICSM'13); 2013.

[4] Perry D, Staudenmayer N, Votta L. People, organizations, and process improvement. IEEE Softw 1994;11(4):36–45.

[5] Singer J, Lethbridge T, Vinson N, Anquetil N. An examination of software engineering work practices. In: CASCON first decade high impact papers (CASCON '10); 2010.

[6] Bailey BP, Konstan JA. On the need for attention-aware systems: measuring effects of interruption on task performance, error rate, and affective state. Comput Hum Behav 2006;22(4):685–708.

[7] http://www.fitbit.com/.

[8] http://www2.withings.com/us/en/products/pulse.

[9] Bravata D, Smith-Spangler C, Sundaram V, Gienger A, Lin N, Lewis R, et al. Using pedometers to increase physical activity and improve health. JAMA 2007;298:2296–304.

[10] Consolvo S, McDonald D, Toscos T, Chen M, Froehlich J, Harrison B, et al. Activity sensing in the wild: a field trial of UbiFit garden. In: Proc. CHI'08; 2008.

[11] Fritz T, Huang EM, Murphy GC, Zimmermann T. Persuasive technology in the real world: a study of long-term use of activity sensing devices for fitness. In: Proc. of the ACM conference on human factors in computing systems 2014 (CHI'14); 2014.

[12] Kersten M, Murphy GC. Using task context to improve programmer productivity. In: Proc. of the ACM SIGSOFT 14th international symposium on the foundations of software engineering 2006 (FSE'06); 2006.

Stack traces reveal attack surfaces

C. Theisen, L. Williams

North Carolina State University, Raleigh, NC, United States

CHAPTER OUTLINE

Stack traces from software crashes have been used for a variety of fault localization purposes. Stack traces in the context of software crashes are a record of the active stack frames, or code, active during the time period of the crash. Liblit and Aiken [1] use stack traces from crashes to build "timelines" of the possible actions a piece of software took right before a crash took place. By stepping backward through the call stack from crashes and building a map of possible paths, the researchers can then summarize the set of nodes common to a set of crashes to determine the possibly flawed path. Paths that appear frequently in multiple crashes are suspects for containing faults.

Wu et al. [2] developed a tool called CrashLocator, which can help practitioners locate a faulty function based on stack traces from crashes of the system under test. By combining the stack traces with information from the static call graph of the system, the tool determines which functions appear most frequently in the set of crashes, and provides this information to the user. The more often a function appears in crashes, the more likely a fault exists in that function. Stack traces were also used in the development of StackMine [3], a tool that uses stack traces to help software development teams discover software performance bugs in use at Microsoft. Industry professionals also recognize the importance of using stack traces; Windows Error Reporting has been in use at Microsoft for years [4], and uses the scale of Microsoft's crash reporting data to identify and fix bugs that would otherwise be missed.

ANOTHER USE OF STACK TRACES?

Take a look at Fig. 1. This graph represents a software system, with individual nodes representing code elements (such as binaries, files, or functions). This graph is pretty dense and difficult to parse, right? If you look at a software system with no prior

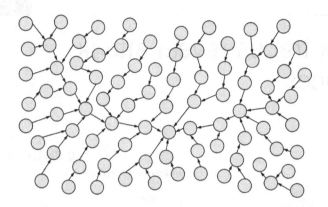

FIG. 1

A tangled web of files. Each node represents a file in a software system, while the edges represent relationships between files, such as function calls.

knowledge and attempt to dive in to find vulnerabilities, you'll feel a similar level of confusion. To combat that effect, security professionals have developed the concept of an attack surface.

Okay, so what is the attack surface? The Open Web Security Project defines it as the paths in and out of a system, the data that travels those paths, and the code that protects both. In short; if someone or something outside the system can send data through it, it's on the attack surface. That's a pretty useful definition to busy security engineers. By focusing on code considered to be on the attack surface, they can prioritize their security hardening efforts, like code review and refactoring, on the code exposed to the outside. That's more important than hardening code in your internal test suites or unreachable areas of your code.

While that all sounds good, explicitly defining the attack surface of a software system is hard. Traditionally, defining the attack surface has meant a lot of manual effort on the part of the security teams. That's obviously an issue, because you want those resources tied up as little as possible. There have been efforts to automate this process, but those efforts were limited to Application program interface (API) scanning techniques and the like; they don't capture the depth areas of the attack surface beyond the API. What sort of new metrics could we use to determine what code in a system is relevant for security professionals? Stack traces, maybe?

Stack traces may have several useful properties for security professionals. They represent user activity that puts the system under stress, and they also allow the security professional to get inside the head of attackers. When attackers are looking for ways into a system, one common technique is to try to get the system to crash, creating a denial-of-service. Not only do crashes indicate where data handling may have flaws, they also give the attacker more information on code flow within the system they're attacking.

ATTACK SURFACE APPROXIMATION

Researchers at North Carolina State University and Microsoft Research have developed a technique called *attack surface approximation* [5]. In this approach, the attack surface of a system is determined by looking at stack traces from crash dumps from the target system. The crash dump stack traces are parsed out into the individual code elements that are seen on each stack trace. Depending on the stack trace in question, these elements could be binaries, files, or functions. Any code element that is seen on at least one stack trace is considered to be on the attack surface of the system, as determined by this approach. Put another way, we color nodes from our original graph in Fig. 2 red if they are seen in at least one stack trace, as seen in the preceding figure. Researchers also explored other metrics, such as the frequency of appearance of code elements, how often code elements appear next to each other, and the shapes that form within the graph representation of the stack traces.

Early results from research into *attack surface approximation* have yielded interesting results. In a study on Windows 8, 48.4% of shipped binaries were identified as appearing in at least one stack trace, while 94.8% of vulnerabilities fixed over the same time period appeared in that same 48.4% of binaries. Busy security professionals can use this information to focus their security testing and hardening efforts on half of the codebase while getting 95% of the vulnerabilities. Attack surface approximation has also been performed on Mozilla Firefox, with 8.4% of files appearing in at least one stack trace. Additionally, 72.1% of vulnerabilities occurred in the files placed on the attack surface [6].

One of the advantages of this approach is its simplicity. If your software system outputs any sort of stack trace when it fails, this approach could apply to you! No additional metrics are necessary to see practical returns; parsing out individual code elements from your stack trace dataset is enough to build your list of code on the attack surface. For organizations without extensive resources, attack surface

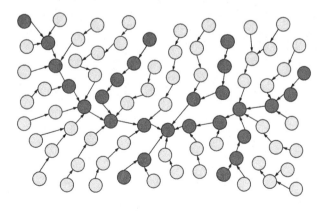

FIG. 2

Making some sense of the tangled web, color files that appear in stack traces.

approximation is a useful first step for determining where to start security hardening efforts. Another advantage of the approach is its scalability. Attack surface approximation can be applied to any software system that generates stack traces, independent of the language used to develop the software. Stack traces are already collected by many software organizations, which means attack surface approximation can make sure of existing data to draw new insights about software systems.

REFERENCES

[1] Liblit B, Aiken A. Building a better backtrace: techniques for postmortem program analysis. Berkeley: University of California; 2002.
[2] Wu R, Zhang H, Cheung S-C, Kim S. CrashLocator: locating crashing faults based on crash stacks. In: Proceedings of the 2014 international symposium on software testing and analysis; 2014.
[3] Han S, Dang Y, Ge S, Zhang D, Xie T. Performance debugging in the large via mining millions of stack traces. In: Proceedings of the 34th international conference on software engineering; 2012.
[4] Glerum K, Kinshumann K, Greenberg S, Aul G, Orgovan V, Nichols G, et al. Debugging in the (very) large: ten years of implementation and experience. In: Proceedings of the ACM SIGOPS 22nd symposium on operating systems principles; 2009. p. 103–16.
[5] Theisen C, Herzig K, Morrison P, Murphy B, Williams L. Approximating attack surfaces with stack traces. In: Companion proceedings of 37th international conference on software engineering; 2015.
[6] Theisen C, Krishna R, Williams L. Strengthening the evidence that attack surfaces can be approximated with stack traces. NCSU technical report.

Visual analytics for software engineering data

Zhitao Hou, Hongyu Zhang, Haidong Zhang, Dongmei Zhang

Microsoft Research, Beijing, China

Many data analysis techniques have been widely used in practice to enable software practitioners to perform data exploration and analysis in order to obtain insightful and actionable knowledge for real tasks around software and services [1]. Although these techniques are effective, they require substantial knowledge and skills and are typically performed by "data scientists." Ordinary users (such as programmers, marketing personnel, service operators, managers, etc.) may find it difficult to apply these techniques to quickly explore the data and obtain insights by themselves. For example, users may have to learn SQL queries in order to extract data from a database, and to learn statistical techniques to analyze the data. Users often need to write programs to analyze data extracted from an Excel/text file. These techniques may increase the cost of data exploration for ordinary users and create high barriers to entry.

Many methods can be designed to democratize data analysis in software engineering. We advocate for incorporating visual analytics techniques into the analysis of software engineering data. Visual analytics is "the science of analytical reasoning facilitated by interactive visual interfaces" [2,3]. It focuses on the interactive exploration and manipulation of the data. Using visual analytics techniques, a user can perform several successive queries and view the data in a variety of formats before satisfactorily identifying the data in which they are most interested.

The Software Analytics group at Microsoft Research Asia developed a visual analytics tool called MetroEyes. MetroEyes can import data from external sources (such as Excel files or SQL databases) automatically. Data are represented as visual objects, such as a slice in a pie chart, a bar in a bar chart, or a series legend in a line chart, etc. MetroEyes provides an interactive graphical interface that enables users to directly click/touch/move all these objects. The visual objects can also be composed to form a new chart. MetroEyes is able to interpret the intentions of the visual operations, extract corresponding data from the data source, and create a new chart.

For example, assume that we have an Excel spreadsheet which contains the app sales data of a multinational software corporation. The corporation has three product teams (code named TeamA, TeamB, and TeamC) developing Game and Education Apps. The data includes yearly app sales in different counties, along with the detailed sales of different teams and categories. There are five columns ("Year," "Team," "Category," "Country," "Sales") in the spreadsheet. Some sample records are shown in the following table.

Year	Team	Category	Country	Sales (M)
2010	TeamA	Game	United States	0.5
2010	TeamC	Game	China	0.5
2010	TeamA	Education	United States	0.1
2011	TeamC	Education	China	0.4
2011	TeamB	Game	United States	0.3
2011	TeamB	Education	China	0.2

In MetroEyes, users can perform data exploration through direct manipulation of the visual objects. Say the users want to explore the sales of TeamA. As illustrated in Fig. 1, users can directly select the TeamA bar from the bar chart representing the contribution of each team to Sales, and drag and drop it into the canvas. The tool can then extract from the data source the app sales data contributed by TeamA, and display it in a new bar chart. This data operation selects a dimension value (Team = TeamA) and finds out its app sales, which is equivalent to the SQL query: SELECT Sales, Team FROM AppSales WHERE Team = "TeamA." Note that each bar in the bar chart is a visual object, which can be touched and moved around. Furthermore, each bar represents the percentage of sales each team contributes (eg, the TeamA bar indicates the percentage of sales of TeamA). The visual operations over the object have semantic meanings and correspond to certain data operations.

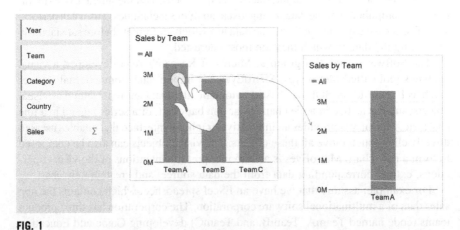

FIG. 1

Explore the sales of TeamA.

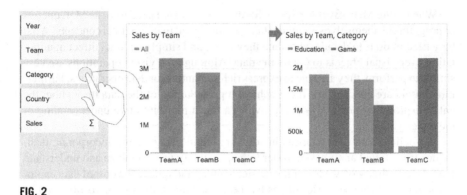

FIG. 2

Explore the sales data by Team and Category.

As another example, say users want to explore the sales data by Team and Category. As illustrated in Fig. 2, users first select the Team dimension and drop it into the canvas. MetroEyes extracts the team data from the data source, and displays a chart that contains the app sales data broken down by Team. Users can then select the Category dimension and drop it into the chart. Finally, MetroEyes displays a chart that shows the Team's sale data, broken down by category. This data operation explores data along multiple dimensions (in this case, the Team and Category dimensions), which is equivalent to the SQL query: SELECT Sales, Team, Category FROM AppSales.

MetroEyes also enables changes from one data visualization format to another, and supports different types of data exploration tasks such as filtering and sorting. For example, data can be sorted through the use of gestures, which is illustrated in Fig. 3.

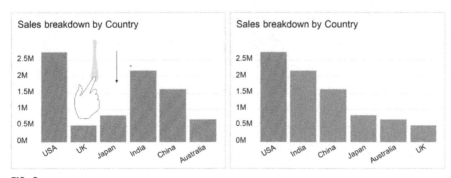

FIG. 3

The gesture for sorting.

When using MetroEyes to explore SE data, users do not need to write SQL queries or programs by themselves, or understand sophisticated mathematical concepts. What they need to do is to decide what data they want, and simply conduct direct manipulation over visual objects to obtain the data. Although the visual operations are very simple to perform, they are able to express rich semantics for data operations. Furthermore, users are able to view the graphical representation of the data throughout the entire exploration process, which provides a much more intuitive understanding of the underlying data.

We believe that data analysis in software engineering should incorporate techniques from visual analytics, in order to help ordinary users analyze and understand their data. In this way, we lower the barrier to entry and reduce the cost of data exploration for ordinary users. MetroEyes has been used internally by Microsoft teams to perform various analytical tasks. We have successfully transferred the main concepts and experiences of MetroEyes to the Microsoft Power BI product (http://www.pow erbi.com), which was officially released in 2015.

REFERENCES

[1] Zhang D, Han S, Dang Y, Lou J, Zhang H, Xie T. Software analytics in practice. IEEE Softw 2013;30(5):30–7.
[2] Kielman J, Thomas J, Guest editors. Special issue: foundations and frontiers of visual analytics. Inf Vis 2009;8(4):239–314.
[3] Thomas J, Cook K. Illuminating the path: research and development agenda for visual analytics. National Visualization and Analytics Ctr; 2005. http://www.amazon.com/Illumi nating-Path-Research-Development-Analytics/dp/0769523234.

Gameplay data plays nicer when divided into cohorts

J. Huang

Brown University, Providence, RI, United States

COHORT ANALYSIS AS A TOOL FOR GAMEPLAY DATA

"Gameplay data" refers to the captured logs that video games generate. It is often used to help with matchmaking or providing players a way to replay their matches. As a software analytics tool, gameplay data provides a broad naturalistic dataset that can be useful for learning about players. However, game histories and replays, while precise and correct, have a lot of inherent noise. This noise comes from players switching accounts, disconnection issues, environmental changes, players not playing to win, and so forth. It is difficult to draw any conclusions from looking at the mix of vastly different players. Additionally, the sheer amount of data collected makes simple descriptive analytics not terribly useful, and because factors are not manipulated as experiments during the game, findings show correlations rather than explain causal effects.

Cohort analysis turns raw player data logs into groups of players, or "cohorts." By having groups include enough players, the variation that occurs during a single player's progression with a game will average out among other players. The assumption is that when players are intentionally divided by a specific game condition, other unrelated conditions will be equally represented in each cohort so they will not affect the analyses.

PLAY TO LOSE

During an internship at Microsoft Research, I worked with a dataset comprising the history of all matches from the first-person shooter game Halo Reach. The team I belonged to was particularly interested in learning what types of players were likely to stick around to play longer, also known as "retention." So one of the things I investigated was what happened to a player in their first 100 matches. Each player's history was completely different from another's. Looking at any individual player revealed no clues about retention because the players were so diverse in what they did. Lumping all the players together didn't do much either, besides producing smooth-looking graphs and uninteresting averages.

But when I grouped the players by skill level at different points in time, I noticed an interesting pattern of how their skill levels changed in the first 100 matches. In every group where players were declining in skill (unbeknownst to themselves), the average player in each group was playing about 15% more matches than the players who were improving. This was the opposite of what our team expected, which was that players would enjoy improving and play more if they got better. It appeared that for many players, improvement was not a relevant condition for them to stick with the game, and this discovery opened up new directions to pursue.

FORMING COHORTS

Cohorts can be formed from any condition, but a few conditions especially make sense for grouping players. A common one used by many games is grouping players who started playing during the same week. So rather than examining all data within a particular calendar date range, a start-based cohort would separate players by when they began playing the game. This approach removes confounding factors due to changes in the game itself (eg, patches or server problems), changes in the game's culture and overall player base (eg, strategies published online or casual players joining later), or even world events like holidays or popular sporting events that can temporarily change the game's demographic. For example, if players in a cohort that started later stick with the game for longer, this may be a signal that the game has become more compelling to play.

Another condition for grouping cohorts can be skill level, or, putting together players who are similar in skill. For competitive games, this is often based on an Elo rating system [1]—a method for calculating the relative skill level among players. These skill levels can be determined after a period of play; when forming these cohorts, players within a skill cohort are comparable no matter how they started the game. Comparing players between skill levels provides clues about what differentiates more skilled players from weaker players.

Note that it is useful, but not crucial, to build cohorts of similar size. As long as each cohort has enough players in it to be statistically relevant, it will be fine in the analysis.

CASE STUDIES OF GAMEPLAY DATA

From the same Halo Reach dataset, we later sought to find out for the players who gained skill the fastest how frequently they played (or essentially, practiced). We formed cohorts of players based on the average number of matches they played per week. From these groupings, we were able to determine that players who played four to eight matches per week on average were the most efficient in gaining skill, more so than players who played more frequently. But we could learn more from forming yet another set of cohorts—groups of players who took breaks; this analysis revealed that week-long breaks from playing Halo Reach required a period of recovery time when the player returned. So consistent and sustained play seemed to be the optimal way to get the most skill out of every match. However, by simply dividing the players into yet another cohort grouping of total number of matches played, players who simply played a greater number of matches (while starting at a lower skill level and gaining skill slowly), still overcame the less-frequent players by playing vastly more matches in the same amount of time [2]. So three ways of forming cohorts each taught us something new.

What about a cohort of the very top players? We formed a cohort of players who ended up with the highest skill ratings after 7 months of play to examine if there was anything particular that led them to become the best at Halo Reach. The highest skilled players consistently improved since the beginning of their play, and showed relatively few dips in skill as they progressed. Since dips are often signals of experimentation and transition to a new strategy, this suggests that the best players already had the habits and tools to succeed from the very beginning.

Unsatisfied with this conclusion, I worked with colleagues to use replays from the real-time strategy game StarCraft 2 to examine the in-game behavioral differences between players of different skill cohorts [3]. Using cohort analysis again, we found that better players are more adept at manipulating many units simultaneously, especially during time-pressure situations. The behavioral data also suggested that these habits are gained from a series of seemingly meaningless warm-up actions of rotating through units that actually develop muscle memory. These were actionable findings that gave us better insight into understanding a pathway to acquire skill in competitive games.

CHALLENGES OF USING COHORTS

There are a few instances where it is easy to end up with wrong conclusions in cohort analysis.

1.   When looking at a particular difference between cohorts, also compare these differences within players of a cohort. If there is a greater difference in that variable within players of a cohort than between cohorts, then that variable might actually not be different between cohorts.

2. Cohorts may be biased in ways you do not expect. For example, a cohort of players that started together after the game's release date may be enthusiasts who jump to new games quickly, so they may tend to play a game for a short period of time. They may also be more experienced with games of this genre, and gain skill faster than a later cohort. As another example, a more skilled cohort may comprise players of a younger demographic because of their better motor control reaction, which is useful in the game; as a side-effect, these players may have more time to play the game compared to older, less-skilled players.

3. Mining data from games, whether with cohort analysis or other methods, still requires care when attempting to make causal claims. It may be overreaching to say that performing more actions per second leads to more wins when these two variables are correlated, because it is possible that there is something that causes both of these conditions.

SUMMARY

Gameplay data is inherently noisy due to many potential environmental factors, but cohort analysis can help extract the signal. Form cohorts to control for different conditions, then compare these cohorts to find differences that may help provide insight about the players. Cohorts based on the install date of the game make it possible to find out whether changes in the software have a long-term effect. Forming cohorts based on some condition of the players, such as skill level, can reveal how these groups are different and why they are different.

REFERENCES

[1] Elo AE. The rating of chess players, past and present. New York: Arco Pub.; 1978.
[2] Huang J, Zimmermann T, Nagappan N, Harrison C, Phillips BC. Mastering the art of war: how patterns of gameplay influence skill in Halo. In: Proceedings of the SIGCHI conference on human factors in computing systems. New York: ACM; 2013. p. 695–704.
[3] Yan EQ, Huang J, Cheung GK. Masters of control: behavioral patterns of simultaneous unit group manipulation in StarCraft 2. In: Proceedings of the 33rd annual ACM conference on human factors in computing systems. New York: ACM; 2015. p. 3711–20.

A success story in applying data science in practice

A. Bener*, B. Turhan[†], A. Tosun[‡], B. Caglayan[§], E. Kocaguneli[¶]

Ryerson University, Toronto, ON, Canada[*]
University of Oulu, Finland[†]
Istanbul Technical University, Maslak Istanbul, Turkey[‡]
Lero, University of Limerick, Ireland[§]
Microsoft, Seattle, WA, United States[¶]

CHAPTER OUTLINE

In software engineering, the primary objective is delivering high-quality systems within budget and time constraints. Managers struggle to make many decisions under a lot of uncertainty. They would like to be confident in the product, team, and the processes. Therefore, the need for evidence-based decision making, a.k.a. data science and analysis, has been growing in the software development industry as data becomes available. Data science involves analytics for using data to understand the past and present, to analyze past performance, and for using optimization and/ or prediction techniques [1].

In the past couple of decades in our research lab (formerly Softlab, now Data Science Lab), we have been working with small- to large-scale software development organizations to conduct data science and analytics projects. These projects involve gaining insights into the daily processes, and building learning-based predictive models to improve resource planning and allocation.

Software analytics must follow a process that starts with problem identification framing both the business problem and the analytics problem. Throughout this process, stakeholder agreement needs to be obtained and/or re-obtained through effective communication. The end goal for any software analytics project should be to address a genuine problem in the industry. Therefore, the outcome of the analytics project could be transferred and embedded into the decision-making process of the organization [1].

We have been collaborating with one of our research partners since 2007 to build a comprehensive metrics and measurement system, and then to build learning-based predictive models for defect prediction, code dependency/missing dependency prediction, issue allocation, technical debt, etc. The company employs an incremental software development process that has new releases every 2 weeks. Therefore, they need an end-to-end measurement and analysis approach to predict defects in order to better organize their testing resources.

This chapter offers an overview of this process.

OVERVIEW

In this work, our client's main software engineering problems were measurement, effective testing, reliability, process and project management, and human resources management. Over the years, we deployed many predictive models addressing these problems. We have constantly been providing software analytics by mining various data repositories of the company. Some of the models we deployed have been successful, and we conducted before and after cost/benefit analyses of the deployed models [2]. In most cases, the output of the analytics has led to process changes and more effective and timely release decision making under uncertainty. We reported successes and failures, lessons learned, as well as direct feedback from the developers and managers of the organization to understand the reasons for failures [2,3].

Phase 1: In the early days of our collaboration, we first tackled the problems of code quality improvement, reducing the testing costs, and decreasing the defect rates. Our solution was an implementation of a bug tracing and matching system, a measurement and data extraction tool (Prest), and a defect prediction model [3–6]. We have done a comprehensive analysis to validate the need for an intelligent oracle (iFitnesse, a learning-based prediction model).

- First we analyzed the raw data by extracting metrics from the source code. We compared metric ranges with the one on NASA datasets [7] as the benchmark. This analysis gave us a picture of common code writing practices in the company. For example, we found out that lines of comment/code, and vocabulary were low, and modularity was high.
- Second, we estimated the testing effort in terms of what amount of code should be reviewed, and how much testing effort we needed to inspect modules. Third, we

constructed a rule-based model as an alternative to a learning-based model. The rule-based model required them to inspect 45% of code in order to detect 15% of defects. This was not practical considering their release cycles. Mining their code repository revealed a hidden factor: static code dependencies as an effective feature leading to defect proneness of the software. We included call graph metrics based on a PageRank algorithm in building the defect prediction model. This increased the information content of the predictive model and resulted in a decrease in testing effort by an additional 4%. Overall, the prediction model that we built was able to detect 70% of the bugs by inspecting only 3% of the code. This has resulted in 95% improvement in the testing effort. We also used the same prediction model to determine candidate software classes for refactoring instead of predicting defects in the upcoming releases by focusing on the complexity metrics [8]. In this case, our predictor was able to detect 82% of the refactored classes with 13% of manual inspection effort on average.

Phase 2: The second phase of the project focused on mining different sources of data and metrics to improve the information content of the prediction model as well as gaining new insights from the data. These new sources of data included mining version histories, and extracting call graphs on the entire code base so that version-based and application-based defect prediction models could be built. In this phase of the project we used churn metrics and call graph metrics to improve the false alarm rates. Mining different data sources and model calibration kept the detection rates constant compared to Phase 1 results of the project; however, it improved the false alarm rates by 15%, translating into a further 25% improvement in testing effort.

Phases 1 and 2 of the project not only fully met their project objectives and provided tangible benefits to the company, there were also additional benefits as a result of new insights gained through data science and analytics: process changes in defect monitoring and matching; development of the metric extraction and analysis tool, Prest [5]; a detailed analysis of different software development of methodologies and their impact on code quality; and refactoring prediction.

Phase 3: This phase of the project focused on building a reliability model, or, as we called it, "confidence factor modeling." The problem was to predict the confidence level of a given release before it is put into production. The company was using a linear formula based on expert biases. In this phase, we built a Bayesian network model to predict the confidence level of a release in preproduction. Such a model enabled the managers to better understand causal relationships using data and algorithms, and make an informed decision on when to stop testing. Our model was able to accurately predict the confidence level of releases based on post-release defect severity [4].

ANALYTICS PROCESS

As we reported in our earlier publications, successful deployments of data science and analytics in this particular project with our industry partner followed a process (Fig. 1) and had the following characteristics. In our previous publications we focused on the aspects of communication with management, and the development teams, to share our experience in terms of lessons learned. In this chapter we tell the story from a data science process point of view.

DATA COLLECTION

Data collection requires identification and prioritization of data needs and available sources depending on the context. Qualitative and quantitative data collection methods may be required, depending on the problem. In some cases, data acquisition demands a tool development first, followed by harmonizing, rescaling, cleaning, and sharing data within the organization.

EXPLORATORY DATA ANALYSIS

The simplest way to get insight from data is through descriptive statistics. Even a simple analysis or visualization may reveal hidden facts in the data. Later, predictive models utilizing data mining techniques may be built to aid the decision-making process in an organization.

MODEL SELECTION

Selection of suitable data mining techniques, depending on the problem, is critical while building the prediction model. Factors such as the definition of the problem, and the maturity of the data collection process in a company and expected benefits from the predictive model may also affect model construction. In addition, insights gained from descriptive statistics may be used in the construction of predictive models [1].

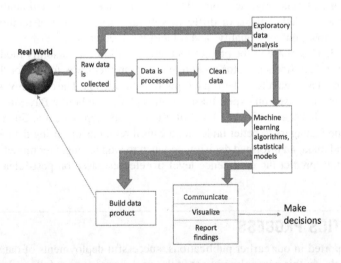

FIG. 1

The data science and analytics process [9].

PERFORMANCE MEASURES AND BENEFIT ANALYSIS

Predictive models need to be evaluated, which requires the definition of certain performance measures, appropriate statistical tests, as well as the effect size analysis [1].

COMMUNICATION PROCESS—BEST PRACTICES
PROBLEM SELECTION

In problem selection, we need to ask the right, or important, questions. It is important to involve the domain expert and/or the practitioner at this stage. We need to make sure that the hypotheses are consistent with questions since these will be the basis of the "statement of problem." Failing to ask the right questions and inconsistencies in hypothesis formulation would also lead to methodological pitfalls such as hypothesis testing errors, issues of statistical power, issues in the construction of dependent/independent variables, and reliability and validity issues.

Tool Support Having automated tool support, such as Prest [5], made it easier and faster to access the data.

MANAGERIAL SUPPORT

As in any project, data science projects need full support of management at all levels.

PROJECT MANAGEMENT

It is important to have a detailed project plan signed off on by all parties. Once the project plan is in place, it needs to be rigorously monitored in order to enable corrective action on a timely basis if there are challenges.

TRUSTED RELATIONSHIP

We have been collaborating with this company since 2007, and it is now a mature and trusted relationship. Such a relationship makes it easier to communicate easily at different levels, and hence, helps the researchers to better understand cause-effect relationships.

SUMMARY

In a period of 9 years, our research lab successfully graduated three PhD, and four MSc students who worked in collaboration with this company. On both sides, we created an open environment to share knowledge, formulate problems, and solve problems as one team. On our part, we made a great effort to understand their problems and help them achieve their goals so that they could see the benefit of the output of our models in their daily processes.

Most of the time, we went beyond our defined research contract/objectives to accommodate a need on their part. Prest and Dione is one good example of a data extraction and analytics tool that we built to provide developer-level support. Over the course of 9 years, there were times that we faced push backs, especially when the company went through major organization changes a few times. Once a push back occurred, we self-reflected and used data science to our benefit. We learned from our own mistakes, and also showed the new team the tangible benefits (before/after analyses) of using our models, tools, and techniques. Trust is built over a period of time by going through difficulties together. In this specific case, the company has continued to collaborate with the new research lab (lead by Prof. Bener), the Data Science Lab in Toronto, by giving us remote access and meeting slots over Skype.

The bottom line of this chapter is to focus better on understanding the data (contrary to classical machine learning applications). Each phase of the project at the end led to a new project and a new collaboration. Although AI techniques may be complex for practitioners, with tool support, and the proper measurement of tangible benefits, the industry can use data science and analytics very effectively [3].

REFERENCES

[1] Bener A, Misirli AT, Caglayan B, Kocaguneli E, Calikli G. Lessons learned from software analytics in practice. In: Bird C, Menzies T, Zimmerman T, editors. The art and science of analyzing software data. Morgan Kaufmann: Elsevier Science; 2015. ISBN 9780124115439. https://books.google.ca/books?id=g-IBAAAQBAJ.

[2] Misirli T, Caglayan B, Bener A, Turhan B. A retrospective study of software analytics projects: in-depth interviews with practitioners. IEEE Softw September/October 2013:54–62.

[3] Tosun A, Bener A, Kale R. AI based software defect predictors: applications and benefits in a case study. AI Mag 2011;32(2):57–68.

[4] Tosun A, Turhan B, Bener A. Practical considerations of deploying AI in defect prediction: a case study within the Turkish telecommunication industry. In: Promise09, May 2009. 18–19, Vancouver, Canada.

[5] Kocagüneli E, Tosun A, Bener A, Turhan B, Çağlayan B. Prest: an intelligent software metrics extraction, analysis and defect prediction tool. In: Proceedings of the 21st international conference on software engineering and knowledge engineering (SEKE 2009), Boston, USA; 2009.

[6] Turhan B, Kocak G, Bener A. Software defect prediction using call graph based ranking (CGBR) framework. In: Proceedings of the 34th EUROMICRO software engineering and advanced applications (EUROMICRO-SEAA 2008); 2008.

[7] Nasa/Wvu IV&V Facility, Metrics data program, available from http://mdp.ivv.nasa.gov, Internet; accessed 2007.

[8] Kosker Y, Bener A, Turhan B. Refactoring prediction using class complexity metrics. In: Proceedings of the 3rd international conference on software and data technologies (ICSOFT 2008); 2008. p. 289–92.

[9] Shut R. Next-gen data scientists. Strata Talk 2013.

There's never enough time to do all the testing you want

K. Herzig

Software Development Engineer, Microsoft Corporation, Redmond, United States

CHAPTER OUTLINE

Software is present in nearly every aspect of our daily lives and also dominates large parts of the high-tech consumer market. Consumers love new features, and new features are what makes them buy software products, while properties like reliability, security, and privacy are assumed. To respond to the consumer market demand, many software producers are following a trend to shorten software release cycles. As a consequence, software developers have to produce more features in less time while maintaining, or even increasing, product quality. Here at Microsoft (as well as other large software organizations [1]) we have learned that testing is not free. Testing can slow down development processes and cost money in terms of infrastructure and human involvement. Thus, the effort associated with testing must be carefully monitored and managed.

THE IMPACT OF SHORT RELEASE CYCLES (THERE'S NOT ENOUGH TIME)

To enable faster and more "agile" software development, processes have to change. We need to cut down time required to develop, verify, and ship new features or code changes in general. In other words, we need to increase *code velocity* by increasing the effectiveness, efficiency, and reliability of our development processes.

Focusing on testing processes, it is important to realize that verification time is a lower bound on how fast we can ship software. However, nowadays this lower bound frequently conflicts with the goal of faster release cycles. As a matter of fact, we simply cannot afford to execute all tests on all code changes anymore. Simply removing tests is easy, the challenge is to cut tests without negatively impacting product quality.

TESTING IS MORE THAN FUNCTIONAL CORRECTNESS (ALL THE TESTING YOU WANT)

Often, testing is associated with checking for functional correctness and unit testing. While these tests are often fast, passing or failing in seconds, large complex software systems require tests to verify system constraints such as backward compatibility, performance, security, usability, and so on. These *system and integration tests* are complex and typically time-consuming, even though they relatively rarely find a bug. Nevertheless, these tests must be seen as an insurance process verifying that the software product complies with all necessary system constraints at all times (or at least at the time of release). Optimizing unit tests can be very helpful, but usually it is the system and integration testing part of verification processes that consumes most of the precious development time.

LEARN FROM YOUR TEST EXECUTION HISTORY

Knowing that we cannot afford to run all tests on all code changes anymore, we face a difficult task: find the best combination of tests to verify the current code change, spending as little test execution time as possible. To achieve this goal, we need to think of testing as a risk management tool to minimize the risk of elapsing code defects to later stages of the development process or even to customers.

The basic assumption behind most test optimization and test selection approaches is that for given scenarios, or context C, not all tests are equally well suited. Some tests are more effective than others. For example, running a test for *Internet Explorer* on the *Windows kernel* code base is unlikely to find new code defects.

However, determining the effectiveness and reliability of tests and when to execute which subset is not trivial. One of the most popular metrics to determine test quality is *code coverage*. However, coverage is of very limited use in this case. First, coverage does not imply verification (especially not for system and integration tests). Second, it does not allow us to assess the effectiveness and reliability of single test cases. Last but not least, collecting coverage significantly slows down test runtime, which would require us to remove even more tests.

Instead, we want to execute only those tests that, for a given code change and a given execution context C, eg, branch, architecture, language, device type, has high reliability and high effectiveness. Independent from the definition of reliability and effectiveness, all tests that are not highly reliable and effective should be executed less frequently or not at all.

TEST EFFECTIVENESS

Simplistically, a test is effective if it finds defects. This does not imply that tests that find no defects should be removed completely, but we should consider them of secondary importance (see "The Art of Testing Less" section). The beauty of this simplistic definition of test effectiveness is that we can use *historic test execution data* to measure test effectiveness. For a given execution context C, we determine how often the test failed due to a code defect. For example, a test T that has been executed 100 times on a given execution context C and that failed 20 times due to code defects has a historic code defect probability of 0.2. To compute such historic code defect probabilities, it usually suffices to query an existing test execution database and to link test failures to issue reports and code changes, a procedure that is also commonly used to assess the quality of source code. Please note that coverage information is partially included in this measurement. Not covering code means not being able to fail on a code change, implying a historic failure probability of 0.

TEST RELIABILITY/NOT EVERY TEST FAILURE POINTS TO A DEFECT

Tests are usually designed to either pass or fail, and each failure should point to a code defect. In practice, however, many tests tend to report so-called *false test alarms*. These are test failures that are not due to code defects, but due to test issues or infrastructure issues. Common examples are: wrong test assertions, non-deterministic (flaky) tests, and tests that depend on network resources that fail when the network is unavailable.

Tests that report false test alarms regularly must be considered a serious threat to the verification and development processes. As with any other test failure, false alarms trigger manual investigations that must be regarded as wasted engineering time. The result of the investigation will not increase product quality, but rather, slow down code velocity of the current code change under the test.

Similar to test effectiveness, we can measure test reliability as a historic probability. Simplistically, we can count any test failure that did not lead to a code change (code defect) as false test alarm. Thus, a test T that has been executed 100 times on a given execution context C and that failed 10 times but did not trigger a product code change has a historic test unreliability probability of 0.1.

THE ART OF TESTING LESS

Combining both measurements for effectiveness and reliability (independent from their definition) allows a development team to assess the quality of individual tests and to act on it. Teams may decide to statically fix unreliable tests or to dynamically skip tests. Tests that show low effectiveness and/or low reliability should be executed only where necessary and as infrequently as possible. For more details in how to use these probabilities to design a system that dynamically determines which test to execute and which to not execute, we refer to Herzig et al. [2] and to Elbaum et al. [1].

WITHOUT SACRIFICING CODE QUALITY

However, the problem is that some tests might get disabled completely, either because they are too unreliable, or because they never found a code defect (in the last periods). To minimize the risk of elapsing severe bugs into the final product and in order to boost the confidence of development teams in the product under development, it is essential to prevent tests from being disabled completely. One possible solution is to regularly force test executions, eg, once a week. Similarly, you can also use a version control branch-based approach, eg, executing all tests on the trunk or release branch, but not on feature and integration branches.

TESTS EVOLVE OVER TIME

Any complex test infrastructure evolves over time. New tests are added, while older tests might become less important or even deprecated. Maintaining tests and preventing test infrastructures from decay can grow to be a significant effort. For products with some history, some of the older tests may not be "owned" by anybody anymore, or show strongly distributed ownership across multiple product teams. Such ownership can impact test effectiveness and reliability, slowing down development speed [3]. Determining and monitoring new test cases being added, or changes to existing tests, can be very useful in assessing the healthiness of the verification process. For example, adding lots of new features to a product without experiencing an increase in a new test being written might indicate a drop in quality assurance. The amount of newly introduced code and newly written or at least modified test code should be well balanced.

IN SUMMARY

Software testing is expensive, in terms of time and money. Emulating millions of configurations and devices requires complex test infrastructures and scenarios. This contradicts today's trend of releasing complex software systems in ever-shorter periods of time. As a result, software testing became a bottleneck in development processes. The time spent in verification defines a lower bound on how fast companies can ship software. Resolving test bottlenecks requires us to rethink development and testing processes to allow new room for newer and better tests and to regain confidence in testing. We need to accept that testing is an important part of our daily development process, but that "There's never enough time to do all the testing we want."

REFERENCES

[1] Elbaum S, Rothermel G, Penix J. Techniques for improving regression testing in continuous integration development environments. In: Proceedings of the 22nd ACM SIGSOFT international symposium on Foundations of Software Engineering (FSE); 2014.

[2] Herzig K, Greiler M, Czerwonka J, Murphy B. The art of testing less without sacrificing quality. In: Proceedings of the 2015 international conference on software engineering; 2015.

[3] Herzig K, Nagappan N. Empirically detecting false test alarms using association rules. In: Companion proceedings of the 37th international conference on software engineering; 2015.

The perils of energy mining: measure a bunch, compare just once

A. Hindle

University of Alberta, Edmonton, AB, Canada

CHAPTER OUTLINE

A TALE OF TWO HTTPs

Shaiful Chowdhury [1] came into the lab and proclaimed, "HTTP/2.0 has significantly better energy performance than HTTP/1.1!" "That's excellent," I exclaimed, "Do you know why?"

The next week Shaiful came back to the lab and said, "I think I was wrong, I don't think there's a difference." He went on to explain that he was happy with the results of the first experiment, but something was bothering him.

To test HTTP/1.1 in Firefox, he had to disable HTTP/2.0 in Firefox's settings, thus his energy consumption test of Firefox for HTTP/1.1 had to do more work than his HTTP/2.0 tests. He investigated the CPU state of the HTTP/2.0 and HTTP/1.1 tests and found that the rigorous button pushing used to disable HTTP/2.0 put the CPU into a higher state: higher frequency, and more voltage. Thus, the CPU state for the HTTP/1.1 started higher and was consuming more than the HTTP/2.0 tests.

Shaiful's solution was to inject some idle time into the HTTP/1.1 test, allowing the CPU to lower its state. He then ensured via manual inspection that the idling did

97

drop down the CPU state. Afterward both tests produced results that were comparable; it turns out that on a fast network there's not much difference between HTTP/1.1 and HTTP/2.0.

The entire experiment was threatened by attributing the change in energy consumption to HTTP/1.1 and HTTP/2.0 code in Firefox, when in fact it was caused by our HTTP/1.1 test inducing the CPU to have a different state than the HTTP/2.0 tests. Misattribution of the root causes of energy consumption is just one of many perils one faces when engaged in Green Mining, energy-aware mining, and software energy consumption measurement.

LET'S ENERGISE YOUR SOFTWARE ENERGY EXPERIMENTS

We want to help prevent experimental accidents when measuring the energy consumption of software systems. The most difficult aspect of measuring and mining software energy consumption is to juggle all of the confounds and potential threats to validity one faces. The first two questions any software energy miner should ask are "What do I want to measure?" and "What am I actually measuring?" The intent is to create a test, or benchmark, that will allow us to compare energy consumption of the task or program in question.

In prior work [2], we proposed a methodology of repeated measurement and comparison of such a test:

1. Choose a product and task to test;
2. Decide on the granularity and level of instrumentation;
3. Choose which versions of the software to test;
4. Develop a test case for the task to be tested;
5. Configure the testbed environment to reduce background noise;
6. For each combination of version, task and configuration, repeat multiple times:
    (i) Setup the testbed to record energy consumption measurements;
    (ii) Run the test;
    (iii) Compile and store the recorded data;
    (iv) Clean up the testbed.
7. Analyze and evaluate.

This methodology can be combined with a simple mnemonic, **ENERGISE** 1. ENERGISE is a checklist of issues, built from prior experience [3], that one should consider when measuring software energy consumption:

- *Environment*—prepare a stable testbed for energy measurement.
- *N-versions*—run a test across more than one version of the software.
- *Energy or power*—do we care about total energy consumed of a task, or the per-second cost of running a service?
- *Repeat*—one run is not enough, we need to run our tests multiple times to address background noise.

- *Granularity*—what level of measurement, how often, and what level of invasiveness of instrumentation can be tolerated?
- *Idle*—how do applications and services react with no load: is energy being wasted?
- *Statistics*—repeat measures call for summary statistics and comparing distributions.
- *Exceptions*—errors happen; how do we address them or notice them?

ENVIRONMENT

The environment is the testbed and the system that will run the software under test. Environments should be representative of realistic platforms and scenarios, yet balanced against noise such as third-party apps or traffic, unneeded applications, or other users. Generally, environments should be as controlled as possible. Even temperature can affect energy measurements.

N-VERSIONS

The first step to any successful attempt at optimization is to measure system performance before optimization. If we are measuring software energy consumption to determine the impact of changing the code, we should measure the system before the modification to allow for comparison. Our work in Green Mining has shown that software does indeed change in energy performance over time, and measuring just one version of the software might not be representative of the versions before or after. It is recommended that multiple versions of the software are measured.

ENERGY OR POWER

Energy is the cost of work, or the capacity to do work, and is typically measured in joules (J). Power is the rate of energy consumption, essentially the derivative of energy consumption, measured in watts (W), where 1 W is equal to 1 Js.

When you measure a task that a system executes, ask your system, does this task have a clear beginning or end? Does this task continuously run? Tasks that do not to run continuously, such as sharpening an image or compressing a video file, can be characterized by the energy consumed. Whereas a task that runs continuously, such a sharpening video images of a surveillance web-camera or streaming video compression, is better characterized by its workload, its power, and the rate of energy consumption.

REPEAT!

While we already recommended measuring multiple versions of software, it is even more important to repeat your measurements. Modern computers are very noisy and active systems, with lots of background processes and lots of states. They have many peripherals and services. It is hard to guarantee what tasks are executing on a modern system and what the current environment is like. If you're running a test using WIFI, your own cellphone could affect the experiment. Furthermore, we're measuring physical phenomena: energy consumption. Our measurement equipment, our test-beds, or energy measurement devices all have errors in them, error is inherent in physical measurement. Thus, we need to take multiple measurements so we can rely upon statistics to give us a more clear picture of what we measured.

GRANULARITY

When designing an energy consumption test, one has to choose the level of granularity. Do you want to measure method calls, system calls, CPU use, memory use, processes, etc., and at what frequency? Many measurement devices and ICs, such as the Watts Up? Pro device or the TI INA-219 IC, are sampling at thousands of times per second, integrating the results and reporting back to you at a fraction of that rate. If you only have 1 s of granularity from a Watts Up? Pro you won't be measuring the cost of a method call unless you explicitly make a benchmark that repeatedly calls it. If you need method call level measurements, the instrumentation overhead will be high.

Granularity is a concern if you measure just a single process or component, or if you measure the whole system. An example scenario is if you asked the sound card to play a sound for 1 s. The request to play a sound might return in 1 ms to the process, for the next second the OS, the sound card driver and sound card will be interacting, playing the requested 1 s of audio. If we measure at the process level, we miss the induced cost on the system of the software. The software commanded work, but we are not measuring that work. If we measure at the entire system level, we will be including a lot of other processes and drivers that will be irrelevant.

IDLE MEASUREMENT

Not all applications or tasks have idle behavior, but many user-facing applications and services run continuously or intermittently in the foreground or background. What programs do when they aren't in direct use is important, because usually their idle operation is a waste of resources, unless work is being executed during idle time. An efficient process can stay asleep until it receives input. The operating system's scheduler is very good at sleeping and waking processes.

Idle use often characterizes baseline energy consumption for an application. If executing tasks and idleness use the same amount of energy, perhaps the idle components can be optimized to use less energy. Measuring idle consumption is useful to determine what impact changes might have on the implementation of nonfunctional requirements.

STATISTICAL ANALYSIS

Repeat measurements cause many problems: there is no longer one measurement, there are many. Thus, summary statistics can be employed to describe the distribution of measurements. There is one saving grace: energy measurements are of physical phenomena, and the Normal (or Gaussian) distribution often models the errors within natural measurements well. Thus, the variance and mean are two reasonable descriptors of our multiple runs. This means we can use parametric tests, such as the Student's T-test, to compare two distributions of measurements to see if they are statistically significantly different. Without statistical tools such as the T-test, we would not have much confidence to determine if distributions were different or not based on random chance.

EXCEPTIONS

To err is human and to throw uncaught exceptions is to execute code. Mobile devices and modern computers still suffer from crashing software. Exceptions happen, core dumps occur, sometimes apps decide to update, sometimes the network goes down, sometimes a remote site is unavailable. Often the software under test is just inherently buggy and only half of the test runs will complete. When developing tests, one should instrument the tests with auditing capabilities such as screenshots, to enable postmortem investigations. Furthermore, outliers should be investigated and potentially re-run. You wouldn't want to attribute a difference in energy consumption to an erroneous test.

SUMMARY

In summary, there are many confounds that one faces when measuring software energy consumption. First and foremost, energy consumption is a physical process, and energy consumption measurement requires repeated measurement and statistical analysis. Thus, remember and use the ENERGISE mnemonic to help evaluate energy measurement scenarios: environment, N-versions, energy or power, repeated measurement, granularity, idle measurement, statistical analysis, and exceptions.

REFERENCES
[1] Chowdhury SA, Sapra V, Hindle A. Is HTTP/2 more energy efficient than HTTP/1.1 for mobile users? PeerJ Preprints 2015; https://peerj.com/preprints/1280/.

[2] Hindle A. Green mining: A methodology of relating software change to power consumption. In: Proceedings of the 9th IEEE working conference on mining software repositories. Zurich, Switzerland: IEEE Press; 2012. p. 78–87.

[3] Hindle A, Wilson A, Rasmussen K, Barlow EJ, Campbell JC, Romansky S. Greenminer: a hardware based mining software repositories software energy consumption framework. In: Proceedings of the 11th working conference on mining software repositories. New York: ACM; 2014. p. 12–21.

Identifying fault-prone files in large industrial software systems

E. Weyuker, T. Ostrand

Mälerdalen University, Västerås, Sweden

A person walks down the street and sees a man on his hands and knees under a lamp post.

What are you doing?
I'm looking for my keys.
You dropped them here?
No, but the light is so much better here than where I dropped them, I thought I'd look here!

A silly old joke, but one that motivated the work that we did on software fault prediction for almost a decade while working at AT&T. A common paradigm used at AT&T to develop large systems was to design and create an initial version, and then continue to maintain it with subsequent releases at roughly 3-month intervals. Each new release might contain added functionality, redesign of existing code, removal of parts no longer needed, and fixes for bugs that had been documented since the last release.

Testing is a critical and expensive step needed to create a software system or new release. Every tester would love to be able to focus their lamp posts exactly where the bugs are so that they could test the relevant program parts most intensively. If only we knew beforehand where the bugs were likely to be, we could test there first, test there hardest, assign our best testers, allocate sufficient time where it's needed, etc. In short, we could use that information to prioritize our testing efforts to find bugs faster and more efficiently, leading to more reliable software. That is exactly what our software fault prediction algorithms aim to do—identify those parts of a software system that are most likely to contain the largest numbers of bugs.

To help identify the parts of a system most likely to contain bugs, we needed to identify which file characteristics correlated most closely with files containing the largest numbers of bugs. We identified both static code characteristics, such as file size and programming language, and historical characteristics, such as the number of recent bugs and the number of recent changes made to each file, that would be used to predict the number of bugs that will be in each file in the next release of the system. As the basis for our research, we looked for real industrial software projects with multiple releases, comprehensive version history, and an accessible bug database.

We needed to work with practitioners and get their interest in the project so that they would give us access to their software and data. As we studied their systems and built our first prediction models, we continued working with practitioners to make sure we were asking the right questions and providing feedback in a form that would be useful to them.

We first looked at an inventory control system containing roughly a half million lines of code that had been in the field for about 3 years. We had data for 12 releases. Like many large industrial systems, this software had been developed using a traditional waterfall model, and had four releases a year. The development team used a proprietary configuration management system that included both version control and change management functionality. Underlying the configuration management system was a very large database that contained all of the information about the system, including the source code and bug repository. That was the primary source of the data used to make predictions.

We identified the most buggy files in each release and looked at what they had in common in order to identify file characteristics that correlated with fault-proneness. We started with characteristics that our intuition, experience, and the folklore told us were most important. For example, everyone knows that "big is bad"—that has been a defining mantra of the software engineering world for the last few decades, and so we looked at file size as a potential characteristic, and found that it did indeed correlate with fault-proneness. Another common belief is "once buggy, always buggy"; files that had bugs in the past are likely to have bugs later. We found, in fact, that while past bugginess was important, it was only the most recent release's status that had a strong influence on bugs in the next release. We continued looking at other characteristics we expected to be most important, and carried out empirical studies to assess the relevance and predictive power of each characteristic we considered. Eventually we determined that by mining the database associated with the configuration management system, five simple file characteristics were sufficient to allow us to build a model that made accurate predictions: file size, the number of changes in the two previous releases, the number of bugs in the most recent previous release, the age of the file in terms of the number of releases the file had been part of the system, and the language in which the file was written.

It took us a number of tries to get a predictive model that seemed to make accurate predictions. We eventually decided to use the statistical method of negative binomial regression. For the initial system, we found that, averaged over the 17 releases of this system, the files predicted to have the largest numbers of bugs did indeed contain a large majority of the bugs. To assess the effectiveness of the predictions, for each release we measured the percent of all real bugs that turned out to be located in the 20% of files that were predicted to have the largest numbers of bugs. Over the system's 17 releases, the percent of real bugs actually detected in the predicted "worst 20%" of files averaged 83%. Armed with these promising results, we were able to attract other projects whose software we could study and for which we could make predictions.

We refined and improved the prediction model while working with three additional projects, eventually settling on a *Standard Model* that uses the five characteristics mentioned above. The basic ideas and method to calculate the predictions are explained in [1], although that paper describes a slightly different early version of the prediction model.

Because easy access to the prediction technology is just as important as the technology itself, we built a tool that provides testers and developers with a simple GUI interface to input the information needed to request bug predictions for their software. Users provide their system name, the types of files they are interested in (Java, C, C++, SQL, etc.), and the release they want predictions for. The tool does the calculations and presents a list of the release's files sorted in decreasing order of the number of predicted bugs. The results can be used to prioritize the order and intensity of testing files, to assign the most appropriate tester(s) to specific files or parts of the system, to help decide which files should be revised or completely rewritten, and to determine whether other quality assurance procedures such as a detailed code review should be carried out. Because a typical run of the tool is very quick, often under 1 min even for a multi-million line system, users could run it repeatedly to get different views, perhaps to restrict their interest to just Java files, or to a subset of the entire system, or to find out if a refactoring of the code changes the expected fault likelihood.

Over the course of several years we studied a total of nine industrial projects and made predictions for a total of 170 releases. All nine systems were in the field for multiple years, all ran continuously (24/7) and ranged from a system with just nine releases over the course of 2 years, to two systems that were in the field for almost 10 years, with each having 35 quarterly releases. The systems performed all sorts of different tasks, were written in different languages, and ranged in size from under 300,000 lines of code to over 2,100,000 lines of code. The prediction accuracy ranged from 75% to 93%.

An unexpected episode at AT&T gave us even more confidence in the usefulness of the prediction models. At a meeting attended by several development managers, we demonstrated the prediction tool and showed the results we had obtained for the last released version of one of the major systems. After seeing this, that system's manager asked whether we could run the model on the version that was currently under development and next in line to be released. On the spot, we were able to access the system's version control and bug database, and generate predictions. The results were highly useful to the manager, as they provided fresh insight to his system. The files that were predicted to be most faulty included several that the manager already knew had potential weaknesses, but also included several that he had not considered problematic. His first action on leaving the meeting was to instruct his testing team to do intensified testing on the files that were previously considered safe.

The Standard Model does not account for some variables that many people (including us!) felt might have an effect on the potential bugginess of code. We experimented with augmented models that included counts of the number of different programmers who had changed the code [2], the complexity of the code's calling structure [3], and detailed counts of the number of lines added, changed or deleted in a file [4]. None of these additional characteristics significantly improved the

Standard Model's predictions, and we even found that augmenting the model with additional variables sometimes made the predictions worse.

A variety of different approaches to software fault prediction have been investigated over the past 20 years, with mixed results. Much of the research has attempted to categorize parts of the software as either fault-prone or not fault-prone, and validation has typically been done using so-called hold-out experiments where predictions were made by training the algorithms on a subset of the files to make predictions on the remaining files *within the same release*. In contrast, our algorithms perform the more ambitious task of ordering the files from most fault-prone to least fault-prone, using data extracted from earlier releases to make predictions for later releases, always using industrial software systems that are running in the field. Our consistent positive results on 170 releases demonstrate that at least for the types of systems and development processes we've studied, accurate prediction results are possible, and can provide useful information to testers, developers, and project managers.

ACKNOWLEDGMENT
This work was supported in part by the Swedish Research Council through grant 621-2014-4925.

REFERENCES
[1] Ostrand TJ, Weyuker EJ, Bell RM. Predicting the location and number of faults in large software systems. IEEE Trans Softw Eng 2005;31:340–55.

[2] Weyuker EJ, Ostrand TJ, Bell RM. Do too many cooks spoil the broth? Using the number of developers to enhance defect prediction models. Empir Softw Eng 2008;13:539–59.

[3] Shin Y, Bell R, Ostrand TJ, Weyuker E. On the use of calling structure information to help predict software fault proneness. Empir Softw Eng 2012;17:390–423.

[4] Bell RM, Ostrand TJ, Weyuker EJ. Does measuring code change improve fault prediction? In: Proceedings 7th international conference on predictive models in software engineering (Promise '11); 2011. This work was supported in part by the Swedish Research Council through grant 621-2014-4925.

A tailored suit: The big opportunity in personalizing issue tracking

O. Baysal

Carleton University, Ottawa, ON, Canada

MANY CHOICES, NOTHING GREAT

Software developers use a variety of powerful tools and repositories in their daily work. Issue tracking is a key element of any software development project. Issue tracking systems (ITS) have long been used by software teams to report, discuss, and track both defects and new features. While issue trackers are good at providing a collaborative facility to developers, some routine tasks are poorly supported; a particular sore point is the weak support provided to developers in building and maintaining a detailed understanding of the current state of their system: what is the current status of the issues? Who is blocking me? How am I blocking others? How many bugs do I need to triage, fix, review, or follow up on?

There are many issue-tracking systems available, both proprietary (eg, JIRA, Google trackers) and open-source (eg, Bugzilla, Trac). However, most issue-tracking systems face several limitations:

- *complexity*: they store an overwhelming amount of usually unused metadata fields (also known as too many pockets in a too-big suit)—the vast majority of which is irrelevant to the task at hand;
- *performance*: they can be unusably slow;

- *usability*: eg, Bugzilla's user interface is unintuitive and wasn't designed to support process management;
- *they're hard to query*: developers are often unable to correctly formulate queries to access and correlate various pieces of metadata; this limitation is like having too-short trousers that leave you in the cold no matter what;
- *they're "one size fits all:"* provide generalized interfaces that can be used by not only developers, but also managers, QA, marketing staff, graphic designers, and artists.

Because issue-tracking systems are complex, general-purpose tools that can provide an immense amount of raw information, developers may feel frustrated when they cannot easily access the particular set of details that they need for a given task. The information they seek is in there, somewhere, but not at their fingertips, and the tools often provide only limited support for their specialized, definable, and recurring information needs.

THE NEED FOR PERSONALIZATION

One way to help developers manage the complexity of issue trackers and the increasing volume of issues is to provide them with *personalized* development tools that work to highlight the most important information for them, while eliminating the rest from view [1]. Our study [2] identified an industrial desire for this kind of personalization for issue-tracking systems. The study captures developers' insights into the strengths, weaknesses, and possible future enhancements of the Bugzilla platform, the primary collaboration platform for Mozilla developers.

Some limitations can be overcome by adding detailed information that is specific to developers and their tasks, and by providing the technical means for developers to create these personalized views themselves. That is, the personalization of issue-tracking systems can help developers better maintain situational awareness about both the issues they are working on and how they are blocking other developers' progress on their own issues [3]. *Situational awareness* is a term from cognitive psychology that refers to a state of mind where a person is highly attuned to changes in their environment. In our context, situational awareness [3] describes how software developers must maintain awareness of what is happening on their project, to be able to manage a constant flow of information as issues evolve, and be able to plan appropriate actions. Developers often find themselves trying to identify the status of a bug—(1) What is the issue waiting on? (2) Who is working on what bug? (3) What are the workloads of others? (4) Who is the best person to review the patch?, as well as trying to track their own tasks—How many bugs do I need to triage, fix, review, or follow up on?

In our study, developers highlighted that customized views of the project's repositories that are tailored to their specific tasks could help them better track their progress and understand the surrounding technical context.

DEVELOPER DASHBOARDS OR "A TAILORED SUIT"

Personalized issue tracking can enable developers to better keep up with the evolution of their issues, and to more easily learn of new issues that may be relevant to them. The concept of personalization can be manifested in custom views of the issue-tracking system via *developer dashboards* that are designed to overcome current limitations and provide developers with better awareness of their working environment. The following Figure 1 illustrates developer dashboards; it shows a custom view of the Bugzilla repository generated for a Mozilla developer. The dashboard serves as a template for displaying information to assist in developers' common tasks. This template contains all the key information elements [2] that are important to the developers—issues and patches. Developers work with both of these on a daily basis. Issues contain bug reports and new features that need to be implemented, while patches contain the reification of issues in source code that can then be reviewed by other developers. Both the management of issues and patches are of key concern to developers.

Developer dashboards can enable developers to better focus on the evolution of their issues in a high-traffic environment, and to more easily learn about new issues that may be relevant to them.

While tailor-made suits can be personalized in any number of ways, customization can lead to overfitting, meaning the tool has to change if we change the process. Therefore, using dashboards is a great way to simply blend out the stuff that the team does not use or need, at least at the moment.

ROOM FOR IMPROVEMENT

1. Development of next-generation issue tracking that is *tailored to individual developers* by equipping them with information *relevant* to their current tasks.
2. *Real-time* analytics are vital as they allow developers to see the "live" picture of what is happening with their issues.
3. Support for *prioritization* by means of enabling developers to set their own or team priorities on issues and tasks and sort them based on their importance.
4. Development of *context-aware* dashboards that are able to anticipate which information is important for a particular developer at a certain time.

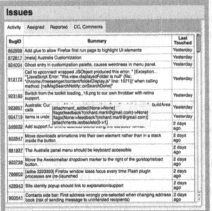
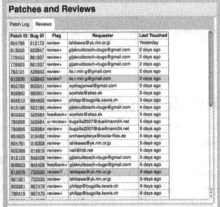

REFERENCES

[1] Storey M-A, Cheng L-T, Bull I, Rigby P. Shared waypoints and social tagging to support collaboration in software development. In: Proceedings of the 20th Conference on Computer Supported Cooperative Work (CSCW); 2006. p. 195–8.

[2] Baysal O, Holmes R, Godfrey MW. No issue left behind: reducing information overload in issue tracking. In: Proceedings of the International Symposium on the Foundations of Software Engineering (FSE); 2014. p. 666–77.

[3] Baysal O, Holmes R, Godfrey MW. Situational awareness: personalizing issue management systems. In: Proceedings of the New Ideas and Emerging Results (NIER) track, the 35th International Conference on Software Engineering; 2013. p. 1185–8.

What counts is decisions, not numbers—Toward an analytics design sheet

G. Ruhe, M. Nayebi

University of Calgary, Calgary, AB, Canada

DECISIONS EVERYWHERE

In the age of app stores, data from users and the market is collected on almost everything: features and their evolution, code and all the changes made, number of downloads, rating of the apps, reviews done by the users, and performance of competitors in the market. In presence of all that, how can analytics support development of highly successful apps?

Decision-making is the process of determining a course of action to achieve a (explicitly stated or not) stated goal, and fulfill given constraints. The variety of product release decisions (What features to release next? When to release them? Focus on functionality versus quality of features?) is just one example of the wide spectrum of decisions that have to be made during the different stages of the software life-cycle. Some of these decisions are related to operational questions (who should fix this bug?), others are more strategic decisions in nature (outsourcing which parts of development? Migration to another platform?). In all these cases, one wants to select the best alternative based on some evaluation criteria. The alternatives need to be feasible in terms of some hard and soft constraints on cost, time, quality or technical conditions.

In the end, all these decisions are made by humans. However, the difference is in how much the human decision makers can rely on insight gained from analytics, and how much of it is just based on intuition. In the context of release decisions for mobile apps, we found that about half of the app owners make rationale-based decisions for releasing their products [1].

THE DECISION-MAKING PROCESS

Russo and Schoemaker [2] recommend that people in business must approach decision making with a clear process and plan. We look at this process from an analytics perspective and define what analytics can provide as far as key steps of the decision-making process:

Step 1 Modeling and scoping: A conceptual model is created describing the scope and context of the decision studied. This includes decision variables, independent variables and context factors to be taken into account.

Step 2 Information gathering: Based on the model created, information from different sources is retrieved and pre-processed. The scope of information gathering should include sources inside and outside the organizational context you are in.

Step 3 Identify and evaluate alternatives: As a form of synthesis, information is explored to determine possible and desirable alternatives. This is a creative process where missing some of the alternatives might be a cause of missing the best possible decision. Having too many alternatives makes the final decision more difficult.

Step 4 Select one alternative: Among the identified alternatives from Step 3, select the one fulfilling potential hard and soft constraints that is ranked highest. This selection is a human-based activity, and all analytics done in previous steps should be in support of this selection.

Step 5 Implement: The selected alternative is implemented as the solution to the original problem.

Step 6 Monitor and adjust to change: The need to adjust to changes is the result of the inherent uncertainties in the actual decision context. Effort, cost, value or market conditions might change, and this implies that a partially implemented solution needs to be adjusted to better match with the new situation.

While Steps 1 and 5 are not directly related to analytics, the other steps mostly benefit from it. In what follows, we describe how to further qualify this process.

THE ANALYTICS DESIGN SHEET

One of the key mistakes in data mining is "Running algorithms repeatedly and blindly" for mining data [3]. We propose the *analytics design sheet* (ADS) as a guide for selecting the right analytics to support decision-making. The ADS consists of four quadrants, Q1 to Q4, devoted to the decision problem specified in the heading of the sheet:

- *Context*: Description of problem context factors and problem formulation (Q1).
- *Decision*: High-level specification of the decision to be made (Q2).
- *Data*: Availability of data (Q3).
- *Analytics*: Selection of helpful analytics techniques (Q4).

In Q1 of the ADS, problem scoping and formulation is addressed. It is important to address the right analytics to properly understand the context and actual real-world problem. Following, the specific decision problem to be tackled needs to be outlined. As such, Q2 represents an informal model of the decision problem under consideration. One way to do this is using an *Influence Diagram* [4], which is a simple visual representation of a decision problem. No perfection or completeness is expected at this stage; data analytics is an adaptive process with an increasing level of detail.

The third quadrant, Q3, evaluates key features of data and their availability. Finally, Q4 provides (human expert-based opinion on) alternatives for selecting the appropriate analytics. This is not meant to be a prescriptive selection, but more like a brainstorming of potential analytical techniques applicable for the stated problem.

EXAMPLE: APP STORE RELEASE ANALYSIS

We illustrate the idea of the ADS by an example taken from the domain of app store analytics. With the mass of available explicit and implicit user feedback, synergies between goal-oriented analytics and human expertise are needed to make good decisions [5]. A team of game app developers decided to gain more visibility for their app in the GooglePlay store by adding new incentives to the game. To this end, a prototype of a new feature is implemented and offered via a beta release. Over a period of time, they further monitor the feature usage (Q1). The actual decision problem is to include or not include the new feature based on the monitored trial usage and the predicted effort for implementing the full functionality of the feature (Q2). For analysis, there is a real-world data set from recording the feature usage (frequency and duration of using the new feature). Furthermore, there is another (historical) data set describing the actual effort from implementing similar features in the past (Q3). Selecting from the variety of techniques outlined by Bird et al. in [6], time-series analysis, predictive modeling and what-if benefit analysis are suggested in Q4. As a result, a recommendation is given on whether the new feature should be included or not. In addition, this suggestion is supported by data analytics. The sample ADS sheet is shown in Fig. 1.

The ADS is a semi-formal approach, leveraging existing knowledge and experience. The sheet is intended to support brainstorming and facilitating discussion among stakeholders. The selection of specific analytical techniques is outside the scope of the sheet. Overall, the proposed approach is intended to facilitate the transition from numbers to support actual decision-making.

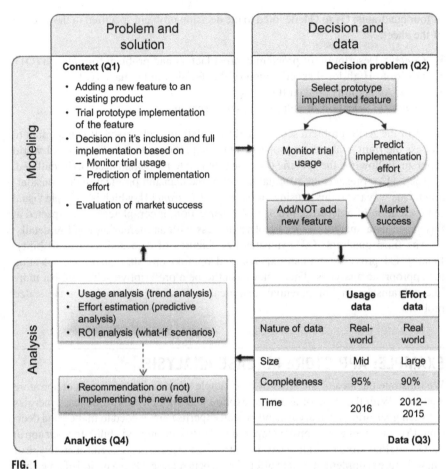

FIG. 1

Sample analytics design sheet in support of the decision to add a new feature.

REFERENCES

[1] Nayebi M, Adams B, Ruhe G. Mobile app releases—a survey research on developers and users perception. In: Proceedings SANER; 2016.

[2] Russo JE, Schoemaker PJ. Winning decisions: getting it right the first time. New York: Doubleday; 2002.

[3] Delen D. Real-world data mining. Upper Saddle River: Pearson Education; 2014.

[4] Shachter RD. Evaluating influence diagrams. Oper Res 1986;34(6):871–82.

[5] Maalej W, Nayebi M, Johan T, Ruhe G. Toward data driven requirement engineering. Special issue on The Future of Software Engineering. IEEE Software 2016;33(1):48–54.

[6] Bird C, Menzies T, Zimmermann T. The art and science of analyzing software data. Burlington: Morgan Kaufman; 2015.

A large ecosystem study to understand the effect of programming languages on code quality

B. Ray*, D. Posnett[†]

University of Virginia, Charlottesville, VA, United States[*] University of California, Davis, CA, United States[†]

CHAPTER OUTLINE

Developers are often tasked with choosing a language for a project. Although such decisions are usually based on prior experiences or legacy requirements, as reported by Meyerovich et al. [1], language choice is in general believed to impact the code quality. For example, statically typed languages catch type errors early, at compile time, while dynamically typed languages catch errors at run time, if the errors at all arise. Other language properties such as strong versus weak typing, procedural versus functional language, managed versus unmanaged memory, etc. can also influence the number of bugs in the resulting code.

In this chapter, we empirically investigate the impact of language choice on code quality. We analyzed the 17 most popular languages from GitHub including C, C++, C#, Objective-C, Go, Java, Ruby, Php, Python, Perl, Javascript, CoffeeScript, TypeScript, Clojure, Erlang, Haskell, and Scala across 728 GitHub projects. Based on our previous study [2] we found that the overall effect of language on code quality is rather "modest."

COMPARING LANGUAGES

Comparing programming languages across multiple projects is a non-trivial task. Language choice may depend on many things. For what purpose are you choosing

115

the language, what are the underlying conditions, how big is your team, or who are the programmers? More than that, though, how can the language itself matter? It is the properties of languages that are important. To estimate the language effect on code quality, all these factors need to be considered.

One method for answering these types of question is the controlled study. For example, recent studies monitored students while programming in different languages and then compared outcomes such as development effort and program quality [3]. Although such controlled studies are precise, they are typically limited in their tasks and context. Studies that employ students to execute tasks that can be completed in a short period are often criticized, sometimes unfairly [4], as not emulating real-world development.

Another alternative is the observational study on a small set of chosen projects. For example, Bhattacharya et al. [5] studied four projects developed in both C and C++ and found that the software components developed in C++ are in general more reliable than C. While less limited than the controlled study, such data often suffers from lack of diversity. Further, if it is collected from the same organization, eg, the Apache Software Foundation, it might be tainted with organizational bias.

What we can do, however, is to seek data sources that naturally capture diversity among software developers, organizations, software languages, and projects [2]. The availability of a large number of open source projects written in multiple languages, and collected in software forges such as GitHub, facilitate the study of questions such as "which language is more defect prone" in an observational setting.

STUDY DESIGN AND ANALYSIS

GitHub projects vary substantially across size, age, and number of developers. Each project repository provides a detailed record, including contribution history, project size, authorship, and defect repair. This is great because we want diversity in our dataset. Diversity helps us make the case for generalizability [6].

This same diversity, however, presents challenges. For example, quality of software may depend on software engineering practices, development environment, developer knowledge, etc. It is important to reduce such unforeseen effects as much as possible. For instance, we focus on projects that are currently under active development, that are widely popular in the open source community, and that are written in somewhat important languages. These choices helped us to mitigate the effect of unmaintained code coming from unskillful development practices. We further excluded some languages from a project that has too few examples within the repository. This ensures that the studied languages have significant activity within the projects.

Finally, we analyzed the 17 most popular languages from GitHub comprising 728 projects, 63 million lines of code, and 1.5 million commits from 29,000 developers. Without such a large software ecosystem, it would be challenging to obtain enough data to statistically compare development across 17 different languages.

To understand the effect of these languages on code quality, we modeled the number of bugfix commits against language. A number of confounding factors including code size, team size, and age/maturity were further included in the study design to capture the variance attributable to them. Failure to include important metrics will lead to spurious relationships with the outcome. The classic example of this is code size. Code that is larger, will, on average, contain more defects. Therefore, languages that are favored in larger projects may appear to be more defect prone than other languages.

Moreover, comparing 17 different languages can be messy. What we want to say is that language X causes N additional defects over language Y. However, attempting to compare all of the languages to each other would complicate interpretation. Instead, we compare each language to a baseline. We weight each language with respect to the number of examples written in each language to compare languages fairly. We then compare it to the average number of defects across all languages in order to compare the impact of each language against a common background.

RESULTS

Finally, using a combination of regression modeling, text analytics, and visualization, we examined the interactions of language, language properties, application domain, and defect type. We found that

1. Functional languages (eg, Clojure, Erlang, Haskell, Scala) produce slightly better results, ie, produce fewer bugs, than procedural languages (eg, C, C++, C#, Objective-C, Java, Go); strong typing (eg, C#, Java, Python, etc.) is somewhat better than weak typing (eg, C, C++, etc.), and static typing (eg, C, C++, C#, etc.) is modestly better than dynamic typing (eg, JavaScript, Python, Perl, etc.).
2. Defect proneness of languages in general is not associated with software domains, ie, the type of project does not mediate this relationship to a large degree.
3. Also, languages are more related to individual bug categories (memory, concurrency, etc.) than bugs overall.

The modest effects arising from language choices on code quality are overwhelmingly dominated by the other process factors that we have controlled for in our regression models. We hasten to caution the reader that even these modest effects might quite possibly be due to other, intangible process factors, eg, developers' expertise, the preference of certain personality types for functional, static and strongly typed languages.

SUMMARY

We have presented a large-scale study of the impact of programming language choice on software quality. The GitHub data we used is characterized by its complexity and the variance along multiple dimensions of language, language type, usage domain, amount of code, sizes of commits, and the various characteristics of the many issue types. We report that programming language choice helps to minimize a certain type of errors like memory errors, concurrency errors, etc. However, as opposed to common belief, in general, a language choice does not impact software quality much.

REFERENCES

[1] Meyerovich LA, Rabkin AS. Empirical analysis of programming language adoption. In: ACM SIGPLAN Notices. vol. 48 (10). ACM; 2013. p. 1–18.

[2] Ray B, Posnett D, Filkov V, Devanbu P. A large scale study of programming languages and code quality in github. In: Proceedings of the 22nd ACM SIGSOFT international symposium on foundations of software engineering. New York: ACM; 2014. p. 155–65.

[3] Hanenberg S. An experiment about static and dynamic type systems: Doubts about the positive impact of static type systems on development time. In: ACM Sigplan Notices. vol. 45 (10). ACM; 2010. p. 22–35.

[4] Murphy-Hill E, Murphy GC, Griswold WG. Understanding context: creating a lasting impact in experimental software engineering research. In: Proceedings of the FSE/SDP workshop on future of software engineering research. ACM; 2010. p. 255–8.

[5] Bhattacharya P, Neamtiu I. Assessing programming language impact on development and maintenance: a study on C and C++. In: 33rd international conference on software engineering (ICSE), 2011. IEEE; 2011. p. 171–80.

[6] Nagappan M, Zimmermann T, Bird C. Diversity in software engineering research. In: Proceedings of the 2013 9th joint meeting on foundations of software engineering. ACM; 2013. p. 466–76.

Code reviews are not for finding defects—Even established tools need occasional evaluation

J. Czerwonka

Principal Architect Microsoft Corp., Redmond, WA, United States

CHAPTER OUTLINE

The process of code reviewing in software engineering is analogous to a plan review in civil engineering or a paper review in academia. In all these, there is the assumption that the quality of output increases by applying differing viewpoints to the subject being reviewed and allowing the author to consider and apply the resulting feedback before finalizing the work.

But output quality is only one of several benefits. And indeed, as software engineers, we often claim the primary goal of code reviewing is to find defects. In fact, we also want reviewing to ensure our code's long-term maintainability; we treat it as a knowledge sharing tool, and an avenue to broadcast ongoing progress [1]. On the surface, these are different purposes, but the common thread is that code reviews allow a group of people to communicate over a shared view of an artefact undergoing a change.

Modern code reviewing traces back its roots to the process of inspection [2]. Inspections were originally conceived as formal meetings, to which participants would prepare ahead of time. Unlike inspections, code reviews do not require participants to be in the same place nor do they happen at a fixed, prearranged time. Aligning with the distributed nature of many software projects, code reviews are now asynchronous and frequently support geographically distributed reviewers. Code review tools are now built with these characteristics in mind and are well-integrated into modern engineering workflows.

119

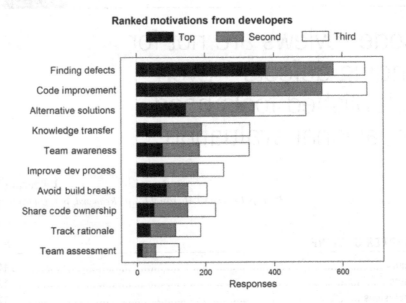

Because of their many uses and benefits, code reviews are a standard part of the modern software engineering workflow. But they come with non-trivial costs. Since they require heavy involvement of people, code reviewing is often the lengthiest part of code integration. On teams where code reviewing is a standard practice, the total time spent by each developer on code reviewing activities is, on average, between two and six hours per week [3,4].

Keeping in mind the significant costs of code reviewing, it is worth asking: do we currently use code reviews in the most efficient way? In what situations do code reviews provide more value than others? What is the value of consistency of applying code reviews equally to all code changes?

The confluence of many goals in one activity does not make it easy to understand where code reviews are most beneficial and how to best inject them into the overall engineering workflow so that the time spent waiting for the opinions of others is always justified. However, with the abundance of data coming from the engineering systems and having a diverse set of projects to observe [5], we finally have an opportunity to understand in detail the costs and benefits of the code review process.

RESULTS

Contrary to the often-stated primary goal of code reviews, they often do not find functionality defects. Only about 15% of comments provided by reviewers indicate a possible defect. Defects that should block a code commit are likely to be even less frequent. Rather, it is feedback related to the long-term code maintainability that comprises a much larger portion of comments provided by reviewers; at least 50% of all.

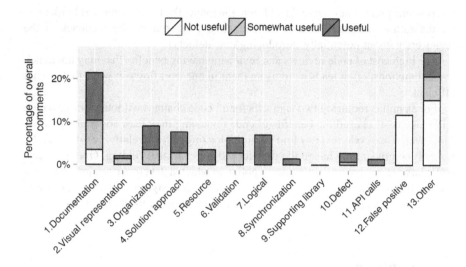

The usefulness of code review comments—as judged by the author of a code change—is positively correlated with reviewers' experience. Without prior exposure to the part of code base being reviewed, on average only 33% of any reviewer's comments are deemed useful by the author of a change. However, reviewers typically learn very fast. When reviewing the same part of code base for the third time, the usefulness ratio increases to about 67% of their comments. By the fourth time, it is equivalent to the project's long-term average [6].

Code review usefulness is negatively correlated with the size of a code review. That is, the more files there are in a single review, the lower the overall rate of useful feedback. The decrease, however, only starts to be noticeable for reviews with 20 or more changed files. In addition, the absolute number of useful comments per review peaks for reviews of around 50 files (6 useful comments), and then starts decreasing for larger reviews.

Code reviews take deliberation and are performed by people with a specific set of skills. The social aspect of code reviews cannot be ignored: people's roles on the team and their standing in the team's hierarchy influence the outcome. Often, it is not only the author of the change, but also the reviewers who find themselves under scrutiny.

EFFECTS

The modern code review process is expensive. Not only does it comprise a significant effort in terms of time spent, but it also it forces the reviewer to switch context away from their current work.

The median time from a review being requested to receiving all the necessary sign-offs is about 24 hours, with many lasting days, sometimes weeks [7]. A long time in review causes process stalls and affects anyone who might be waiting to take a dependency on the new code. In addition, the longer the review time, the harder it is for the author to switch back to the change and incorporate the feedback of the reviewers without potentially introducing new defects.

The high cost of code reviews and reviewing having benefits that may not match the assumptions, often leads us to using them in our workflows in ways that are not efficient.

For example, requiring two sign-offs for all code changes without discrimination will make costs exceed the benefits of code reviewing in at least some of the cases. Moreover, since code reviews find commit blocking defects relatively infrequently, it might be prudent to change the practices to better fit that finding. One of Microsoft's large teams recently instituted a policy in which a developer is allowed to proceed with a commit after the very first code review sign-off. If there are more comments coming after that, another commit can be made to finalize the change.

CONCLUSIONS

Code reviewing is an example of a software engineering process with established norms and expected outcomes. Its usage patterns and policies are often a result of combining the industry's collective learning and a specific team's culture. Past experiences of decision makers often dictate and reinforce policies. Even with such a well-established practice, it is useful to review its outcomes and verify if it applies to the specific context in which it is used, and if so, whether it still delivers the assumed results.

REFERENCES

[1] Bacchelli A, Bird C. Expectations, outcomes, and challenges of modern code review. In: Proceedings of the 2013 international conference on software engineering (ICSE '13). Piscataway, NJ, USA: IEEE Press; 2013. p. 712–21.

[2] Votta Jr. LG. Does every inspection need a meeting? SIGSOFT Softw Eng Notes 1993;18(5):107–14.

[3] Internal Microsoft code review active usage study.

[4] Bosu A, Carver J. Impact of peer code review on peer impression formation: a survey. In: Proceedings of the 7th ACM/IEEE international symposium on empirical software engineering and measurement (ESEM), 2013. Baltimore, MD, USA; 2013. p. 133–42.

[5] Czerwonka J, Nagappan N, Schulte W, Murphy B. CODEMINE: building a software development data analytics platform at microsoft. IEEE Softw 2013;30(4):64–71.

[6] Rigby PC, Bird C. Convergent contemporary software peer review practices. In: Proceedings of the 2013 9th joint meeting on foundations of software engineering (ESEC/FSE 2013). New York, NY, USA: ACM; 2013. p. 202–12.

[7] Bosu A, Greiler M, Bird C. Characteristics of useful code reviews: an empirical study at microsoft. In: Proceedings of the international conference on mining software repositories (MSR 2015); 2015.

Techniques

Interviews

C. Bird

Microsoft Research, Redmond, WA, United States

CHAPTER OUTLINE

WHY INTERVIEW?

Two years ago I was investigating code review latency at Microsoft. In the process of analyzing data from code reviews, I found something odd in the data for a team in Bing. Many of their code reviews were signed off in just minutes (sometimes *under* a minute) after the code review was created. That couldn't be right! I meticulously looked at the data collection code to see if there was an error. I manually looked at the reviews in question to try to see how and why the reviews were signed off so fast. I conducted a number of statistical tests on the data based on guesses that I had. As a last resort, I contacted one of the developers on the team and scheduled an interview. When we talked, he explained that the reason for the lightning fast reviews was that they often conduct code reviews in person with two or three reviewers huddled around the developer's screen as he explained the change. Once the reviewers were happy, the author would create the code review in the review system and the reviewers would immediately sign off on the review. The code review in the system didn't actually reflect how the code review was being done by the team. It hadn't occurred to me that this might be the reason for my data anomaly, and if I hadn't taken the time to actually ask the developer, I still wouldn't know. In just a few minutes, he had answered a question that I hadn't been able to answer after hours of testing hypotheses on data. In my view, this is one of the primary benefits of doing interviews. Unlike approaches based purely on recorded data where you must have some idea or hypothesis ahead of time (you can't compute a metric or run a t-test without first deciding what you want to measure or test), you can learn things in an interview that you would never have thought of yourself.

We have found that interviews can be wonderful tools for exploratory investigation and they often can drive the formation of theories and hypotheses. We can then use complementary quantitative methods to further investigate and support these hypotheses. Interviews allow rich engagement and follow up questions. You can collect historical data that is not recorded anywhere, as well as elicit opinions and impressions in richer detail than people would provide through written communication. Information from interviews can be triangulated with other data sources. In addition, interviews can be used to clarify things that have already happened (especially following an observation). In short, the interview can be an important tool that you should have in your research toolbox.

Interviews are not a panacea, however. Drawbacks of using interviews for research include the usually small sample size, the time required for each individual interview, the challenge of finding appropriate interviewees and scheduling a time that works for all parties, potential bias introduced by the interviewer during the interviewer (word choice, tone of voice, or even body language can potentially affect responses), and the time required for transcription and subsequent analysis. The pros and cons of the approach should always be weighed when making a decision about whether to interview.

In this chapter, I'll provide a description and best practices for the different phases of interview research based on experiences that we have had conducting interviews for software engineering research at Microsoft.

THE INTERVIEW GUIDE

Creating an interview guide helps interview research in a number of ways. An interview guide is simply a list of the high level topics that you plan on covering in the interview with the high level questions that you want to answer under each topic. We usually limit the guide to one page so that it's easy to refer to and to make sure that we're not getting too low level. The process of creating such a guide can help to focus and organize your line of thinking and therefore questioning.

When conducting the interview, we always bring a fresh copy of the guide so that we can easily cross off questions or topics as they are covered. Often we find that some questions are answered during the course of our conversation with the interviewee without even asking. Using the guide, I can check off the question on the guide so that we don't ask it explicitly later. It is important to remember that the interview guide really is only a *guide*. You don't have to follow the exact ordering and there's nothing wrong with "going off script" at times if a particular line of questioning that you hadn't anticipated seems worthwhile. You may also decide partway through that an entire line of questioning isn't appropriate for a particular interviewee. However, the guide can help you with pacing during an interview. If you're ten minutes into a thirty minute interview and you realize that you've only covered one topic out of the five on your guide, then you still have time to get back on track.

SELECTING INTERVIEWEES

While random sampling of a population is a good choice when doing quantitative analysis with a large sample, it is not the best approach when selecting interviewees. Due to the time and effort required in conducting interviews, it is unlikely that you would be able to get a large enough sample. Instead, I focus on capturing in my sample as much variation as possible along the dimensions that I believe may have an effect on the topic of my research.

As an example, I recently was trying to understand how people were using code review data at Microsoft. If I had selected a random sample, my interviewees would mostly be male software developers in their mid-twenties at low levels of seniority working in Redmond on shipping products. If I focused mostly on this demographic, I may have only gotten a narrow view of the ways that the data is used. Instead, we interviewed (among others) contracted developers in Asia, a program manager responsible for the education of a development team, an older female development lead from the Bay Area, and two senior managers making plans for a cloud product. By intentionally selecting a diverse set of interviewees with respect to seniority, age, role, geography, business responsibility, and product, we were able to capture a large number ways that the data was used.

You may not always be fortunate enough to be able to pick and choose your interviewees. In that case, you can take a *saturation*-based approach. Once you reach the point where you have not received any new answers to your questions after the last few interviews, you have likely reached *saturation* and further interviews are unlikely to provide much value.

RECRUITMENT

Once you have determined who you want to recruit for interviews, you need to contact them. We've found that it is helpful to do the following things when making contact, whether via email or some other means.

- Introduce yourself and explain your job or role.
- Tell them what the goal of your research is and how conducting an interview with them will help you accomplish that goal.
- Describe how what you are doing can potentially benefit them.

- Explain how long you estimate that the interview will take.
- Let them know if you'd like them to do anything to prepare for the interview. As an example, I once asked developers to open up a recent code review they had taken part in and look over it before I arrived.
- Tell them how they were selected. Did you select them because they fit some criteria, or were they selected at random?
- Share any information they need and ask for any information you need to be able to conduct the interview, such as Skype name or office location.

Often, research involving humans will need a consent form. Sending that in email during or soon after recruitment is important so that you don't forget it at the interview and you can answer any questions the interviewee might have.

COLLECTING BACKGROUND DATA

Depending on your goal, you may need to collect information specific to the interviewee prior to conducting the interview. As an example, a few years ago we were investigating the value of categorizing source code commits [1]. As part of this, once a developer had accepted an interview invitation, we categorized their commits and created graphs for each category over time so that we could ask them about the peaks and valleys of activity. Even if you don't need to collect specific artifacts or conduct analysis prior to the interview, learning a bit about the team, project, and processes that the interviewee is associated with can help you to be more effective during the interview.

CONDUCTING THE INTERVIEW

The most important phase of interview research is actually conducting the interview. Here are some suggestions.

When possible, we have two people conduct the interview together. One can focus on taking notes while the other manages the conversation (looks at the interview guide, maintains eye contact, etc.). Both people are listening, so they are more likely to notice comments or answers that require follow up questions and either interviewer can ask a question at any time. The two will likely notice different things during the interview so they can discuss what they noticed immediately afterward. We've found that more than two interviewers can create problems, as too many interviewers at once may be perceived as threatening and may also require finding a larger meeting space than a typical office.

We usually record the interview so that we can capture everything verbatim, but one of us is still tasked with taking copious notes during the interview. It's much easier to refer to notes than it is to find a particular place in a recording.

Remember that the purpose of the interview is to listen to the interviewee, not make them listen to you. It's easy to fall into the trap of talking too much in your interview. Often questions will require the interviewee to think for a while or recall events. Don't feel the need to fill that silence; it means they're trying to provide accurate and valuable responses.

Face to face interviews are ideal, even if the interview happens over the internet. By being able to see the interviewee and let them see you, you can have a richer, more engaging conversation. This allows you to pick up on non-verbal cues indicating enthusiasm, hesitance, confusion, or boredom and adjust your questions appropriately.

Be aware of time. Time passes more quickly during interviews than you expect. If I can tell that the interviewee is engaged and wants to share information, there's not a problem letting the interview run over time, but as a courtesy I usually let him or her know when the normal time slot has elapsed in case they need to go.

We usually bring a small token of appreciation and give it to the interviewee at the end of the interview. Often this is something small like a $5 Starbucks gift card. While the monetary value may be small, it shows that you appreciate them and leaves a positive impression.

When leaving, let them know if and how they'll hear from you in the future. I let people know that I'll pass along the final report or paper. I also ask if I can email them if I need any clarification on anything.

POST-INTERVIEW DISCUSSION AND NOTES

There are a number of things that we try to do as soon as possible after the interview while the interview is fresh in our minds.

We talk about the things that we noticed in the interview while it is fresh in our minds. This can include things that were surprising, things that we have heard before from other interviewees, and things that did or did not go well during the interview. We also talk about whether we've reached saturation and if our interview guide should be modified.

Based on these conversations and my own thoughts and impressions from the interview, I try to write down post-interview notes. I use the notes taken during the interview as part of the basis for this, but the post-interview notes are more coherent, organized, and thoughtful because they are not as constrained by time as in-interview notes.

TRANSCRIPTION

The decision about whether and how to transcribe an interview can be a difficult one. Services can be expensive, transcription software often doesn't work well, and doing it yourself can take a very long time, but all of these options have their benefits as well. One alternative is what I call "chunked transcription." This entails listening to a 10–30 second chunk of a recording, writing down the main point or idea in the chunk, and then moving to the next chunk. The advantage is that this doesn't need to be as precise as verbatim transcription, but still is able to capture the majority of the valuable content. These chunks end up being quite amenable to card sorting, the most common form of interview data analysis that we use.

ANALYSIS

The most fruitful method we have found for analyzing interview responses is *card sorting*. This entails literally printing off the individual answers to interview questions onto paper that we then cut into (often hundreds of) cards. We then group these cards into themes which can be used to organize reporting, can inform additional research methods such as creating surveys for quantitative support, or can be analyzed individually. Card sorts are beyond the scope of this chapter and can be used for almost any form of qualitative data such as open survey responses. For details, please take a look at the chapter *Card-sorting: From Text To Themes*.

REPORTING

There are a number of ways to report the results of interviews in papers, and I think the best way to learn is by reading a number of interview-based research papers. Work by Murphy-Hill et al. [2], Guzzi et al. [3], Singer et al. [4], and Li et al. [5] are good examples of such papers.

Here are a few things that you should consider including in a report or publication:

- The number of interviewees, how they were selected, how they were recruited.
- The duration and location of interviews as well as how they were conducted (eg, online or in person).
- A link to any interview guides or other artifacts used during the interviews.

Providing quotes directly in the paper can help tell a story, provide concrete evidence to support a point, or add engaging detail. However, be careful when providing quotes from interviews in a publication. It can be tempting to cherry-pick a controversial quote or take a quote out of context. I've heard more than a few quantitative leaning researchers make skeptical comments about quotes, so don't be guilty of their suspicions! One best practice used in many research papers is to use a quote that accurately captures the sentiment of a group of interviewees.

Finally, resist the temptation to apply quantitative methods to interview results. It's fine to say that only one person mentioned some topic, or almost everyone answered a particular question in the same way, but calculating confidence intervals from interview data is probably not a good idea.

NOW GO INTERVIEW!

Those who haven't conducted interviews before are often hesitant to try. You may feel more comfortable looking at raw data in the comfort of your own lab. Numbers can't put you on the spot or make you feel awkward. I can honestly say that I've learned more about how software engineering takes place by conducting interviews than I have through all of the other research methods I've used combined and I started with *much* less information about how to do it than is in this chapter. I hope this chapter has provided a few techniques to help you include interviews in your own research.

REFERENCES

[1] Hindle A, Bird C, Zimmermann T, Nagappan N. Relating requirements to implementation via topic analysis: do topics extracted from requirements make sense to managers and developers? In: Proceedings of the 28th IEEE international conference on software maintenance; 2012.

[2] Murphy-Hill ER, Zimmermann T, Nagappan N. Cowboys, ankle sprains, and keepers of quality: how is video game development different from software development? In: ICSE; 2014.

[3] Guzzi A, Bacchelli A, Riche Y, van Deursen A. Supporting developers' coordination in the IDE. In: Proceedings of CSCW 2015 (18th ACM conference on computer-supported cooperative work and social computing); 2015. p. 518–32.

[4] Singer L, Figueira Filho F, Storey M-A. Software engineering at the speed of light: how developers stay current using twitter. In: Proceedings of the 36th international conference on software engineering. New York: ACM; 2014.

[5] Li PL, Ko AJ, Zhu J. What makes a great software engineer? In: Proceedings of the 37th international conference on software engineering. Vol. 1. Piscataway: IEEE Press; 2015.

Look for state transitions in temporal data

R. Holmes
University of British Columbia, Vancouver, Canada

CHAPTER OUTLINE

BIKESHEDDING IN SOFTWARE ENGINEERING

A group of scientists sit down on a nice sunny day to examine a large tabular data set they have experimentally gathered. The first order of business is to figure out what program they should use for analysis; should they use Excel? OpenOffice? R? An online collaborative spreadsheet? Resolving the matter to everyone's satisfaction takes 1 h. Next they tackle the column names: should they be all caps? Can they contain spaces? Should they be short, or should they be descriptive? Agreeing to a naming scheme takes another 3 h.

Throughout this time, the data is just sitting there. Row upon row. Waiting to give insight. But the volume is overwhelming; it is more comfortable to tackle issues that are easy to reason about and have less technical baggage. This phenomenon is known as "bikeshedding," or Parkinson's law of triviality. Rather than exploring the data itself, the meeting gets derailed by administrative minutiae. This phenomena is also related to "analysis paralysis," whereby transitioning from *talking* about something to actually *doing* it is overwhelming and inhibits progress.

SUMMARIZING TEMPORAL DATA

As in the preceding bikeshedding example, it is easy to be overwhelmed with the complexity of large datasets. Faced with a daunting data set (once of course it is appropriately formatted and named), we often want to build some form of summarization. Given the tabular form of the data, it is often tempting to count events or to build distributions because these are easy to think about; however, in data sets that are temporal in nature it is possible to find interesting relationships between data points by noting how they are related through time. One possible quick summarization approach that can often reveal interesting insights that are difficult to spot with a more tabular approach are state-transition diagrams.

To create a state-transition diagram, first identify the "states" that are possible (for instance, for a test execution you could have a pass, error, or fail; for a code review you could have the review request, a positive review, or a negative review). Next, iterate through the data and figure out at each point in time what state is appropriate in each instance in time. Finally, draw a state-transition diagram where each node is a state and edges represent transitions between the states. Annotate each edge with a count representing the number of times it occurred in the data. Two important things are often visible in these diagrams. First, the most dominant transitions are instantly visible and can help to guide future investigations. Second, unexpected edges are often present.

While any expected edge confirms your understanding of the data, unexpected edges provide insight into how your model of the data could be incorrect. These unexpected transitions are therefore a great place to start a qualitative investigation of the individual data points they represent and provide a concrete way to move from a summarization to an in-depth examination of specific rows in your data.

A concrete example is shown in the following figure. In this work, we compared code review practices between Webkit and Firefox. The possible states a code review can be in are shown in the rectangles. The shaded rectangles represent terminal states for a code review. The only distinction between states that are terminal and those that are transitory is that reviews do not transition out of terminal states; a patch that is updated and resubmitted for a new review is considered as if it were new. We next examined how the code reviews move between the states; the annotations on the edges describe these. A request review is annotated with an r?, while a positive review is r+ and a negative review is r−. The Firefox project also uses a super-review for some patches, which accounts for the sr+ and sr− edges. The percentage labels correspond to number of patches flowing across each state transition divided by the total number of total starting edges (review requests, in this case). For example, 7.9% of the 34,749 patches in Webkit (or 2745) were resubmitted for additional review, even though they had been accepted.

By examining the summarization of the tens of thousands of data points provided by the state-transition diagram, we can see some huge differences between the two projects. The most notable of these is the edge between submitted and resubmitted for Webkit; while at first we thought this was an error in our data, it gave us a concrete question to approach the Webkit developers about and greatly contributed to our understanding of the Webkit code review process (it turns out Webkit runs automated analyses on patches; if an analysis turns up a problem, the developer will "obsolete" their own patch and resubmit a new one).

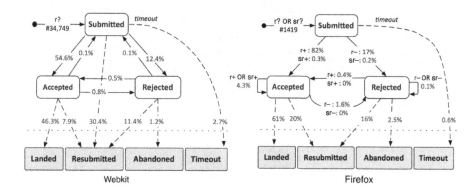

Webkit   Firefox

RECOMMENDATIONS

(1)   Data can be overwhelming; while tabular summarization is often tempting, this can abstract away important relationships between data points.

(2)   The flows between implicit states in the data are often hard to identify and can provide tremendous insight into what the data represents.

(3)   Starting a qualitative investigation from events captured by unexpected transitions often highlights conceptual misunderstandings which can be used to refine and improve the initial model or suggest future research ideas.

REFERENCE

[1] Baysal O, Kononenko O, Holmes R, Godfrey MW. Investigating technical and non-technical factors influencing modern code review. J Empir Softw Eng 2015;1–28, http://dx.doi.org/10.1007/s10664-015-9366-8.

Card-sorting: From text to themes

T. Zimmermann
Microsoft Research, Redmond, WA, United States

CHAPTER OUTLINE

Suppose you just ran a survey with the question "What problems are stopping us from meeting our deadlines?" Since you didn't know the problems in advance, you asked participants to simply write the problems into a textbox. This type of question is called an open-ended question; in contrast to closed-ended questions, which limit participants to a list of predefined answer choices. Your survey was very successful and you received hundreds of responses. Now you want to make sense of the data. How can you do this in a systematic way?

I've frequently used card sorting to derive themes from text. Card sorting is widely used to create mental models and derive taxonomies from data and to deduce a higher level of abstraction and identify common themes. The idea is simple: *print text on index cards and sort them into groups* that correspond to themes. This has several advantages compared to, say, annotating text in Excel. With physical cards it's easy to split and merge groups or simply just read the cards of a group. You also build up spatial memory of the groups, which helps with remembering the groups.

Over past years I used card sorting in dozens of projects for the analysis of survey data and software artifacts. Here are two examples:

- Andrew Begel and I used card sorting to analyze the responses to a survey question "Please list up to five questions you would like (a team of data scientists who specialize in studying how software is developed) to answer." We received 679 questions, which we sorted into 12 themes such as Bug Measurements, Development Practices, and Productivity. We then distilled the responses (raw questions) into descriptive questions, which led to a final catalog of 145 questions.

- Silvia Breu, Rahul Premraj, Jonathan Sillito, and I used card sorting to identify frequently asked questions in bug reports. We extracted 947 questions from a random sample of 600 bug reports which we then sorted into eight themes such as Missing Information, Triaging, and Status Inquiry. For each question we had additional statistics such as when the question was asked, whether it was answered, and how long the response took. This allowed us to combine the card sort with a quantitative analysis.

There are two basic types of card sorts. *Open* card sorts have no predefined groups; the groups emerge and evolve during the sorting process. *Closed* card sorts have predefined groups; they are typically used when the themes are known in advance. In some cases, *hybrid* card sorts can work well too, you start with a representative sample of cards to identify themes, and then later sort the remaining cards into those themes. Most times I've used open card sorts.

Cart sorting has three phases: in the *preparation phase*, we create cards for each response; in the *execution phase*, cards are sorted into meaningful groups with a descriptive title; finally, in the *analysis phase*, abstract hierarchies are formed in order to deduce general categories and themes.

PREPARATION PHASE

To create the cards, I use the Mail Merge feature of Microsoft Word. The input is simply an Excel spreadsheet with one row per card and all the relevant information separated into columns (with column headers). Word allows you to customize the layout of the cards by using the Mail Merge fields.

It is important to have one thought/comment per row. For *surveys*, the best approach is to design the survey in a way that allows different thoughts to be entered separately. For example, instead of having one text box for all five responses, Andrew Begel and I provided one text box for each response: "Please enter your first response." TEXTBOX. "Please enter your second response." TEXTBOX. And so on. Unfortunately, it is not always possible or practical to design surveys in such a way. In that case, you might have to split responses manually (sometimes with support from your survey tool), ideally before you print your cards. For *large documents* like webpages, interview transcripts, or PDF files, quantitative coding tools such as Atlas. TI or QDA Miner (which has a free Lite version) can be used to extract relevant pieces of text from large documents.

On each card, I print demographics, if available, and always a card identifier to uniquely label the card. The *demographics* provide you with a better context during sorting. The *identifier* allows you to combine the results of the card sort with additional data, which can enable additional analysis later on (see the following for an example). I simply number the cards to get my identifiers, eg, 100, 101, 102. I typically start at higher numbers (like 100 or 1000) so that all identifiers have the same number of digits; I found that this helps to enter card numbers more easily into the computer later on.

I usually prints cards 4-up on a letter page. Print the text in a large font (at least 20 point); the larger the better, and the easier it is to read. After the mail merge, you can manually reduce the font size for any cards that don't fit. A trick I recently discovered is to sort the Excel sheet by response length (put longer responses in the first rows to prevent Excel from cutting off text). That way, you have to only go through some cards to reduce the font size, or you could split the responses into two or more sets (eg, one set for short responses in a large font, one set for long responses in a smaller font).

EXECUTION PHASE

Get a large room for your card sort. Besides the cards, bring pens, sticky notes, markers, envelopes, and rubber bands. Use the pens and sticky notes to create descriptive titles once you have several cards in a group. Use the markers to highlight important text, for example, when the text is very long. Plan about 2 hours for a card-sorting session, but not more than three hours. Longer sessions give you brain freeze. If you have a large number of cards you will need multiple sessions. Don't forget to take breaks.

The first card is the easiest one to sort. It always starts its own group. For the second card, decide if it is similar to the first group. If it is similar, put it in the first group, if not start a new group. Repeat for each of the following cards: decide if it fits an existing group, and if not start a new group. Keep going until you run out of cards.

Don't overthink where to put a card. If it's difficult to decide where to put a card, put it at the end of the pile and come back to it later. The groups are not fixed and can change during the course of the card sort. It is fair game to split, merge, or even resort groups. For example, when a group gets very big, you might want to revisit the cards and see if there are important subthemes. While sorting, you might discover some cards that make no sense or are off-topic; I put those in a special Discard group.

Card sorting in teams can help you derive better themes and sort a larger number of cards. Jointly sort the first few cards with the entire team (calibration phase), then divide up the cards, but still communicate while sorting. Let others know when you start a new group. When you have an ambiguous card, read the card out loud and ask others for feedback. Avoid having more than four or five people for a card sort. Too many cooks spoil the broth. Always have one team member lead the card sort.

Don't forget to take photos of your card sort. That will help you to later reconstruct the spatial layout of the cards. Photos are also great to impress friends or to explain the process in a presentation. Please refer to Fig. 1.

After you are done with the card sort, use the envelopes and rubber bands to store the cards. I put the sticky note to the side of the top card and then pile up the groups. Have the sticky note stick out a little from the top card. That helps you to later separate the pile of cards into the individual groups.

FIG. 1

A card sorting session.

ANALYSIS PHASE

After you are done with the card sort, it's a good idea to go through the cards one more time to check for consistency within the groups. It's still okay to move cards around, though at some point you want to freeze the groups.

As the last step, take a look at the groups and see if you can deduce more general categories and themes, especially if you have many groups. In the card sort of data science questions, Andrew Begel and I ended up with 60 groups... too many to make sense of the data! We then used affinity diagrams to find general themes. The result was a hierarchy of themes and categories. Each group from the card sort was a category. We then combined categories into themes. For example, the groups "Productivity Measures," "Measuring the Individual," "Impact on Productivity from Build and Process Tools," and "Tradeoffs between Vendors and Full Time Employees" all became part of the theme "Productivity."

If you have extra data, you can do a quantitative analysis of the themes. For example, for the card sort of bug reports questions, we had the response time for each question. With the identifier, we could tie back the response time to the different themes and check for differences. Before you can do the analysis, you need to enter the results of the card sort into the computer. Always enter card numbers in pairs: one person reads out the numbers, the other types in the numbers. Both check for errors. To combine card sort categories with the original data, I use the VLOOKUP function in Excel.

Last, a word of caution. A common mistake is to give more importance to themes that have more cards; however, quantifying inherently qualitative data is dangerous. Here's a simple example for the question from the beginning "What problems are stopping us from meeting our deadlines?" If someone does not mention the slow build system as a problem, it does not automatically mean that they are happy with the build system. They might not have recently worked with the build system or they just did not think of it when they took the survey.

That's all you need to get started with your first card sort. Good luck!

REFERENCES

[1] Begel A, Zimmermann T. Analyze this! 145 questions for data scientists in software engineering. In: Proceedings of the 36th international conference on software engineering (ICSE 2014). New York, NY: ACM; 2014. p. 12–23.

[2] Breu S, Premraj R, Sillito J, Zimmermann T. Information needs in bug reports: improving cooperation between developers and users. In: Proceedings of the 2010 ACM conference on computer supported cooperative work (CSCW 2010). New York, NY: ACM; 2010. p. 301–10.

[3] Mail merge for email, http://office.microsoft.com/en-us/word-help/use-word-mail-merge-for-email-HA102809788.aspx.

[4] Affinity diagram, https://en.wikipedia.org/wiki/Affinity_diagram.

Tools! Tools! We need tools!

D. Spinellis

Athens University of Economics and Business, Athens, Greece

TOOLS IN SCIENCE

In 1908, Ernest Rutherford won the Nobel Prize in Chemistry "for his investigations into the disintegration of the elements, and the chemistry of radioactive substances." In support of his candidacy, the Nobel Committee for Chemistry wrote about the elegant experiments he performed to show that alpha particles were in fact doubly-charged helium atoms. Rutherford was able to show this through a simple but ingenious device. He had a glassblower create a tube with an extremely thin wall that allowed the alpha particles emanating from the radon gas it contained to escape. Surrounding that tube was another from which he had emptied the air. After some days he found that the material accumulated in the outer tube produced the spectrum of helium [1].

Science has always progressed mightily through the use of tools. These are increasingly designed by scientists, but built by engineers and technicians. Telescopes allow us to see stars at the edge of our universe, imaging satellites uncover the workings of our Earth, genome sequencers and microscopes let us examine cells and molecules, and particle accelerators peer into the nature of atoms. Currently the world's largest single machine is a tool explicitly built to advance our scientific understanding of matter: CERN's 27 km-round Large Hadron Collider, which more than 10,000 scientists and engineers from over a 100 countries built over a period of 10 years.

THE TOOLS WE NEED

The availability and use of large data sets associated with software development has transformed software engineering in ways described in other chapters of this book. A key element for the application of data science in software engineering is the availability of suitable tools. Such tools allow us to obtain data from novel sources, measure processes and products, and analyze all that data to derive insights that can advance science and everyday practice. By definition, scientific advancement happens through work beyond the state of the art, so it should come as no surprise that a lot of effort in data science involves building and refining tools. In the following paragraphs I outline important types of tools and best practices for building them. In order to provide insights on the building of tools, the description is mostly based on personal experience.

First we need tools for **obtaining metrics**. Although software metrics have been with us for decades, tools for obtaining them reliably are often hard to come by. I've seen research work where the collection of metrics was treated as an afterthought, apparently delegated to inexperienced undergraduate students. This is often evident from the quality of the corresponding tools, which may not scale, may produce erroneous results, or may be difficult to build upon.

Partly as a result of such problems, in 2005 I built *ckjm*,[1] a tool that derives Chidamber and Kemerer metrics from Java programs [2]. These are the weighted methods per class, the depth of the inheritance tree, the number of children per class, the coupling between object classes, the response for a class, and the lack of cohesion in methods [3]. Designing *ckjm* to work as a Unix-style filter allowed it to analyze arbitrarily-large projects, an advantage appreciated by many of its users.

Also during 2000–10 I built *CScout*,[2] a source code analyzer and refactoring browser for collections of C programs. It can process workspaces of multiple projects (a project is defined as a collection of C source files that are linked together) mapping the complexity introduced by the C preprocessor back into the original C source code files. *CScout* takes advantage of modern hardware advances (fast processors and large memory capacities) to analyze C source code beyond the level of detail and accuracy provided by current compilers, linkers, and other source code analyzers [4]. The analysis *CScout* performs takes into account the identifier scopes introduced by the C preprocessor and the C language proper scopes and namespaces. After the source code analysis *CScout* can:

- perform accurate cross-project identifier renames,
- process sophisticated queries on identifiers, files, and functions,
- locate unused or wrongly-scoped identifiers,
- identify header files that don't need to be included, and
- create call graphs spanning both C functions and function-like macros.

---

[1] www.spinellis.gr/sw/ckjm/
[2] www.spinellis.gr/cscout/

The implementation of *CScout* required developing a theory behind the analysis of C code in the presence of the preprocessor [5], and the detailed handling of many compiler extensions and edge cases. I used *CScout* to compare four operating system kernels [6] and later look at the optimization of header-file included directives [7]. Both tasks required months of work in order to adjust *CScout* to the requirements of the analysis task. Despite its sophistication, *CScout* has seen considerably less use than *ckjm*, probably because of the considerable work required to put it to work.

More recently, in order to analyze the use and evolution of C language constructs and style, I adopted a simpler approach, and built *qmcalc*:[3] a tool that will perform lexical analysis of C source code and calculate and print numerous metrics associated with it. The program reads a single C file from its standard input and outputs raw figures and diverse quality metrics associated with the code. These include the number of functions, lines, and statements; the number of occurrences of various keywords; the use of comments and preprocessing; the number and length of identifiers; the Halstead and cyclomatic complexity per function; the use of spacing for indentation; a measure of style inconsistency; and numbers associated with probable style infractions. What *qmcalc* lacks in sophistication, it offers in versatility, as it can process any code thrown at it, including code with errors or obscure undocumented constructs. This made it easy to analyze millions of lines of diverse code [8].

A second category of tools are those we use to **obtain or synthesize data** from processes and running products, which can then be distilled into metrics. Such tools bridge the gap between the utilitarian data formats used to support software developers and the needs of data science for software engineering. Given that computers are reflective machines, the possibilities for data collection are endless. One example in this category is GHTorrent,[4] a system that obtains data through GitHub's event API (whose raison d'être is the automation of software development processes) and makes them available as a database [9,10]. Another is a set of tools[5] used to synthesize a Git repository[6] containing 44 years of Unix evolution from software distribution snapshots and diverse configuration management repositories [11]. The development of both tools demonstrated the difficulties associated with processing big, incomplete, and fickle data sets. The associated tools must be able to handle perverse cases, such as dates lying several years into the future or several-kilobytes-long file names. Other interesting data generation tools are those that instrument integrated development environments to obtain usage details [12]. These can give us valuable insights on how developers actually work, minimizing the risk of self-report bias. Instrumenting programs, libraries, and middleware can also provide valuable data. For example, by modifying memory allocation functions and a call graph profiler's function call processing code, I obtained data to illustrate memory fragmentation and stack size variability [13].

---

[3] https://github.com/dspinellis/cqmetrics
[4] http://ghtorrent.org/
[5] https://github.com/dspinellis/unix-history-make
[6] https://github.com/dspinellis/unix-history-repo

Finally, a third category of tools are those we use to **analyze data**. Thankfully in this segment there are many general-purpose mature tools and libraries that we can readily use. These include R, Python's data tools,[7] and relational database management systems often (mis)used to perform online analytical processing. Skimping on the effort required to master these tools in favor of ad hoc approaches is a mistake. Then, there are also specialized platforms, such as *Alitheia Core* [14], *Evolizer* [15], and *Tesseract* [16], that can analyze software engineering data. These can be very helpful if the research question matches closely the tool's capabilities. Otherwise, their complexity often makes tailoring them more expensive than developing bespoke tooling.

RECOMMENDATIONS FOR TOOL BUILDING

Given the importance of tools in conducting software engineering research, the most important piece of advice is to **hone your tool-building skills**. I have written tools in Perl, the Unix shell, C++, and Java. C++ can be beneficial when extreme performance is required (in some cases I have run processing jobs that took many months to complete). Java can be useful when interacting with other elements in its ecosystem, for example the Eclipse platform. Perl has the advantage of a huge library of mature components that can cover even the most specialized needs, such as processing legacy SCCS (source code control system) files, but the underlying language shows its age. Using the Unix shell benefits from the power of the hundreds of tools available under it, and can be a particularly good choice when the heavy lifting will be performed by such tools. Otherwise, a modern scripting language, such a Python or Ruby, can offer the best balance between versatility, programmer efficiency, and performance. Choose the language that appeals to your taste and requirements, and sharpen your skills in its use.

Given that many of the tools used are bespoke contraptions rather than mature software, **testing** them thoroughly is a must. Thankfully, the practice of unit testing provides methods for performing this task in an organized and systematic fashion. According to the software's change logs, when developing *qmcalc*, 130 unit tests uncovered more than 15 faults. Without these tests some of these faults might have resulted in erroneous results when the tool was used. Given the large data sizes processed, testing can often be optimized through appropriate sampling. This allows the data input and output to be carefully inspected by hand in order to validate the tool's operation.

Finally, when developing tools consider **sharing** the results of your efforts as open source software and contributing to other similar endeavors. This allows our field to progress by standing on each other's shoulders rather than toes. It is also a practice that aids the reproducibility of research, as others can easily obtain and reuse the tools used for conducting it. In addition, the knowledge that your tool will

---

[7]http://pydata.org/downloads/

be shared as open source software where the whole world will be able to see and judge it, puts pressure on you to develop it from the beginning, not as a quick and dirty throwaway hack, but as the high-quality piece of software it deserves to be.

Historians have commented that when Rutherford's glassblower, Otto Baumbach, was interned during the First World War, experimental physics at the University of Manchester where he had set up shop were brought to a halt [17]. Such is the power of tools to advance great science.

REFERENCES

[1] Rutherford E, Royds T. The nature of the alpha particle from radioactive substances. Philos Mag 1909;17(6):281–6.

[2] Spinellis D. Tool writing: a forgotten art? IEEE Softw 2005;22(4):9–11. http://dx.doi.org/10.1109/MS.2005.111.

[3] Chidamber SR, Kemerer CF. A metrics suite for object oriented design. IEEE Trans Softw Eng 1994;20:476–93.

[4] Spinellis D. CScout: a refactoring browser for C. Sci Comput Program 2010;75(4):216–31. http://dx.doi.org/10.1016/j.scico.2009.09.003.

[5] Spinellis D. Global analysis and transformations in preprocessed languages. IEEE Trans Softw Eng 2003;29(11):1019–30.

[6] Spinellis D. A tale of four kernels. In: Schafer W, Dwyer MB, Gruhn V, editors. ICSE'08: proceedings of the 30th international conference on software engineering. New York: Association for Computing Machinery; 2008. p. 381–90. http://dx.doi.org/10.1145/1368088.1368140.

[7] Spinellis D. Optimizing header file include directives. J Softw Maint Evol Res Pract 2009;21(4):233–51. http://dx.doi.org/10.1002/smr.369.

[8] Spinellis D, Louridas P, Kechagia M. An exploratory study on the evolution of C programming in the Unix operating system. In: ESEM'15: proceedings of the 9th international symposium on empirical software engineering and measurement. New York, USA: IEEE; 2015. p. 54–7.

[9] Gousios G, Spinellis D. GHTorrent: Github's data from a firehose. In: Lanza M, Di Penta M, Xie T, editors. Proceedings of the 9th IEEE working conference on mining software repositories (MSR). New York, USA: IEEE; 2012. p. 12–21. http://dx.doi.org/10.1109/MSR.2012.6224294.

[10] Gousios G. The GHTorrent dataset and tool suite. In: MSR'13: proceedings of the 10th working conference on mining software repositories; 2013. p. 233–6.

[11] Spinellis D. A repository with 44 years of Unix evolution. In: MSR'15: proceedings of the 12th working conference on mining software repositories. New York, USA: IEEE; 2015. p. 13–6. http://dx.doi.org/10.1109/MSR.2015.6.

[12] Murphy GC, Kersten M, Findlater L. How are Java software developers using the Eclipse IDE? IEEE Softw 2006;23(4):76–83.

[13] Spinellis D. Code quality: the open source perspective. Boston, MA: Addison-Wesley; 2006.

[14] Gousios G, Spinellis D. Conducting quantitative software engineering studies with Alitheia Core. Empir Softw Eng 2014;19(4):885–925. http://dx.doi.org/10.1007/s10664-013-9242-3.

[15] Gall HC, Fluri B, Pinzger M. Change analysis with evolizer and changedistiller. IEEE Softw 2009;26(1):26–33.

[16] Sarma A, et al. Tesseract: interactive visual exploration of socio-technical relationships in software development. In: ICSE 2009: IEEE 31st international conference on software engineering. New York, USA: IEEE; 2009.

[17] Gall A. Otto Baumbach—Rutherford's glassblower. Newsletter published by History of Physics. Group of the Institute of Physics (UK & Ireland); 2008; (23). p. 44–55.

Evidence-based software engineering

T. Dybå*, G.R. Bergersen[†], D.I.K. Sjøberg*,[†]

SINTEF ICT, Trondheim, Norway* *University of Oslo, Norway*[†]

CHAPTER OUTLINE

INTRODUCTION

> *I believe in evidence. I believe in observation, measurement, and reasoning, confirmed by independent observers. I'll believe anything, no matter how wild and ridiculous, if there is evidence for it. The wilder and more ridiculous something is, however, the firmer and more solid the evidence will have to be.*
>
> **Isaac Asimov**

A decade ago, Kitchenham, Dybå and Jørgensen coined the term and provided the foundations for *evidence-based software engineering* (EBSE). A trilogy of papers was written for researchers [1], practitioners [2], and educators [3]. They suggested that practitioners consider EBSE as a mechanism to support and improve their technology adoption decisions, and that researchers should use systematic literature reviews as a methodology for performing unbiased aggregation of empirical results. This spurred significant international activity, and a renewed focus on research methods and theory, and on the future of empirical methods in SE research [4].

THE AIM AND METHODOLOGY OF EBSE

EBSE aims to improve decision making related to software development and maintenance by integrating the best current evidence from research with practical experience and human values.

Based on the stages in evidence-based medicine, EBSE involves five steps [2]:

1. *Ask an answerable question.* The main challenge in this step is to convert a practical problem into a question that's specific enough to be answered, but not so specific that you don't get any answers. Partitioning the question into the main intervention or action you're interested in, the context or specific situation of interest, and the main outcomes or effect of interest, makes it easier not only to go from general problem descriptions to specific questions, but also to think about what kind of information you need to answer the question.
2. *Find the best evidence.* Finding an answer to your question includes selecting an appropriate information resource and executing a search strategy. There are several information sources you can use. You can, for example, get viewpoints from your customers or the software's users, colleagues or an expert, use what you've learned as a student or in professional courses, use your own experience, or search for research-based evidence.
3. *Critically appraise the evidence.* Unfortunately, published research isn't always of good quality; the problem under study might be unrelated to practice, or the research method might have weaknesses such that you can't trust the results. To assess whether research is of good quality and is applicable to practice, you must be able to critically appraise the evidence.
4. *Apply the evidence.* To employ the evidence in your decision-making, you integrate it with your practical experience, your customers' requirements, and your knowledge of the concrete situation's specific circumstances, and then you apply it in practice. However, this procedure isn't straightforward and, among other things, depends on the type of technology you're evaluating.
5. *Evaluate performance.* The final step is to consider how well you perform each step of EBSE and how you might improve your use of it. In particular, you should ask yourself how well you're integrating evidence with practical experience, customer requirements, and your knowledge of the specific circumstances. You must also assess whether the change has been effective.

It's important to note that recommendations on evidence-based medicine tend to be context independent and implicitly universal, while software engineering prescriptions are contingent and sensitive to variation in the organizational context.

CONTEXTUALIZING EVIDENCE

What works for whom, where, when, and why is the ultimate question of EBSE [5]. Still, the empirical research seems mostly concerned with identifying universal relationships that are independent of how work settings and other contexts interact with the processes important to software practice. Questions of "What is best?" seem to prevail. For example, "Which is better: pair or solo programming? Test-first or test-last?"

However, just as the question of whether a helicopter is better than a bicycle is meaningless, so are these questions, because the answers depend on the settings and goals of the projects studied. Practice settings are rarely, if ever, the same. For example, the environments of software organizations differ, as do their sizes, customer types, countries or geography, and history. All these factors influence engineering practices in unique ways. Additionally, the human factors underlying the organizational culture differ from one organization to the next, and also influence the way software is developed.

We know these issues and the ways they interrelate are important for the successful uptake of research into practice. However, the nature of these relationships is poorly understood. Consequently, we can't a priori assume that the results of a particular study apply outside the specific context in which it was run. Taking something out of context leads to misunderstanding; for instance, "I am attached to you" has very different meanings for a person in love and a handcuffed prisoner.

STRENGTH OF EVIDENCE

Several systems exist for making judgments about the strength of evidence of a body of knowledge. Most of these systems suggest that the strength of evidence can be based on a hierarchy with systematic reviews and randomized experiments at the top and evidence from observational studies and expert opinion at the bottom. The inherent weakness such evidence hierarchies is that randomized experiments are not always feasible and that, in some instances, observational studies may provide better evidence.

To cope with these weaknesses of evidence hierarchies, the GRADE working group ([6], see Table 1) grades the overall strength of evidence of systematic reviews as high, moderate, low, or very low.

According to GRADE, the strength of evidence can be determined on the basis of the combination of four key elements: study design (there were only two randomized trials in the review), study quality (how well methods were described, how issues of bias, validity, and reliability were addressed, and how methods of data collection and

Table 1 Definitions used for grading the strength of evidence [6]

High	Further research is very unlikely to change our confidence ibvn the estimate of effect
Moderate	Further research is likely to have an important impact on our confidence in the estimate of effect and may change the estimate
Low	Further research is very likely to have an important impact on our confidence in the estimate of effect and is likely to change the estimate
Very low	Any estimate of effect is very uncertain

analysis were explained), consistency (the similarity of estimates of effect across studies), and directness (the extent to which the people, interventions, and outcome measures are similar to those of interest). Combining these four components, Dybå and Dingsøyr [7] found that the strength of the evidence regarding the benefits and limitations of agile methods, and for decisions related to their adoption, was *very low*. Hence, they concluded that any estimate of effect that is based on evidence of agile software development from research is very uncertain. However, their systematic review was published in 2008, and many more empirical studies of agile software development have been published since then.

EVIDENCE AND THEORY

Consider, for example, the "reversing effect theory" (Cf. Sjøberg et al. this book). Why would this theory be worthy of being believed by contemporary software engineers? A plausible answer is that the evidence possessed by contemporary software engineers strongly suggests that it is true. Paradigmatically, those theories that are worthy of being believed enjoy such status in virtue of the availability of evidence sufficient to justify belief in their truth.

Evidence that supports or tells in favor of a given theory *supports* that theory. On the other hand, evidence that tells against a theory *weakens* that theory. Of course, a given piece of evidence might confirm or disconfirm a theory to a greater or lesser degree. "Verification" signifies the maximal degree of confirmation: evidence may *support* a theory in the sense it conclusively establishes that the theory in question is true (even though one can never be absolutely certain). At the opposite end of the spectrum, *falsification* signifies the maximal level of disconfirmation: evidence falsifies a theory just in case it conclusively establishes that the theory in question is false [8].

In considering questions about how a given body of evidence bears on a theory, it is crucial to distinguish between the *balance* of the evidence and its *weight*. Intuitively, the balance of the evidence concerns how decisively the evidence tells for or against the theory. On the other hand, the weight of the evidence is a matter of how substantial the evidence is. However, for any body of evidence, there will always be alternative theories that constitute equally good explanations of that evidence [8].

REFERENCES

[1] Kitchenham BA, Dybå T, Jørgensen M. Evidence-based software engineering. In: Proc. 26th international conference on software engineering (ICSE 2004), Edinburgh, Scotland, 23–28 May; 2004. p. 273–81.
[2] Dybå T, Kitchenham BA, Jørgensen M. Evidence-based software engineering for practitioners. IEEE Softw 2005;22(1):58–65.

[3] Jørgensen M, Dybå T, Kitchenham BA. Teaching evidence-based software engineering to university students. In: Proc. 11th international software metrics symposium (Metrics 2005), Como, Italy, 19–22 September 2005; 2005.

[4] Sjøberg DIK, Dybå T, Jørgensen M. The future of empirical methods in software engineering research. In: Briand L, Wolf A, editors. 29th international conference on software engineering (ICSE'07), Minneapolis, Minnesota, USA, 20–26 May. Future of software engineering. Los Alamitos, CA: IEEE Computer Society Press; 2007. p. 358–78.

[5] Dybå T. Contextualizing empirical evidence. IEEE Softw 2013;30(1):81–3.

[6] Grades of Recommendation, Assessment, Development, and Evaluation (GRADE) Working Group. Grading Quality of Evidence and Strength of Recommendations. BMJ 2004;328(7454):1490–4.

[7] Dybå T, Dingsøyr T. Empirical studies of agile software development: a systematic review. Inf Softw Technol 2008;50(9–10):833–59.

[8] Kelly T. Evidence: fundamental concepts and the phenomenal conception. Philos Compass 2008;3(5):933–55.

Which machine learning method do you need?

L.L. Minku

University of Leicester, Leicester, United Kingdom

CHAPTER OUTLINE

LEARNING STYLES

An unarguable fact in teaching is that people do not all learn in the same way. Some of us spend hours reading instructions, whereas others just start trying things out to learn from the outcome. Some of us quickly adjust to new situations and technologies, whereas others tend to stick to the traditions. People also tend to use different approaches to learn different tasks. If we try to use an approach that is unsuitable for us, we will not be able to learn well or will take a much longer time to learn.

This is no different in machine learning for software data analytics. There is a plethora of learning algorithms that can be used for several different purposes. Learning algorithms can give us insights into software processes and products, such as what software modules are most likely to contain bugs [1], what amount of effort is likely to be required to develop new software projects [2], what commits are most likely to induce crashes [3], how the productivity of a company changes over time [4], how to improve productivity [4], etc.

The right learning algorithm depends on the data and the environment being modeled. In order to create good data models, it is important to investigate the data analytics problem at hand before choosing the type of learning algorithm to be used. Here are a few useful questions to ask.

DO ADDITIONAL DATA ARRIVE OVER TIME?

Databases containing software project data may not have a static size—they may grow over time. For example, consider the task of predicting whether commits are likely to induce crashes [3]. New commits and new information on whether they have induced crashes may become available over time. When additional data are produced over time, it is desirable to use such incoming data to improve data models. Online learning algorithms are able to update data models with incoming data continuously. Chunk-based learning algorithms wait for a new chunk of data to arrive, and then use it to update the data models. Different from offline learning algorithms, online and chunk-based learning algorithms do not need to reprocess old data or completely rebuild the data model once new data becomes available [5]. In this way, they are able to update data models faster. Given that rebuilding data models several times can be painfully slow when data sets are not small, this is particularly useful for larger data sets.

ARE CHANGES LIKELY TO HAPPEN OVER TIME?

Environments that produce data may suffer changes over time. For example, consider the data analytics tasks of software effort estimation [6] and software bug (defect) prediction [7]. Software companies may hire new employees, may change their development process, may adopt new programming languages, etc. Such changes may cause old data to become obsolete, which in turn would cause old software effort estimation and software bug prediction data models to also become obsolete. Such changes may also bring back situations that used to occur in the past, but were not occurring recently. Therefore, simply using all available data together can lead to contradictory and misleading data models. When temporal information about the data is available, change detection techniques can be used in combination with online or chunk-based learning algorithms [5] to handle changes. For instance, they can be used to (1) identify when a change that affects the adequacy of the current data model is occurring [8], (2) determine which existing data models best represent the current situation [6], and (3) decide how to update data models to the new situation [4,6,8]. When an environment has the potential to suffer changes, it is essential to collect additional data over time to be able to identify such changes and adapt data models accordingly.

IF YOU HAVE A PREDICTION PROBLEM, WHAT DO YOU REALLY NEED TO PREDICT?

In prediction/estimation problems, we wish to predict a certain category or quantity based on features describing an observation. It is important to decide what the target to be predicted really is, because this may affect both the predictive data models' accuracy and its usefulness. For example, we may wish to estimate the number of bugs in a software module based on features such as its size, complexity, number of commented lines, etc. For that, we should use a regression learning algorithm. Or, we may wish to predict whether or not a certain software module contains bugs. For that, we should use a classification learning algorithm. Or, we may wish to estimate the ranking of modules based on their bug-proneness. For that, we should use a rank learning algorithm. Depending on data availability, estimating the precise number of bugs may be more difficult than simply predicting whether or not a module is likely to contain bugs, and less informative. If we do not really need to know the exact number of bugs, rank learning algorithms [9] may be able to provide a balance between predictive accuracy and informativeness.

DO YOU HAVE A PREDICTION PROBLEM WHERE UNLABELED DATA ARE ABUNDANT AND LABELED DATA ARE EXPENSIVE?

In order to create predictive data models, it's helpful to use supervised learning algorithms to review data whose quantity/category to be estimated is known (labeled data). These learning algorithms are considered "teachers." Even though the existence of a teacher can help us create good predictive data models, it is sometimes expensive to hire such a teacher, ie, it is sometimes expensive to collect labels. This may result in few labeled data despite the existence of abundant unlabeled data, potentially causing supervised learning algorithms to perform poorly. An example of a problem that results from this issue is software effort estimation, where the actual effort required to develop software projects is costly. However, other features describing software projects may be collected in an automated manner [10,11], which would be less costly.

Semisupervised learning algorithms are able to use unlabeled data in combination with labeled data in order to improve predictive accuracy [10,12]. They typically learn the structure underlying the data based on the unlabeled data, and then combine this structure with the available labels in order to build predictive data models. If it is possible to request specific observations to be labeled, one may also opt for active learning algorithms. These learning algorithms are able to determine which observations are most valuable if labeled, instead of requiring all data to be labeled [11].

ARE YOUR DATA IMBALANCED?

In some cases, there may be abundant data representing certain aspects of an environment, but little data representing other aspects. Software bug prediction is an example of an imbalance problem, where there are typically fewer buggy software modules than nonbuggy ones. When the data are imbalanced, learning algorithms tend to be biased toward the more common aspects and completely fail to model the less common ones. Learning algorithms specifically designed for imbalance learning should be used to deal with that [13].

DO YOU NEED TO USE DATA FROM DIFFERENT SOURCES?

Even though there may be little data from within the targeted environment, there may be more data available from other environments. Such data may be useful to improve data models for the targeted environment. For example, in software bug prediction, there may be little data telling whether modules within given software are buggy, despite a lot of data from other software. Learning algorithms able to transfer knowledge among environments can be used in these cases [4,6,14,15].

DO YOU HAVE BIG DATA?

Certain data analytics tasks may need to process large quantities of potentially complex data, causing typical learning algorithms to struggle in terms of computational time. This may be the case, for example, when modeling developers' behavior based on software repositories hosting hundreds of thousands of projects. Online learning algorithms able to process each observation only once can help to build data models faster [5,8].

DO YOU HAVE LITTLE DATA?

When there is not so much data to learn from, learning algorithms tend to struggle to create accurate data models. This is because the available data are not enough to represent the whole environment well. This is typically the case for software effort estimation data, but other software engineering problems may suffer from similar issues. When there is not much data, simpler learning algorithms that do not have too many parameters to be learned tend to perform better [16].

IN SUMMARY...

...examine your data analytics problem first, then choose the type of learning algorithm to consider! Given a set of learning algorithms to consider, it is also advisable to run experiments in order to find out which of them is best suited to your data.

REFERENCES

[1] Hall T, Beecham S, Bowes D, Gray D, Counsell S. A systematic literature review on fault prediction performance in software engineering. IEEE Trans Softw Eng 2012;38(6): 1276–304.

[2] Dejaeger K, Verbeke W, Martens D, Baesens B. Data mining techniques for software effort estimation: a comparative study. IEEE Trans Softw Eng 2012;38(2):375–97.

[3] An L, Khomh F. An empirical study of crash-inducing commits in Mozilla Firefox. In: Proc. 11th international conference on predictive models and data analytics in software engineering; 2015 [article no. 5, 10 pp.].

[4] Minku L, Yao X. How to make best use of cross-company data in software effort estimation?. In: Proc. 36th international conference on software engineering; 2014. p. 446–56.

[5] Gama J, Gaber M. Learning from data streams. Berlin: Springer-Verlag; 2007.

[6] Minku L, Yao X. DDD: a new ensemble approach for dealing with concept drift. IEEE Trans Knowl Data Eng 2012;24(4):619–33.

[7] Ekanayake J, Tappolet J, Gall HC, Bernstein A. Tracking concept drift of software projects using defect prediction quality. In: Proc. 6th IEEE international working conference on mining software repositories; 2009. p. 51–60.

[8] Minku L, Yao X. Can cross-company data improve performance in software effort estimation?. In: Proc. 8th international conference on predictive models in software engineering; 2012. p. 69–78.

[9] Yang X, Tang K, Yao X. A learning-to-rank approach to software defect prediction. IEEE Trans Reliab 2015;64(1):234–46.

[10] Kocaguneli E, Cukic B, Menzies T, Lu H. Building a second opinion: learning cross-company data. In: Proc. 9th international conference on predictive models in software engineering; 2013 [article no. 12].

[11] Kocaguneli E, Menzies T, Keung J, Cok D, Madachy R. Active learning and effort estimation: finding the essential content of software effort estimation data. IEEE Trans Softw Eng 2013;39(2):1040–53.

[12] Chapelle O, Scholkopf B, Zien A. Semi-supervised learning. Cambridge, MA: MIT Press; 2006.

[13] Wang S, Yao X. Using class imbalance learning for software defect prediction. IEEE Trans Reliab 2012;62(2):434–43.

[14] Nam J, Pan S, Kim S. Transfer defect learning. In: Proc. international conference on software engineering; 2013. p. 382–91.

[15] Turhan B, Menzies T, Bener A, Distefano J. On the relative value of cross-company and within-company data for defect prediction. Empir Softw Eng 2009;14(5):540–78.

[16] Kocaguneli E, Menzies T, Bener A, Keung J. Exploiting the essential assumptions of analogy-based effort estimation. IEEE Trans Softw Eng 2012;38(2):425–38.

Structure your unstructured data first!

The case of summarizing unstructured data with tag clouds

A. Bacchelli

Delft University of Technology, Delft, The Netherlands

UNSTRUCTURED DATA IN SOFTWARE ENGINEERING

Anyone who has never worked on a real software project might mistakenly believe that software engineers spend all their time reading and writing source code.

But software engineers do much more than just read and write code. Their day-to-day reality is that they spend much time writing a wide range of material—little of which is source code (we see this happening even in open-source software projects, where there is not really a paper-driven or manager-mandated development process). Accordingly, it is very important to discuss methods for handling data that is not source code, particularly unstructured software data: data written mostly in natural language to exchange information with other people.

Look, for example, at Fig. 1. It represents the volume of emails exchanged *monthly* in the Linux kernel mailing list, from Jun. 1995 to Mar. 2010. With a constantly growing trend, we see that in the last month we consider, developers exchanged 13,657 emails, or 440 emails *per day*.

And emails are just one of the types of documents that software engineer produce and read daily. They also write and read issue reports, design documents, commit messages, code review messages, etc. All of these form the so-called *unstructured*

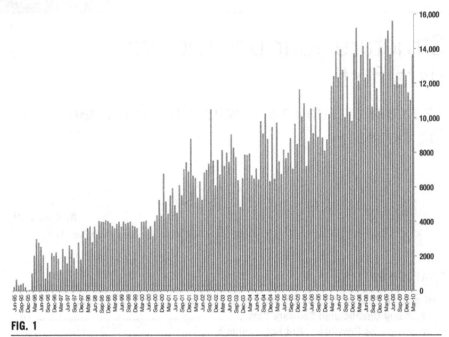

FIG. 1

Number of emails exchanged in the development mailing list of the Linux Kernel, by month.

software data, ie, data written in natural language by people for other people (as opposed to source code, which is written for a computer, or log messages, which are generated by a computer for a human).

SUMMARIZING UNSTRUCTURED SOFTWARE DATA

With that much information available, it is doubtful that engineers have the chance to read all the documents and get the right information out of them. For this reason, researchers in software engineering looked into various techniques to summarize, or aggregate, the various types of information available in unstructured software data.

AS SIMPLE AS POSSIBLE… BUT NOT SIMPLER!

The first reasonable approach for unstructured software data summarization is to tap into the methods devised by the community of Information Retrieval, whose target is exactly to retrieve information from natural language documents, and to combine them with some basic visualization techniques.

So, let us say we want to summarize the email information produced in just a single discussion thread on the mailing list of an open-source software project. A common solution would be to collect all the terms present in those emails and display them in a tag cloud [1] where the most frequently occurring terms are represented in larger fonts and the less frequently occurring ones are represented in smaller fonts. The more visible a term is in the tag cloud, the greater should be its semantic value. Terms are defined as single words, divided by space or punctuation, or some special characters.

Let us take the content of the following email in Fig. 2, adapted from a real email sent to the mailing list of an open-source system (ArgoUML).

```
Alice wrote:
> On Mon 23, Bob wrote:
> > Dear list,
> > When starting up ArgoUML on my MacOS X system (Java 2)
> > it throws a NullPointerException very soon. You'll find the
> > trace below. I hope someone knows a solution. Thanks a lot!

> > Exception in thread "main" java.lang.NullPointerException
> > at
> > javax.swing.event.SwingSupport.fireChange(SwingChange.java)
> > at javax.swing.AbstractAction.setEnabled(AbstractAction.java)
    [...]
> > at uci.uml.Main.main(Main.java:148)

> I'm sorry I can't help you Bob but thanks for sharing the stack...
> Alice.
> --
> "Beware of programmers who carry screwdrivers." --L. Brandwein

Alice, I believe the flawed Explorer class generates Bob's issue:
 public void setEnclosingFig(Fig each) {
  super.setEnclosingFig(each);
  if (each != null || (each.getOwner() instanceof MPackage)) {
   m = (MPackage) each.getOwner(); }

The problem is the if condition, see the diff:
--- src/org/argouml/ui/explorer/Explorer.java    (revision 14338)
+++ src/org/argouml/ui/explorer/Explorer.java (working copy)
@@ -147,1 +147,1 @@
[...]
  super.setEnclosingFig(each);
- if (each.getOwner() instanceof MPackage) {
+ if (each != null && (each.getOwner() instanceof MPackage)) {
  m = (MPackage) each.getOwner(); }

Probably ModelTree is also affected, if so, please change it :)
Cheers, Carl.
-- I used to have a sig, but it took up much space so I got rid of it!
------------------------------------------------------------------
To unsubscribe, e-mail: dev-...@argouml.tigris.org
For additional commands, e-mail: dev-...@argouml.tigris.org
```

FIG. 2

A development email sent to the development mailing list of an open-source software.

FIG. 3

A tag cloud directly generated from a development email, without pre-processing.

If we had to summarize the content, we could say that there are three people involved and the content refers to a bug affecting OS X, which is solved by patching the class "Explorer." How good would a tag cloud represent this threaded email? If we create a tag cloud directly from it, we obtain the following (see Fig. 3).

The tag cloud already gives us some interesting information, but it also contains a lot of noise, which reduces the visibility of what really matters. Apparently, taking "off-the-shelf" methods from information retrieval and data visualization is quick and simple, but it is probably a "too simple" solution, not good enough to solve our problem.

YOU NEED STRUCTURE!

Why did the preceding method not work well? Because most off-the-shelf techniques are prepared to work on a very specific kind of data. If we took newspaper articles and followed the same approach, we would probably have obtained more interesting results. But documents generated by software engineers are substantially different from those generated by writing professionals, such as newspaper journalists. Developers might use jargon more often and have a more terse language, and there is a lot of implicit knowledge not expressed. Then, emails contain text that is not relevant for analyzing their content, such as authors' signatures. Finally, and perhaps most important, software engineers often mix languages: natural language is mixed with source code, stack traces, and patches.

If we really want to extract useful information, which can be summarized, from unstructured software data, we first have to find the latent structure it has and exploit it correctly.

How can we give structure to a wall of text, such as an email? We first can realize that there is a simple underlying structure we can and should take advantage of, and build on top of it. We should take into account that threaded emails already give us information about how many people are involved in the discussion (the starting ">"s tell us about the indentation level). Then we can exploit a structure that is already there: emails are divided by authors in lines; our previous research showed that this is a very good starting point in finding the structure of a message [2]. Considering these two aspects, we obtain the following version of the same email (see Fig. 4), which visually already gives us much more information (this is what every good email client would do).

```
(1)     Alice wrote:
(2)     ┃ On Mon 23, Bob wrote:
(3)     ┃ ┃ Dear list,
(4)     ┃ ┃ When starting up ArgoUML on my MacOS X system (Java 2)
(5)     ┃ ┃ it throws a NullPointerException very soon. You'll find the
(6)     ┃ ┃ trace below. I hope someone knows a solution. Thanks a lot!

(7)     ┃ ┃ Exception in thread "main" java.lang.NullPointerException
(8)     ┃ ┃ at
(9)     ┃ ┃ javax.swing.event.SwingSupport.fireChange(SwingChange.java)
(10)    ┃ ┃ at javax.swing.AbstractAction.setEnabled(AbstractAction.java)
        ┃ ┃ [...]
(11)    ┃ ┃ at uci.uml.Main.main(Main.java:148)

(12)    ┃ I'm sorry I can't help you Bob but thanks for sharing the stack...
(13)    ┃ Alice.
(14)    ┃ --
(15)    ┃ "Beware of programmers who carry screwdrivers." --L. Brandwein

(16)    Alice, I believe the flawed Explorer class generates Bob's issue:
(17)      public void setEnclosingFig(Fig each) {
(18)        super.setEnclosingFig(each);
(19)      if (each != null || (each.getOwner() instanceof MPackage)) {
(20)        m = (MPackage) each.getOwner(); }

(21)    The problem is the if condition, see the diff:
(22)    --- src/org/argouml/ui/explorer/Explorer.java    (revision 14338)
(23)    +++ src/org/argouml/ui/explorer/Explorer.java (working copy)
(24)    @@ -147,1 +147,1 @@
        [...]
(25)       super.setEnclosingFig(each);
(26)    - if (each.getOwner() instanceof MPackage) {
(27)    + if (each != null && (each.getOwner() instanceof MPackage)) {
(28)       m = (MPackage) each.getOwner(); }

(29)    Probably ModelTree is also affected, if so, please change it :)
(30)    Cheers, Carl.
(31)    -- I used to have a sig, but it took up much space so I got rid of it!
(32)    ------------------------------------------------------------------
(33)    To unsubscribe, e-mail: dev-...@argouml.tigris.org
(34)    For additional commands, e-mail: dev-...@argouml.tigris.org
```

FIG. 4

A development email with line numbers and information about quotation levels.

Once we have this basic structure, the next step is realizing that, in most of the cases, the different languages used in emails are used in different lines. In this way, we simplified our problem into a *classification* problem: how can we assign each line to the language it belongs to? From our email, we would like to have a categorization that looks like the following (see Fig. 5).

Is it possible to automatically tag each line with the language it is written in? Yes! Researchers developed a number of methods to classify text in different categories. A classical example is the case of classifying a whole email into "spam" or legitimate. In the case of development emails, we developed simple methods to recognize lines of code from other text [2] and more complex ones to recognize more complex languages, such as those used in signatures, from natural language content [3]. As an example, here we describe how the lines of Java source code can be recognized in the content of an email, with a very simple, yet effective approach, and see what its impact is on a final tag cloud summary.

If we consider lines 17–20 and 25–28, we note a peculiarity present in many programming languages (eg, Java, C, C#, Perl): the developer must end each statement with a semicolon or a curly bracket (mainly used to open or close a block). Based on this intuition, a simple approach that verifies whether the last character of a line is a semicolon or a curly bracket might be a good way to detect source code. Plus, we can

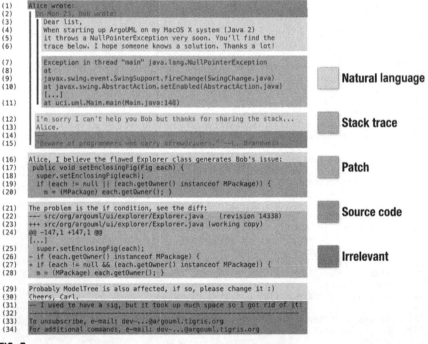

FIG. 5

A development email in which the different used "languages" are visible recognized.

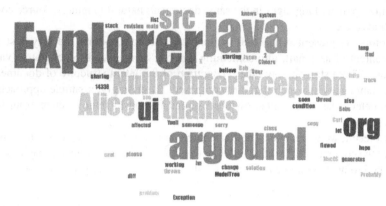

FIG. 6

A tag cloud generated from preprocessed email content.

write a simple regular expression to recognize the lines of a stack trace (9–11), as they have a very clear structure, without any nested blocks.

We tested this approach on thousands of emails from five Java source systems and we found that it is working well in practice and can be used as a basis for further data analysis on emails [2].

Now, if we take our initial email, we remove the signatures (by for example, eliminating everything at the end after the dashes) and apply the source code detection approach, we can generate a new tag cloud, as the one depicted below (see Fig. 6). Now we see that more important terms (such as "Explorer" and "NullPointerException") started to emerge, thus creating a summary that gives a much better idea of the content.

With more sophisticated approaches [3], we can even *parse* the different parts of the content of a development email and remove more noise, thus making the most important content emerge and creating better summaries.

CONCLUSION

In this brief chapter, we made everybody aware that developers do not only write source code, but many other artifacts, such as issue reports, design documents, and emails.

We showed that the amount of these artifacts can be overwhelming (as in the case of development emails for the Linux mailing list), so we need some way to summarize the information they contain for a faster, yet still useful consumption. We made the case that, unfortunately, the best candidate techniques from information retrieval do not work well in the case of software engineering documents, because unstructured software data has a very special language. In particular, software engineers often mix up many languages in the same document: natural language, source code, stack traces, etc.

For this, we presented the steps that one can take to transform the very unstructured content of an email, into something that can be analyzed to generate a valid summary. These steps involve the recognition of the latent structure of documents and the languages in which they are composed. Surprisingly, a simple approach is able to detect reasonably most of these languages and to remove them from text if necessary.

As a result, we were able to obtain a much more informative tag cloud that summarizes the content of a threaded email, thus giving ideas on how an approach can be developed to analyze and summarize similar unstructured software documents.

REFERENCES

[1] Tag cloud. Wikipedia, the free encyclopedia. Retrieved from https://en.wikipedia.org/w/index.php?title=Tag_cloud&oldid=678980330 [accessed 01.09.15]

[2] Bacchelli A, D'Ambros M, Lanza M. Extracting source code from e-mails. In: Proc. 18th IEEE international conference on program comprehension (ICPC 2010); 2010. p. 24–33.

[3] Bacchelli A, Dal Sasso T, D'Ambros M, Lanza M. Content classification of development emails. In: Proc. 34th international conference on software engineering (ICSE 2012); 2012. p. 375–85.

Parse that data! Practical tips for preparing your raw data for analysis

P. Guo

University of Rochester, Rochester, NY, United States

CHAPTER OUTLINE

Use Assertions Everywhere 170
Print Information About Broken Records 170
Use Sets or Counters to Store Occurrences of Categorical Variables 171
Restart Parsing in the Middle of the Data Set 171
Test on a Small Subset of Your Data 172
Redirect Stdout and Stderr to Log Files 172
Store Raw Data Alongside Cleaned Data 172
Finally, Write a Verifier Program to Check the Integrity of Your Cleaned Data 172

Data analysis is a central task in the workflow of data scientists, researchers, software engineers, business analysts, and just about every professional who needs to work with data. The first mundane step in data analysis is *preparing raw data*, which can originate from a diverse variety of sources such as:

- logs from a web server,
- outputs from a scientific instrument,
- exported data from an online survey,
- data dump from a 1970s government database, or
- reports prepared by external consultants.

What all of these sources of raw data have in common is that you have no control over their format or quirks. You need to work with what you have been given, which is often:

- incomplete (not all fields are present in all records),
- inconsistent (field names and schemas change throughout the data set), and
- corrupted (some records are malformed in unusual ways).

Thus, you must often write computer programs to parse the raw data and transform it into a form that is more friendly for analysis. This often-unglamorous chore is sometimes called *data munging* or *data wrangling*. In certain domains, you can use

169

specialized tools to ease this process. But if you do not have access to those tools, or your needs are more complex, then you will need to write your own parser.

This chapter presents a collection of practical tips for writing reliable and effective data parsers. These tips can be implemented in any programming language (eg, Perl, Python, R).

USE ASSERTIONS EVERYWHERE

Here is the most important tip: write lots of assertions in your parsing code. Write down every assumption you have about your data's format in the form of assertions, and then revise those assertions as you find out which parts of the data violate them.

For instance, should all records be in chronological order? If so, assert it. Should there be exactly seven fields per record? If so, assert it. Should the first field always be an even integer between 0 and 26? If so, assert it!

In a perfect world, all records would be cleanly-formatted and abide by an elegant and fixed schema. But the real world is far from perfect.

If you write good assertions, then your parsing code *will crash a lot*. This is great news, since every crash (due to assertion failure) means that you have just discovered one more way in which the raw data violated your original assumptions. Keep refining your assertions until your code successfully parses the entire raw data set. But keep them as stringent as possible, or else they are not doing their job. The worst-case outcome is data sneaking through your parser in a format that you did not originally expect.

PRINT INFORMATION ABOUT BROKEN RECORDS

Some records in the raw data will be broken in unfixable ways, so your program has no choice but to skip over them when parsing. A bad idea is to simply skip them silently, since you will not know what parts of the data set are corrupted. Instead, always:

- print a warning to stderr (the error output stream) along with the raw record itself so that you can inspect it later to find out what is wrong and
- keep a running count of how many records your program has skipped so far, along with how many records were successfully parsed. Doing so will give you a sense of how unclean your raw data was. For instance, if your program is skipping only 0.5% of the raw data, then it is probably not a big deal. But if your program is skipping 35% of the raw data, then you need to take a closer look to find out what is wrong.

USE SETS OR COUNTERS TO STORE OCCURRENCES OF CATEGORICAL VARIABLES

Some of your fields will represent categorical variables. For instance, in a medical data set, blood type can be either A, B, AB, or O. It is a good idea to assert that blood type must be one of those values, since there are only four of them. But what if a category contains many more possible values, especially those that you did not know about beforehand? In that case, you cannot write a meaningful assertion.

Instead, use a set or counter data structure in your favorite programming language to keep track of which values appear in your data set as it is being parsed.

By following this idiom, you can:

- print out a message whenever you encounter a new kind of value for that categorical variable in the raw data, to make sure it does not come as a surprise and
- inspect the full set of values when your parser finishes to see if any of them look unusual. For instance, if someone entered C for a blood type record, that would immediately stand out as an error.

RESTART PARSING IN THE MIDDLE OF THE DATA SET

If you have a lot of raw data, your parsing program will probably take a long time to process all of it: maybe 5 min, maybe 10 min, maybe an hour, maybe even a few days. Chances are, it will often crash mid-way through parsing.

Say that your raw data has 1 million records and your program crashes on record number 325,392. If you fix your code and re-run it, chances are it will still work fine on records 1–325,391, so you will just be waiting around needlessly for minutes or even hours until your code tries to parse record 325,392. Instead:

- make your program print out which record it is currently parsing so that you can see where it failed and
- make it possible to pass a parameter to your program to specify a starting point, so that you can tell it to start at, say, record 325,392. Your program will keep parsing along and probably crash again at a later record. Then you can fix the code, re-run starting at that record, and keep fixing bugs until it successfully parses all 1 million records.

Making your programs able to restart by parsing in the middle of your data set will save you lots of time when debugging. Finally, after everything parses properly, re-run your code on all 1 million records to double-check, since your edits might have led to regression errors on earlier records.

TEST ON A SMALL SUBSET OF YOUR DATA

Do not try to parse the entire data set at once. When you are in the early stages of developing and debugging your program, start testing on a small, random subset of the data. Then make that subset bigger as you gain more confidence. The main reason for using a subset is that your program will terminate much faster, preferably within a few seconds, which will tighten your iteration cycle and help you debug faster.

However, note that by testing on only a subset of your data, you are less likely to pick up on rare quirks in the data set since they are, by definition, rare.

REDIRECT STDOUT AND STDERR TO LOG FILES

When running your program, redirect the stdout and stderr streams to log files so that you can inspect them later using a text editor, `less`, or `tail -f` (for real-time streaming updates). On most Mac and Linux terminals, you can use the > operator to redirect stdout to a file, and 2> to redirect stderr to a file.

STORE RAW DATA ALONGSIDE CLEANED DATA

This tip is most applicable when you have plenty of storage space. In that case, consider storing each record of raw data *inside of* the corresponding record in the cleaned data set. That way, if you find an abnormal record in your cleaned data set, you can immediately see what raw data it came from, which will make it easier to debug.

However, doing so will double your storage requirements and make certain analysis operations a bit slower, so use this technique only when you can stand the loss in efficiency.

FINALLY, WRITE A VERIFIER PROGRAM TO CHECK THE INTEGRITY OF YOUR CLEANED DATA

Along with your parser, also write a verifier program that walks over the cleaned data and checks (asserts) that it conforms to the format that you expect. You have no control over the quality of the raw data, but you have *all the control* over the cleaned data, since your program parsed it. Thus, make sure that it does, in fact, conform to your own schema and expectations.

This final step is *very important* because after you finish parsing, you will be working solely with the cleaned data. Chances are, you will not even touch the raw data again unless something catastrophic happens. Thus, you want to make sure that your cleaned data is in top shape before starting your analyses. Otherwise, you might get misleading results that are ultra-hard to diagnose since they originated from a long-ago parsing mistake, and your raw data is no longer in front of you.

In sum, these tips may seem like a lot of up-front work, but the good news is that the time you invest in writing a robust parser will make your actual analysis work-flow much more pleasant. I have learned this from years of hard-earned experience. Happy parsing!

Natural language processing is no free lunch

S. Wagner

University of Stuttgart, Stuttgart, Germany

CHAPTER OUTLINE

Today's operating systems, with their personal assistants *Siri* or *Cortana*, show the impressive progress natural language processing (NLP) has made. They make it seem like all technical and methodological challenges of NLP have been solved. As many artefacts in software engineering are full of natural language, the applications are endless. As it turns out, however, using NLP is no free lunch. We offer a brief check on how and how not to apply NLP in software analytics in this chapter.

We recently applied NLP on the documentation of software systems. Our starting point was that the likes of JavaDoc and Doxygen allowed software developers to document source code in a structured and versatile way. This led to a considerable amount of documentation, especially of interfaces in many programs today. The documentation focuses, however, on the level of functions/methods and classes. Documentation on the component level is often missing.

So why can't we use the lower-level documentation to generate the component documentation? One problem is that most of this documentation is in natural language (apart from some annotations for authors or return values). How can we decide what from the class and method comments is important for describing the component they are a part of?

I decided to team up with a NLP expert and colleague, Sebastian Padó, and to explore this issue in a master thesis [1]. While we could apply topic modeling to the comments on the class level and generate meaningful topics, the practical usefulness of the results is unclear. For example, for the Java package *java.io* it showed us the following topic to be most probable: "buffer, stream, byte, read, method, field, data, write, output, class, serial, input, written…". It gives an idea what the package is about. Yet, it cannot replace a description created by a human.

Let us discuss what it takes to create such results and how we could improve them.

NATURAL LANGUAGE DATA IN SOFTWARE PROJECTS

Most data we deal with in software projects is somehow textual. The central artefact in a software project is the source code, which is textual, in a formal language, and how to analyse it has been thoroughly studied. Beyond the source code, however, we find a lot of natural language data in today's software projects. For example, we have textual documentation for the user, or of the software architecture. We also find textual data in commit messages and issue descriptions. Even in the source code, as we saw before, we have natural language in the comments. We need to make more use of this rich source of information to support developers and guide projects. Yet, how can we deal with data that is as fuzzy as natural language?

NATURAL LANGUAGE PROCESSING

NLP has made huge progress over the last decades. NLP researchers have developed a wide range of algorithms and tools to deal with large text corpora and give various insights into the meaning of the natural language texts. For example, *part-of-speech tagging* gives you the grammatical use of each word (verb, noun, or determiner) and *topic modeling* extracts the most probable topics for documents in a text corpus. The access to the research results in NLP is easy as there are several great text books (eg, [2]) and open-source libraries (eg, from the Stanford NLP group: http://nlp.stanford.edu/software/) available. They provide us with the means to analyse the natural language data from our software projects.

HOW TO APPLY NLP TO SOFTWARE PROJECTS

But how are we going to apply that in a software project? The first thing to do is to understand the used algorithms and tune them so they fit to the problem. Binkley et al. [3], for example, provide insights and an interesting discussion on how to tune parameters of the topic modeling algorithm Latent Dirichlet allocation (LDA) in the context of software artefacts. Yet, as the natural language data, as well as the goals of its analysis, are diverse and specific to your context, I will focus on four further good practices to follow in general.

DO STEMMING FIRST

The first step in any analysis is extracting and cleaning the data. This is also the case with natural language data. Often, we need to extract it from Microsoft Word documents or PDFs. As soon as we have the plain text data, it is usually a good idea to use a stemmer. Stemming is the process of removing morphological and inflexional endings from words. This allows an easier analysis as all words from the same word stem can be treated equally. For example, in most cases I don't care for the difference between "read" and "reading." In the topic modeling example, it should lead to the same topic.

In my experience, a simple stemming algorithm such as the one by Porter [4], as implemented in the library from the Stanford NLP group mentioned herein, is sufficient for texts in English. In some applications and for other languages, stemming might not be enough. For those cases, you should look into *lemmatization*, which employs dictionary and morphological analysis to return the base form of a word. More details can be found, for example, in Manning et al. [2].

CHECK THE LEVEL OF ABSTRACTION

As natural language texts do not follow formal grammar and do not have formal semantics, the level of abstraction can be diverse in text documents, even if we look at the same type of artefact. This became very apparent when we applied clone detection to natural language requirements specifications [5]. The intention was to find parts of the specifications that were created by copy&paste. We found that the level of cloning was extremely diverse from several specifications with almost none up to specifications with more than 50% clones. The main reason was the level of detail in which the specification described the system. The specifications with high cloning described very concrete details such as messages on a network. The specifications with low cloning described the functionality in an abstract way. It is probably not a good idea to further analyse these textual data in the same way. So be sure to know what you are looking for. It might be helpful to cluster artefacts even if they are of the same type.

For example, we might be interested in whether the topics that are used in our requirements specifications differ. This could give us hints about whether we usually specify similar aspects. Yet, as we learned herein, the levels of abstraction are quite different in typical requirements specifications. An analysis of the topics of all of those specifications might not be very insightful. Yet, using the degree of cloning to cluster them with a clustering algorithm such as *k-means* could help us in grouping them in useful levels of abstraction. Inside of each of these clusters, the topics are probably more homogeneous. For example, specifications with a low level of abstraction might include topics such as protocols, messages, and hardware platforms, while high-level specifications might talk more about use cases, features, and interactions.

Besides using a clustering algorithm, it can also be a good idea to apply manual analysis here (see also Section "Don't Discard Manual Analysis of Textual Data", which follows). An experienced requirements engineer is probably able to quickly cluster the specifications along their level of abstraction. While this takes more effort, it would be a more direct analysis of abstraction than the degree of cloning and could provide further insights as well.

DON'T EXPECT MAGIC

Even though the methods, algorithms, and tools in NLP are of impressive quality today, don't expect that everything can be used out of the box and provide perfect results. It is still necessary to try alternative algorithms and tune them during the analysis. More importantly, however, the algorithms can only give you results as good as the text that already contains them. We found in the master thesis [1] that we can generate topics with useful terms, but rely strongly on the quality of the Java-Doc comments. The analysis of the official Java library worked well, as those classes are well documented. But the analysis of other open source code with fewer comments also showed less usable topics. Being able to provide such additional use of comments might encourage better commenting and create a self-enforcing loop. Yet, often we find missing, outdated, or sparse documentation in practice. Hence, don't expect too much up front, but also, don't be discouraged. Continued analysis could pay off in the longer term.

DON'T DISCARD MANUAL ANALYSIS OF TEXTUAL DATA

So what can we do if the automatic NLP analysis does not give us fully satisfactory results? I believe it is often helpful to keep the human in the loop. This could mean a fully qualitative analysis of the natural language data [6] to create a full human interpretation. Great insights can come from such an analysis. Humans can make connections based on their own knowledge and experience not available to computers. Furthermore, they are able to formulate the results in a way that is easily accessible to other humans. Yet, such an analysis is very elaborate. A middle ground could be to use manual feedback early and often [7]. We applied topic modeling to user stories to classify them. Initially, our automatic analysis had rather poor precision, but two feedback rounds with practitioners increased it to 90%. Hence, I believe such a combination of automatic analysis with manual feedback could be beneficial in many contexts.

So what does a systematic manual analysis look like? Generally, we apply well-proven techniques of qualitative analysis from areas such as sociology. In its most basic form, this means a simple *coding* of the textual data. You can attach a *code* or *tag* to a piece of the complete text to analyse. This can be single word, a sentence, or whole paragraphs. For example, we have analyzed a part of a survey on problems in requirements engineering with such methods [6]. Practitioners gave free-text answers on what problems they experience in requirements engineering, how they manifest in their development process, and what they consider causes for these problems.

First, we added codes to pieces of text describing each of these aspects (problem, cause, and effect) with very little abstraction. With several reviews and revisions, we grouped the low-level codes to more abstract ones to come up with more general problems, causes, and effects. For example, we coded the answer "The communication to customer is done not by technicians, but by lawyers." as the problem *Weak Communication*. This brought us to a deep understanding of the answers an automated technique would hardly be able to achieve. Yet, the manual analysis must be accompanied by continuous discussion and reviews by other people to avoid too much subjectivity. Furthermore, one has to weigh the high degree of insight against the large amount of effort necessary.

SUMMARY

Natural language data is omnipresent in software projects and contains rich information. NLP provides us with interesting tools to analyse this data fully automatically. Yet, as always, there is no free lunch. The textual data must be extracted and cleaned, potentially clustered according to the level of abstraction, and the analysis often has to be complemented with human analysis and feedback to be practically useful. Nevertheless, I am certain we will see much more interesting research in this area in the future.

REFERENCES

[1] Strobel PH. Automatische Zusammenfassung von Quellcode-Kommentaren. MSc thesis. University of Stuttgart; 2015.
[2] Manning C, Raghavan P, Schütze H. Introduction to information retrieval. New York: Cambridge University Press; 2008.
[3] Binkley D, Heinz D, Lawrie DJ, Overfelt J. Understanding LDA in source code analysis. In: Proc. international conference on program comprehension (ICPC 2014). ACM; 2014. p. 26–36.
[4] Porter MF. An algorithm for suffix stripping. Program 1980;14(3):130–7.
[5] Juergens E, Deissenboeck F, Feilkas M, Hummel B, Schätz B, Wagner S, et al. Can clone detection support quality assessment of requirements specifications? In: Proc. 32nd international conference on software engineering (ICSE'10). ACM; 2010.
[6] Wagner S, Méndez Fernández D. Analysing text in software projects. In: Bird C, Menzies T, Zimmermann T, editors. Art and science of analysing software data. Waltham: Morgan Kaufmann; 2015.
[7] Vetrò A, Ognawala S, Méndez Fernández D, Wagner S. Fast feedback cycles in empirical software engineering research. In: Proc. 37th international conference on software engineering (ICSE'15). IEEE; 2015.

Aggregating empirical evidence for more trustworthy decisions

D. Budgen

Durham University, Durham, United Kingdom

CHAPTER OUTLINE

WHAT'S EVIDENCE?

We all make rational decisions that are based upon evidence, don't we? After all, the last time we ate a pepperoni pizza for supper we had bad dreams, so that's clearly good evidence that in the future we should avoid eating pepperoni after 6 pm! Except, of course, that it obviously isn't good evidence. What else did we eat that evening, and did the dreams occur because of something entirely different? Yet, in everyday life much of our "evidence" is rather like that, anecdotal in nature, far from objective, and likely to be rather selective.

That doesn't matter too much when deciding which pizza to order, since that sort of decision is not one that needs to be objective, and there will be many other factors that will influence it. However, if we are planning to run the local half-marathon in a month's time, perhaps we do need some sound nutritional information so that we can develop the necessary stamina and develop our training plan.

So when the stakes get higher, for both personal and professional decisions, then we may (should) seek out good quality evidence that can be used to help make a choice. The evidence may take many forms, but usually we will want to find the best and most reliable sources wherever possible, and prefer evidence that is based upon objective measurements rather than "gut feel."

WHAT DOES DATA FROM EMPIRICAL STUDIES LOOK LIKE?

When we need information about physical properties (weight, energy consumption, brightness of illumination, etc.) to help with a decision, then taking a single measurement will usually be sufficient. However, when our decisions relate to information about how humans behave and react, as occurs in clinical medicine, education, psychology, as well as software engineering, then we need rather more than individual measurements and have to turn to empirical studies.

Why is this so? Well, experimental studies (trials) in these subjects make extensive use of human participants. And in such studies, we can expect to find quite a wide spread of values in the results obtained when measuring the effect of some "intervention," even when a study is performed rigorously. This "spread" largely stems from the natural variation that occurs between humans, whether it be physiological (affecting clinical studies) or differences of experience and ability (affecting computing studies). Because of this, it is necessary to collect measurements from many people. In contrast, for experiments in the natural sciences, if we repeat our measurements, any variation in the results is usually small, and can be attributed to measurement errors.

This variation is often illustrated by the use of box plots for reporting the outcomes from a study that involves humans. A box plot "groups" the results in quartiles, each containing 25% of the values and then plots these to show how the data is distributed. The range covered by the middle 50% of values is shown as a "box," and the outer "quartiles" as long lines. Within the box, a line indicates the value of the median (the middle value). Fig. 1 shows a simple example, where the vertical axis measures the outcome variable (in this case time) and there are separate plots for the results obtained with and without the "intervention" being studied. (The width of the boxes is arbitrary.)

As we can see from Fig. 1, the participants allocated to the group who were using the intervention (a software tool) mostly took a shorter time to perform their task than those in the "control" group, although a few did take longer. So the box plot showing

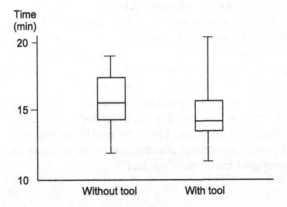

FIG. 1

Example of Box plot.

the time taken when using the tool has a wider spread of values, and is also rather skewed.

Box plots provide a useful visualization of how the results may vary across the different participants. However, it is still necessary to employ statistical tests to determine whether or not any differences between the two datasets is meaningful, or could simply have occurred randomly.

As well as this naturally occurring variability, there may also be some possible experimental errors that might bias the results of a study. So we can see that relying upon the results of a single trial of an intervention in order to make decisions may be somewhat risky. This, however, was how medicine was often practiced in the past, with doctors making clinical decisions about a patient's treatment that were based on the results of those trials that they were aware of, or that were recommended by experts as being most appropriate. Unfortunately though, expert judgment is itself an unreliable way of identifying relevant evidence, although it may be useful when interpreting it. Experts will have opinions, which can bias their selections.

THE EVIDENCE-BASED PARADIGM AND SYSTEMATIC REVIEWS

What is now considered to be the "model" for evidence-based decision-making first became established in clinical medicine. Much of the stimulus for this came from the work of Archie Cochrane (1909–1988) who was a pioneer in seeking ways to determine the best evidence about treatments. He was highly critical of the lack of sound evidence for many commonly used medical interventions and particularly encouraged the use of greater rigor in clinical trials ("randomize till it hurts") to reduce bias. In honor of this, the not-for-profit organization that now oversees the clinical review process was named after him (the Cochrane Collaboration, http://www.cochrane.org).

A key step in developing an evidence-based approach was realizing that aggregating the results from a set of studies could help reduce the effects of both natural variability and also of any bias that might occur in individual studies. But to be really effective, this process of aggregation needs to be performed in a rigorous and systematic way. At this point, we need to shift from the medical past to the software engineering present and discuss what we do in computing. Before doing so, though, we should note that should you have to consult your doctor, it is highly likely that he or she will consult knowledge derived through this process of aggregation.

For computing, the evidence-based process used to derive sound and unbiased evidence from empirical studies consists of five steps [1].

1. Convert a need for information about some intervention (typically, a software engineering technique such as pair programming) into an answerable question. This helps determine which studies are going to be of use.
2. Track down the best evidence relating to the question in a systematic, objective, and unbiased way. This might be by using specialist search engines such as IEEExplore that search through publishers' databases to search for papers reporting the outcomes of relevant studies.

3. Critically appraise the evidence for validity, impact, and applicability (how useful it is). This commonly involves developing a checklist of factors related to quality and to the question being addressed, using this to score each study found, and then aggregating the outcomes from the studies.
4. Integrate the critical appraisal with domain expertise about the given topic and the needs of any stakeholders. Having aggregated the data, we then seek to use it to provide guidelines about when we should use the intervention within a particular organizational structure.
5. Evaluate the outcomes and use to improve the preceding steps. This final step is really related to how we can improve the overall process.

The first three of these steps form what we term a systematic review, while the fourth involves a process usually termed knowledge translation (KT) that is concerned with interpreting the review outcomes. A systematic review is also termed a secondary study, since it does not involve any direct activity with participants, as occurs in a primary study. A secondary study is therefore one that aggregates the results from a set of primary studies.

A really important aspect of a systematic review is that it should be planned in advance, as it is important to avoid the risk of "fishing" for useful patterns in any results. Particularly important elements to specify in advance are the search terms used for identifying relevant primary studies, and the criteria used to determine which studies should be used as inputs to the review. Because the application of these criteria does require some expertise about both the topic of the review and also the conduct of systematic reviews, it is also common to make decisions about which primary studies to include by using two analysts, carefully resolving any differences in their decisions [2]. It is worth noting that the "reduction factor" is often quite high; it is quite normal to begin with several thousand candidate studies, and end up using around 20–50 of these. The example in the side box illustrates this more fully.

The way that the outcomes of the eventual set of primary studies is synthesized is also important, since it helps influence the quality of the eventual data from the review as well as any decisions made using this [3]. While statistical meta-analysis is the most powerful form, this can rarely be used in computing studies due to the widely different forms of the primary studies typically found, so less powerful and more qualitative procedures usually need to be employed.

HOW FAR CAN WE USE THE OUTCOMES FROM SYSTEMATIC REVIEW TO MAKE DECISIONS?

So, if your doctor can make decisions about how best to treat you using the outcomes of a systematic review, can we make our technical decisions in the same way? In principle, the answer is yes, although in practice it is rather less clear-cut for software engineering. This is largely because the form of a clinical study usually involves making comparisons between the effects of the treatment and some placebo, and with the participants being recipients of the treatment, making it possible to use statistical meta-analysis to synthesize the outcomes. In contrast, computing studies usually have a range of forms, and the participants are often asked to perform skilled tasks within organizational contexts that may introduce many other "confounding factors," and so complicate eventual synthesis.

In a recent study we examined 216 systematic reviews, published between 2004, when the use of systematic reviews began to be adopted in software engineering, and the end of 2014, to see if they contained material that might be used to support the teaching of core software engineering ideas as well as to provide advice about practice. From these, we identified 59 studies that were considered to provide useful experience about such topics as cost modeling, requirements elicitation, model-driven engineering, agile methods, the needs of start-up companies, etc. (see the Appendix in [2]).

In computing, it is unusual for the adoption of a new or different technical practice (eg, pair programming) to make a large difference when compared with the effect of using another. So none of the studies had definitive results showing that one technique was always better than another, although a number embodied useful experiences about the situations in which it might be appropriate to employ a particular technique.

We should not be too surprised at this. Back in 1987, Fred Brooks Jr. explained why the nature of software made it unlikely that the "silver bullet" solutions desired by managers could ever be feasible for software development activities [4]. So, when it comes to making decisions in computing, consulting the outcomes of a systematic review is unlikely to make the decision for you, but it is likely to provide you with some important insight into what does work, when it is most likely to work, and possibly why, depending on the degree of knowledge translation provided. And knowing what factors may be important can still usefully make it possible to come to an evidence-informed decision. (Given that every patient the doctor sees has their own set of personal factors, clinical decisions are usually evidence-informed too.)

Will things change in the future? Well, this is still early days for secondary studies, with experience from only little more than a decade of performing systematic reviews in software engineering, much of which has been a learning process. With this growing experience, it is likely that more and better systematic reviews will be performed. We may also expect better primary studies, performed to meet needs identified by systematic reviews.

So, evidence-informed decision making is now increasingly possible, and is likely to become used more and more widely in the future. However (the inevitable caveat), to employ it effectively, users of evidence also need to understand how to use it and adapt it to their contexts. Systematic reviews are no more of a silver bullet than any other software engineering practice, but their use forms an important step toward putting software engineering education and practice on to a much sounder basis, by providing more objective knowledge about our practices.

EXAMPLE OF A SYSTEMATIC REVIEW: VISUALIZING SOFTWARE ARCHITECTURE

To illustrate what a systematic review in software engineering might involve, this summarizes a recently published review [5]. Systematic reviews are complex procedures, so we just provide a very simple outline of what is involved, to give some idea about the nature of the process.

The study examined how software architecture visualization techniques were employed, and the purposes for which they were used. Like many systematic reviews in software engineering, this is partly a mapping study (identifying the scope of the primary studies, with only limited synthesis), although it does provide some analysis of the outcomes. In the rest of this box, we simply describe the first steps of the study process as the outcomes are too detailed to be easily summarized.

Research Questions: There were five main questions. A good example is RQ5: "Which are the architecture visualization techniques mostly used in industry?". This is a typical "mapping study" question, giving limited scope for synthesis.

Period Covered by searches: February 1999—July 2011.

Searching: Manual + Electronic (see the following).

Electronic Search String: (architecture OR architectural OR architecting OR structure) AND (visual OR visualize OR visualization OR visualizing OR diagram OR picture OR graphic OR graphical).

Number of studies used for analysis: 53.

Manual searching involved looking through the index pages of over 30 journals and conferences, while the electronic search, using seven search engines, found a further 2887 publications. From the initial inclusion/exclusion step based on looking at titles and keywords, they retained 300 as "possibles." Looking at the abstracts of these reduced this number to 89, but checking the references used in this set (this is termed "snowballing") identified another 14 papers not found by the searches. After reading the 103 papers in full, they selected the final set of 53 that were used for the analysis.

This study used a particularly thorough approach to searching, and we should note that many studies employ electronic searching alone, or use just a modest amount of manual searching to check the reliability of the search strings.

REFERENCES

[1] Kitchenham B, Dybå T, Jørgensen M. Evidence-based software engineering. In: Proceedings of ICSE 2004. IEEE Computer Society Press; 2004. p. 273–81.

[2] Kitchenham B, Budgen D, Brereton P. Evidence-based software engineering and systematic reviews. Chapman & Hall; 2015.

[3] Cruzes DS, Dybå T. Research synthesis in software engineering: a tertiary study. Inf Softw Technol 2011;53(5):440–55.

[4] Brooks Jr. FP. No silver bullet: essences and accidents of software engineering. IEEE Comput 1987;20(4):10–9.

[5] Shahin M, Liang P, Babar MA. A systematic review of software architecture visualization techniques. J Syst Softw 2014;94:161–85.

If it is software engineering, it is (probably) a Bayesian factor

A. Bener*, A. Tosun[†]

Ryerson University, Toronto ON, Canada* Istanbul Technical University, Maslak Istanbul, Turkey[†]

CHAPTER OUTLINE

For more than two decades, we have witnessed how software is developed in the industry and later conducted empirical research in academia to build predictive models, mine software repositories, and perform various software analytics tasks to help software development teams make evidence-based decisions.

As we discussed in our previous work, over the years we have come to the conclusion that in the software engineering domain, we need different approaches to solve problems in the field in a real-time fashion. These approaches may be modifications of existing Artificial Intelligence (AI)-based algorithms that go beyond the capabilities of human reasoning, are evolved through iterative user feedback, and that can present the results in a simple, easy to interpret way [1]. In different contexts such as big data, researchers argue that next-generation models with AI should not only be capable of identifying relationships from observed data and "predicting the future" but also should be "causing the future" by studying all possible scenarios (relations and their effects on final outcome), and determining the best future scenarios in terms of cost, accuracy, and time [2].

CAUSING THE FUTURE WITH BAYESIAN NETWORKS

Bayesian Networks (BN) offer a unique solution to the next generation of AI usage on real data since they have the ability to encode causal relationships (for predicting the future) and to go one step further with its property of "information propagation through the network." This property makes it possible to understand the entire system, such as how a change in one variable can affect the others, and how important certain variables in a network are, and start gaming over the network to see which scenarios would give the best outcome (what is called "causing the future"). Thus, BNs provide real-time solutions that are beyond the capabilities of human reasoning and present them in simple, easy to interpret graphical models [3].

Causal relationship is formed based on two processes in which one of them ("cause") is partly responsible for the occurrence or change of the other ("effect"). The direction of a causal relationship is not two-sided as in correlations. For example, smoking increases the risk of cancer, but patients who are diagnosed with cancer do not have to be smokers. There could be other factors such as genetics that cause cancer. If there are several factors involved in a causal relationship, BNs provide an efficient and easier way to define this relationship, observe how a change in each one of the factors causes the others, and infer the future (the outcome) based on the historical knowledge (on the inputs).

THE NEED FOR A HYBRID APPROACH IN SOFTWARE ANALYTICS

BNs have been rigorously used in many disciplines such as healthcare and medicine that are more mature disciplines in terms of research design and guidelines. Similar to healthcare, evidence-based software engineering must put this research approach into practice in order to support and improve the decisions made by software practitioners on the usage and adaptation of a specific technology [1]. Earlier work on BNs in software engineering included validating dependability of software-based systems, estimating system reliability, making resource decisions, modeling project trade-offs, and estimation of software effort [4–9].

We need to recognize the fact that software intelligence provided by academia in the form of prediction models, software analytics, etc. should aim to help practitioners explain large volumes of data, understand what works and what does not, in practice, that would also let them make better decisions. These models should use the power of AI techniques, produce fact-based, faster, error-free solutions, and hence, help practitioners by reducing their workload during decision making and analysis. However, none of these models replace practitioners; instead they evolve via iterative feedback by practitioners. So a hybrid approach considering both the output of AI-based models and user knowledge is essential.

In our previous work we used the power of BNs to solve a specific problem of predicting software reliability, to combine the power of Bayesian statistics and expert knowledge, and to build hybrid models that can easily adapt to the environment, depending on the amount of local data in software organizations [1]. We observe that existing models in the literature were often built based on expert knowledge. Metrics were defined through surveys with experts, and metrics' distributions and their causal relationships were also determined by senior developers/

researchers. But this approach causes building models that are highly dependent on human judgment. We overcame this limitation by introducing a hybrid data collection and model construction process, and utilizing a suitable inference methodology. We collected both qualitative (expert knowledge) and quantitative (local data repositories) data in forming the nodes of BN. The proposed network models the processes of the software development life cycle (SDLC) and their relationships with software reliability. Using this causal network, we estimated the reliability of consecutive releases of software projects before a release decision, in terms of their residual (post-release) defects.

Collecting artifacts and defining metrics from all software processes may not be feasible. On the other hand, quantifying processes with survey data also has a bias due to subjective judgments of the software team, as their experience and qualifications are diverse. Therefore, we need a hybrid data collection approach by using quantitative data extracted from the organization's software repositories and qualitative data collected through surveys.

A hybrid BN is necessary to handle a mixture of continuous and categorical variables in a single model, such that categorical variables can also be parents of continuous variables. A hybrid BN also handles continuous variables without transforming them (ie, discretization). This also helps to avoid potential biases due to discretization in small-state spaces, such as software engineering datasets.

In this work, our industry wanted to decide "when to stop testing and release the product." Therefore, we aimed at predicting software reliability by learning the probability of residual defects given observations from software metrics. This probability is computed, ie, "inferred," from the BN via several techniques. We used Gibbs sampling, a well-known Monte Carlo technique on approximation of the joint probability distribution over conditional distributions. Gibbs sampling is well-suited for inferring the posterior distribution in a BN formed with a mixture of continuous and categorical variables, some of which also have missing data. Missing data in surveys is a common problem, and we had missing data in our surveys as well.

Our findings in this study showed that the effects of software processes and their causal relationships on software reliability are worth the investigation. Construction of a BN gave us some insights into understanding process factors in detail and their effect on software reliability. We used different factors/metrics to cover the 3Ps (people, process, product) of an SDLC. We have seen that causal models are better at predicting software reliability than generalized linear models, which treat each factor independently. The BN model in our industry partner predicts 84% of post-release defects with less than a 25% Mean Relative Error.

USE THE METHODOLOGY, NOT THE MODEL

Software organizations need predictive models to make release decisions. Using estimated post-release defects and the company's pre-determined threshold for software reliability, it is possible to estimate a release readiness level for each release. This threshold helps managers to make a decision either to release the software, or to delay the release, or to cancel the release. Measuring/quantifying software processes helps software organizations build a measurement repository and monitor trends of development practices in a systematic way. Our experience in building BNs in different organizations showed that there are not a specific set of metrics that should be used in any software development organization to predict reliability in terms of post-release defects. Causal relationships also change from one model to another based on local data collected from the organization. Hence, we suggest that practitioners follow a methodology rather than using same metric sets with the same causal relationships among each other.

Our experience in industry as well as the findings of our systematic review in [3] showed that there is a need for a systematic approach in building BNs. The dataset characteristics, source of data, and types of input and output variables would be important in:

1. identification of structure learning techniques to model cause-effect relationships between variables, and the rationale of choosing the selected technique, and in
2. identification of parameter learning, with respect to
    o   how to set the prior distributions, and
    o   how to estimate the final parameters of the model (inference), and the rationale of choosing the selected technique.

As always, the tool support and tool selection is also an important consideration for adoption and sustainability of a given technique/model in the industry.

Similar to computational biology and healthcare, we need to make decisions under uncertainty using multiple data sources. As we understand the dynamics of BNs and the techniques used for model learning, and inference, these models would enable us to uncover hidden relationships between variables, which cannot be easily identified by experts [1]. BNs will help us determine how scientific belief is modified by data. In the software engineering/software analytics community (both academia and practice), we should embrace BNs as a method for evidence-based statistics to be used in inference and decision making.

REFERENCES

[1] Misirli AT, Bener A. Bayesian networks for evidence-based decision-making in software engineering. IEEE Trans Softw Eng 2014;40(6).
[2] Schutt R. 10 important data science ideas; 2012. Available at http://columbiadatascience. com/2012/10/15/10-important-data-science-ideas/.
[3] Tosun A, Bener A, Akbarinasaji S. A systematic literature review on the applications of Bayesian networks to predict software quality. Software Qual J published online, 2015. http://dx.doi.org/10.1007/s11219-015-9297-z.
[4] Littlewood B, Verrall J. A Bayesian reliability growth model for computer software. Appl Stat 1973;26:332–46.

[5] Fenton N, Neil M, Marquez D. Using Bayesian networks to predict software defects and reliability. Proc Inst Mech Eng Part O—J Risk Reliab 2008;222(4):701–12.

[6] Fenton N, Marsh W, Neil M, Cates P, Forey S, Tailor M. Making resource decisions for software projects. In: Proceedings of the 26th international conference on software engineering. ICSE 2004. IEEE; 2004. p. 397–406.

[7] Fineman M, Fenton N, Radlinski L. Modelling project trade-off using Bayesian networks. In: International conference on computational intelligence and software engineering. 2009. CiSE 2009. IEEE; 2009. p. 1–4.

[8] Mendes E. Predicting web development effort using a Bayesian network. Proc EASE 2007;7:83–93.

[9] Mendes E, Mosley N. Bayesian network models for web effort prediction: a comparative study. IEEE Trans Softw Eng 2008;34(6):723–37.

Becoming Goldilocks: Privacy and data sharing in "just right" conditions

F. Peters

Lero - The Irish Software Research Centre, University of Limerick, Limerick, Ireland

CHAPTER OUTLINE

If we forget that Goldilocks trespassed, ate food, as well as used and broke furniture that did not belong to her—we can appreciate her sense of figuring out what was *just right* for her. Baby Bear's porridge was neither too hot nor too cold. Baby Bear's chair was not too big. Baby Bear's bed was neither too hard nor too soft. Finding that middle ground, that balance between two extremes or conflicting goals, such as privacy and utility, is the basis of research in data privacy and data sharing.

THE "DATA DROUGHT"

One of the facets of data science is reproducible reporting [1]. To do this, data used for analysis must be shared, but this is not always possible. Extracting project data from organizations is often very difficult due to its business sensitivity. For example, during his 11-year stint at NASA's software IV&V center, Tim Menzies observed that NASA divides its IV&V work among multiple contractors who all work on similar projects. Every three years, all the contracts are subject to competitive bidding. Hence, those contractors are very reluctant to share data about (say) the effort associated with finding mission-critical errors in manned spacecrafts, lest that data be used against them during the bidding process. Consequently, researchers and NASA managers suffer from a "data drought" that inhibits their ability to learn effective defect detection models for life-threatening software errors [2].

One way to convince data owners to share their data is to offer them a means to obfuscate their data in a way that is "just right" for both the data owners and researchers. In other words, the shared data should not allow the competition to learn specific sensitive information and remain useful for research purposes such as cross-project defect prediction. This was echoed by Sebastian Elbaum et al. in 2014 when they released Google testing results data online. These results contain 3.5 million test suite execution results. When questioned about sharing source code being tested and details on the failures, their response was:

> Sharing industrial datasets with the research community is extremely valuable, but also extremely challenging as it needs to balance the usefulness of the dataset with the industry's concerns for privacy and competition [3].

Since 2009, we have accepted the challenge of *Becoming Goldilocks* for privacy research in the domain of Cross-Project Defect Prediction. Our evaluations were conducted using static code defect data [4]. Each instance in these data represented a source code class and consisted of two parts: 20 independent static code attributes and the dependent attribute labeled "defects," indicating the number of defects in the class. We sought to protect this data from *sensitive attribute disclosure*, a privacy threat that can occur when an instance in the data is associated with information about their sensitive attributes, such as software code complexity. The defect data used in our work contains attributes that can be considered sensitive, for example, lines of code (LOC) are seen as a function of code complexity, where higher numbers for LOC indicate higher complexity, which can make understanding and maintaining code more difficult for developers and testers to find defects.

Our aim was, and is, to create privacy algorithms that produce "just right" data that offer data owners their prescribed privacy level and that are still useful for researchers and other users. Along the way, we learned some valuable lessons.

CHANGE IS GOOD

When we first started research into data privacy for software engineering, we focused on the literature for privacy-preserving data publishing [5,6]. Four main issues stood out:

1. Privacy could not be 100% guaranteed;
2. Obfuscating data could damage the usefulness (utility) of the data;
3. There are many different ways to measure privacy;
4. The question of whether the privacy of one matters, when the utility of the data provides benefits for all.

With these issues in mind, our first effort at generating "just right" data was MORPH, an instance mutator for obfuscating numerical data [7]. The intuition behind MORPH is to change the data enough to avoid privacy breaches, but not enough to degrade utility. To generate MORPHed instances, we first find for each original instance, its *nearest unlike neighbor*, that is, if an instance is defective, then its nearest unlike neighbor is non-defective. We then apply the following equation:

$$y_i = x_i \pm (x_i - z_i) \times r,$$

where y is the MORPHed instance generated when we find the difference between the values of the original instance (x) and it's nearest unlike neighbor (z). The random value (r) can be set to between 0 and 1 and represents the boundary between the original instance and its nearest unlike neighbor, which the MORPHed instance must not cross. A small r value means the boundary is closer to the original instance, while a large r value means the boundary is farther away from the original instance.

To measure the privacy of MORPHed data compared with the original data, we use an Inverse Privacy Ratio [7]. The Inverse Privacy Ratio models an attacker's background knowledge of a source code class in the form of queries. In an example with static code metrics, if our sensitive attribute is LOC, the attacker's query could be the values for *number of children* and *weighted methods per class*. When the query is applied to the original data, they will know the exact LOC value. However, when data has been MORPHed, the value for LOC is likely to be different from the original result. Therefore, if the same query applied to the original data and the MORPHed data yields the same result (LOC), then we say that there has been a privacy breach, or else there is no privacy breach.

When MOPRH was applied to our static code defect data [7], it offered four times more privacy than the original data, along with comparable utility for cross-project defect prediction.

This is lesson one: Little changes in your data can offer privacy and comparable utility.

DON'T SHARE EVERYTHING

This next lesson came as a side effect of work in data minimization, with the focus on dealing with the drawbacks of the k-Nearest Neighbor algorithm. These drawbacks include: (1) the high computation costs; (2) the storage required to hold the entire dataset in memory; (3) the effects of outliers; (4) the negative effect of data with non-separable and/or overlapping classes; and (5) the effects of noise on k-Nearest Neighbor inference [8].

We overcame these drawbacks with CLIFF, an algorithm which retains the subset of data that are the better representatives of the dependent variable of the data. CLIFF operates by ranking the sub-ranges of values for each non-sensitive attribute, by calculating the how often values from a sub-range appear for defective instances versus how often they appear for non-sensitive instances, and vice versa. We then find the product of the ranks for each instance and keep those instances that are ranked in the top 20% for both defective and non-defective instances.

The result was that with just 20% of the original data, utility could be maintained. Recognizing the potential of this result for privacy where 80% of the data could be protected because it does not have to be shared, we combined CLIFF with MORPH to form a powerful privacy algorithm [9]. We generated obfuscated data from only 20% of the original data.

This is lesson two: Don't share all your data. Some of your data are better at representing the dependent variable than others. Only share that data—keep the rest in your possession.

SHARE YOUR LEADERS

Once we had privacy algorithms, we realized that there was another factor that affected privacy and data sharing, ie, repeated data from different projects. We surmised that the reason for this is software code reuse in multiple projects. Selby [10], did a study and found that in a set of programs, 32% were comprised of reused code (not including libraries). Therefore, in a scenario of multiple data owners working together to share an obfuscated version of their combined data, there may be some repetition that would allow them to share less of their data.

We adapted the Leader Follower algorithm [11] to bring this scenario to life. The algorithm is an online, incremental technique for clustering data. The cluster centers are the "leaders," and all other data are the "followers." The basic algorithm works as follows: randomly select an instance from the data to be the first leader, then for every other instance in the data, find its nearest leader. If the distance to the leader is less than a user-defined distance, then update the cluster. Otherwise, create a new cluster with the instance as the leader. These steps are repeated until each instance has either updated a cluster or become a leader. We were only interested in the leaders. In this way, we avoided data repetition by not allowing data owners to share what others had already shared.

Fig. 36.1 shows an example with three data owners, Alice, Bob, and Eve, going through the leader sharing process, which we liken to a game of "pass the parcel." In our rendition of the game, the parcel starts empty, and as it is passed around, each player (data owner) adds leaders to the parcel. In the end, we found that privacy levels of the shared data by each data owner increased because they shared less data (~5%) while maintaining the utility of the data [12].

This is lesson three: Don't share what others have already shared. Instead, share your *leaders*, data that is unique to the population of shared data.

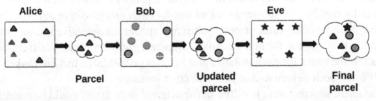

FIG. 36.1

An example of multiple data owners working together to share an obfuscated version of their combined data. As the parcel is passed around, each data owner adds leaders to the parcel.

SUMMARY

The lessons we learned since 2009 have helped us to generate obfuscated data that demonstrate the "just right" balance between privacy and utility of defect data. We recognize that there are a variety of different data types that could be shared in software engineering, and that each type may require different approaches. However, the lessons learned can be considered when developing or using other privacy algorithms for different types of software data.

ACKNOWLEDGMENTS

This work was partially funded by a National Science Foundation CISE medium grant (#1302169), Science Foundation Ireland grant 10/CE/I1855 and by the European Research Council (Advanced Grant 291652—ASAP).

REFERENCES

[1] Peng RD. The reproducibility crisis in science: a statistical counterattack. Significance 2015;12(3):30–2.
[2] Menzies T, Benson M, Costello K, Moats C, Northey M, Richarson J. Learning better IV&V practices. Innov Syst Softw Eng 2008;4(2):169–83.
[3] Elbaum S, Mclaughlin A, Penix J. The Google dataset of testing results. https://code.google.com/p/google-shared-dataset-of-test-suite-results; 2014.
[4] Jureczko M. Significance of different software metrics in defect prediction. Softw Eng Int J 2011;1(1):86–95.
[5] Brickell J, Shmatikov V. The cost of privacy: destruction of data-mining utility in anonymized data publishing. In: Proceedings of the 14th ACM SIGKDD international conference on knowledge discovery and data mining (KDD 2008). New York, NY, USA: ACM; 2008. p. 70–8.
[6] Li T, Li N. On the tradeoff between privacy and utility in data publishing. In: Proceedings of the 15th ACM SIGKDD international conference on knowledge discovery and data mining (KDD 2009). New York, NY, USA: ACM; 2009. p. 517–26.
[7] Peters F, Menzies T. Privacy and utility for defect prediction: experiments with morph. In: Proceedings of the 2012 international conference on software engineering, ser. ICSE 2012. Piscataway, NJ, US: IEEE Press; 2012. p. 189–99.
[8] Wilson DR, Martinez TR. Reduction techniques for instance-based learning algorithms. Mach Learn 2000;38:257–86.
[9] Peters F, Menzies T, Gong L, Zhang H. Balancing privacy and utility in cross-company defect prediction. IEEE Trans Softw Eng 2013;39(8):1054–68.
[10] Selby R. Enabling reuse-based software development of large-scale systems. IEEE Trans Softw Eng 2005;31(6):495–510.
[11] Duda R, Hart P, Stork D. Pattern classification. USA: Wiley; 2012.
[12] Peters F, Menzies T, Layman L. LACE2: better privacy-preserving data sharing for cross project defect prediction. In: 2015 IEEE/ACM 37th IEEE international conference on software engineering (ICSE), vol. 1, 16–24 May; 2015. p. 801–11.

The wisdom of the crowds in predictive modeling for software engineering

L.L. Minku

University of Leicester, Leicester, United Kingdom

CHAPTER OUTLINE

THE WISDOM OF THE CROWDS

The "wisdom of the crowds" phenomenon has long been observed in cognitive, social, and political sciences. The idea is that the combination of the judgments given by a large group of people on a certain matter is often better than the judgment given by any individual within this group.

Classically, the wisdom of the crowds was studied in continuous estimation problems, even though it has also been studied in other types of problems. A landmark study was performed in 1906, when a contest was set up in a country fair in Plymouth (UK) to estimate the weight of a slaughtered and dressed ox. The person whose guess was the closest to the actual weight of 1198 pounds would win a prize. Around 800 people, including both experts and people with no expertise in judging the weight of cattle, participated in the contest. The interesting fact was that, even though people gave several different and wrong estimations, statistician Francis Galton found that the average guess of all the participants was 1197 pounds. The collective "wisdom" of the Plymouth crowd was remarkably close to the actual weight of the ox, and better than the estimations given by any of the experts [1]!

The reason why the combined guess was so close to the actual weight was that, even though individual guesses were frequently completely wrong, the overestimations of

199

the weight given by some people cancelled out the underestimations given by others, resulting in an excellent combined guess.

SO... HOW IS THAT RELATED TO PREDICTIVE MODELING FOR SOFTWARE ENGINEERING?

Existing data on software projects and processes can be used to create predictive models able to help us with several different software engineering tasks, such as prediction of the effort required to develop software projects, prediction of whether a given software module is likely to contain bugs, prediction of whether a commit is likely to induce a crash, prediction of the energy likely to be consumed by a software program, etc. However, the accuracy of the predictions given by single models is sometimes not ideal.

Similar to the wisdom of the crowds, in order to improve predictive accuracy, we can combine the predictions given by a crowd (ensemble) of different models, instead of using a single model! Numeric predictions (eg, effort or energy estimations) given by different individual models can be combined by taking their average, allowing errors to cancel each other out. Categorical predictions (eg, whether or not a software module is likely to be buggy, or whether or not a commit is likely to induce a crash) can be combined by choosing the category "voted" on by the majority of the individual models. In this case, the correct categories predicted by some of the models can compensate for the incorrect categories predicted by the others.

EXAMPLES OF ENSEMBLES AND FACTORS AFFECTING THEIR ACCURACY

The predictive accuracy of an ensemble tends to improve more if individual models are not only themselves accurate, but also diverse, ie, if they make different mistakes. Without diversity, the combined prediction would make similar mistakes to the individual predictions, rather than individual mistakes canceling each other out, or correct predictions compensating for incorrect ones. Therefore, algorithms for creating ensembles of models consist of different techniques to create diverse (and not only accurate) individual models.

An example of an ensemble learning algorithm is bagging [2]. Given a learning algorithm for creating single predictive models and a data set, bagging creates diverse predictive models by feeding different uniform samples of the data set to the learning algorithm in order to create each model. Another example of ensembles are heterogeneous ensembles, where each individual model is created based on a different learning algorithm in order to produce different models [3]. Both of these ensembles have been shown to help improve predictive accuracy (and stability) in software engineering tasks [4,5].

Besides individual models' predictive accuracy and diversity, another factor that can influence the predictive accuracy of ensembles is their size, ie, the number of individual models composing the ensemble. A too-small ensemble size (eg, two models) may not be enough to improve predictive accuracy. A large ensemble size may use extra computational resources unnecessarily, or even cause reductions in predictive accuracy if too large, eg, 10,000+ models [6]. Even though some early studies suggested that ensembles with as few as 10 models were sufficient for improving predictive accuracy [7], other studies suggested that predictive accuracy can be further improved by using more than 10 models, eg, 25 modes [8]. The minimum ensemble size before further improvements in predictive accuracy cease to be achieved is likely to depend both on the predictive task and the learning algorithms involved.

CROWDS FOR TRANSFERRING KNOWLEDGE AND DEALING WITH CHANGES

Sometimes there is not much data for building predictive models within a given environment, hindering the accuracy of predictive approaches. There may be more data available from other environments, but these data are not always directly relevant for predictions in the targeted environment. For example, the effort required to develop a certain software project within a given company may be different from the effort required to develop the same project in another company because these companies adopt different management strategies. So, a software effort estimation model created with data from one of these companies may not be directly applicable to the other.

Even though data from different environments are not always compatible, they may become more or less relevant over time. This is because environments may change over time, becoming more or less similar to other environments. Changes in the environment are referred to as "concept drifts" by the machine learning community. They may affect how well predictive models represent the environment, triggering the need for updating predictive models. As an example, a software company may adopt a new software development process, resulting in its productivity becoming more similar to the productivity of other companies that adopt this process. If the company wishes to keep its software effort estimation models accurate, it must update them to reflect the new situation. If we can identify *when* data from other environments become useful and *how much more useful* they are, we can benefit from them to obtain better and more up-to-date predictive models.

Ensembles are useful in this context because they can maintain several different models representing different environments. When changes affect the adequacy of a given model to the targeted environment, we can identify which other models would be most adequate for the new situation, based on a few new data examples from the targeted environment. We can then emphasize the predictions of the most appropriate models. This is useful for improving predictive accuracy when there are not enough new examples from the targeted environment to create a whole new model representing the new situation of this environment. Given that it may take a lot of time and effort to collect enough new data from the targeted environment, ensemble approaches can be particularly useful to transfer knowledge from different models in changing environments [9].

Moreover, it is possible to use a few incoming examples from the targeted environment to learn functions that are able to map the predictions given by models representing different environments to the context of the targeted environment. An ensemble of such mapped models can transfer knowledge from models representing environments that do not directly match the targeted environment. This can greatly reduce the number of examples that need to be collected from within the targeted environment, being particularly useful when data collection is expensive within the targeted environment [10].

CROWDS FOR MULTIPLE GOALS

Ensembles of models can also be used to deal with different goals in software engineering predictive tasks. For example, in software bug prediction, one may wish to identify the largest possible number of software components that contain bugs at the same time as making very few mistakes in terms of pointing out a non-buggy software module as buggy. These are two different and often conflicting goals. In order to deal with different goals, we can create models that emphasize different goals. Combined, these models can provide a good trade-off among different goals [11].

A CROWD OF INSIGHTS

Ensembles have the potential to provide several insights into software engineering. Besides the insights given by the predictions themselves, different models representing different environments can give us insights into the differences between these environments. In particular, when used for software effort estimation, ensemble models can themselves be visualized in order to reveal how a company's productivity compares to the productivity of other companies [10]. This can then be used to monitor how the productivity of a company changes over time in comparison to other companies and help identify areas where improvement is needed. The differences between the predictions given by different models to different sets of input values can also potentially lead to insights into how best choices vary from one environment to another, and whether it is worth trying to migrate from one environment to another.

ENSEMBLES AS VERSATILE TOOLS

In summary, ensembles are versatile tools that can help us to deal with different issues in predictive modeling for software engineering. They can help us to improve predictive accuracy (and stability) across data sets, to deal with changes and transfer knowledge, to handle different goals, and to gain insights into software processes.

Even though some ensemble approaches have potential drawbacks, depending on the problem at hand, other ensemble approaches can actually help us to overcome these drawbacks. For example, a potential drawback of ensembles is the possible increase in the computational resources (eg, running time and memory) required for creating ensembles in comparison to single models. Even though many ensemble approaches do not increase the time and memory *complexity* of the learning algorithms used by their individual models, their increase in required computational resources may still become a problem for very large data sets. That said, several other ensemble approaches are specifically designed to reduce the computational resources that would be required by single models when data sets are very large. This can be easily achieved, for example, by creating individual models with disjointed subsets of the data, as done by chunk-based incremental learning ensembles [12].

Another potential drawback of ensembles is lack of explanatory power. As the ensemble size increases, it becomes difficult to "read" ensembles in order to explain how exactly their predictions are made. This is not a problem if practitioners are more interested in how helpful the predictions themselves are, rather than in how the predictions are made. However, if practitioners wish to understand the models behind the predictions, lack of explanatory power can become a problem. Even though lack of explanatory power is a drawback of many ensemble approaches, some ensemble approaches do not hinder explanatory power, or can even help us to understand certain conditions better. For example, ensembles where a single model is created for each different environment can be useful for understanding the relationship and the differences between environments [10].

To learn more about ensembles and their applications to software engineering, I recommend Polikar's [13] and Menzies et al. [14] manuscripts, respectively.

REFERENCES

[1] Galton F. Vox Populi, Nature 1907;450–1. http://galton.org/essays/1900-1911/galton-1907-vox-populi.pdf [accessed 04.01.16].
[2] Breiman L. Bagging predictors. Mach Learn 1996;24(2):123–40.
[3] Perrone MP, Cooper LN. When networks disagree: ensemble methods for hybrid neural networks. In: Mammone RJ, editor. Neural networks for speech and image processing. UK: Chapman Hall; 1993. p. 126–42.
[4] Kocaguneli E, Menzies T, Keung J. On the value of ensemble effort estimation. IEEE Trans Softw Eng 2012;38(6):1403–16.

[5] Minku LL, Yao X. Ensembles and locality: insight on improving software effort estimation. Inform Softw Technol 2013;55(8):1512–28.

[6] Grove AJ, Schuurmans D. Boosting in the limit: maximizing the margin of learned ensembles. In: Proceedings of the fifteenth national conference on artificial intelligence; 1998. p. 692–9.

[7] Hansen LK, Salamon P. Neural network ensembles. IEEE Trans Pattern Anal Mach Intellig 1990;12(10):993–1001.

[8] Opitz D, Maclin R. Popular ensemble methods: an empirical study. J Artif Intellig Res 1999;11:169–98.

[9] Minku LL, Yao X. Can cross-company data improve performance in software effort estimation? In: Proceedings of the 8th international conference on predictive models in software engineering (PROMISE'2012); 2012. p. 69–78.

[10] Minku LL, Yao X. How to make best use of cross-company data in software effort estimation? In: Proceedings of the 36th international conference on software engineering (ICSE'14); 2014. p. 446–56.

[11] Minku LL, Yao X. Software effort estimation as a multi-objective learning problem. ACM Trans Softw Eng Methodol 2013;22(4)article no. 35.

[12] Nick Street W, Kim WS. A streaming ensemble algorithm (SEA) for large-scale classification. In: Proceedings of the 7th ACM SIGKDD international conference on knowledge discovery and data mining; 2001. p. 377–82.

[13] Polikar R. Ensemble based systems in decision making. IEEE Circ Syst Mag 2006;6(3):21–45.

[14] Menzies T, Kocaguneli E, Minku LL, Peters F, Turhan B. Sharing data and models in software engineering, part IV: sharing models. USA: Morgan Kaufmann; 2014.

Combining quantitative and qualitative methods (when mining software data)

M. Di Penta

University of Sannio, Benevento, Italy

CHAPTER OUTLINE

PROLOGUE: WE HAVE SOLID EMPIRICAL EVIDENCE!

In recent years, empirical research in software engineering has gained a lot of maturity. This is in part thanks to the availability of a large amount of data from different kinds of software repositories, as well as of techniques to mine them, eg, for tracing data from heterogeneous sources, summarizing changes, or mining unstructured and semi-structured data sources. Noticeably, the analysis of data from software repositories has also gained a lot of attention in industry, where developers rely on software data to make important decisions. The roles, competencies, and working styles of data scientists in software development has been recently investigated by Kim et al. [1].

Suppose we are software engineering researchers and we have developed a new recommendation tool that identifies certain kinds of code's bad smells. We want to convince practitioners to adopt our tool. Also, suppose that, by using data from software repositories, and by using appropriate statistical methods, we are able to show that our new code smell detector achieves 90% precision and 60% recall, and that classes affected by such smells tend to be significantly more defect-prone than others. Hopefully, such findings can be useful to provide practitioners with convincing arguments about the performance of our novel tool and its potential usefulness. Is this sufficient to convince them to adopt the tool? Does it show that detecting code's bad smells is relevant and useful? What are we missing?

CORRELATION IS NOT CAUSATION AND, EVEN IF WE CAN CLAIM CAUSATION...

No matter how we carefully conduct our (quantitative) empirical study, it would not tell us the whole story. Let us assume that, by doing a quantitative study, we know that our tool is very precise and has a good recall, better than an alternative tool. Let us also assume that we conduct a controlled experiment to study the relation between smells and code defect-proneness. In a controlled experiment, we observe one or more dependent variables (in our case defect-proneness) while varying the level of some independent variables (eg, separating classes containing bad smells from others) and controlling others (eg, determining whether the class size could influence our results). Results of the experiments show that classes containing code smells identified by our tools are more fault-prone than others. However, this does not tell us the whole story.

Specifically, we still do not know *why* our recommender worked better (or worse) than the baseline, *how* developers have used it during their tasks, and *whether* there are clear directions for improvement. More than that, there are problems in claiming the causation of our findings. Imagine our tool is able to highlight potentially defect-prone classes based on the presence of some code smells, and it seems to exhibit a very good precision and recall. Is the presence of code smell really what causes defects? Or, maybe, defective code is subject to more patches and then becomes "smelly"? Or, perhaps a specific module of our projects is just too complicated to become smelly and defect-prone? While in some cases, a purely quantitative analysis may have results sufficient to determine the direction of a causality relation (eg, smells are always introduced in the code before defects occurs, therefore we could claim that smells may cause defects and not vice versa, ie, defect fixes make source code smelly). In some other cases this is not possible, either because it is not possible to determine a temporal precedence between two phenomena, or because causation depends on factors we are ignoring.

Other than that, quantitative findings might tell us how good our approach is, but tells us little on how to improve it. Why is my smell detector producing so many false positives, especially when applied on certain (sub)systems? And, why does it fail to detect some true smells?

In some other circumstances, it can happen that a quantitative study does not show the effect of a factor we are not observing. A typical example is a study by Bird et al. [2] on the effect of developers' geographical distribution. Quantitative results showed a limited effect of geographical distribution, though developers suggest this is because of countermeasures they have taken (not observable in the study).

What are the recipes to properly complement the gained quantitative evidence? In short, you should try to complement quantitative findings with qualitative ones.

While, as exemplified herein, quantitative studies will provide you with empirical evidence in terms of numerical relations between variables, qualitative studies will help you to interpret and explain a phenomenon by observing it in its context. This is often achieved through the analysis of people observations, interviews, and documents [3].

COLLECT YOUR DATA: PEOPLE AND ARTIFACTS

To complement our quantitative findings with qualitative insights, we can rely on at least two precious sources of information: (i) artifacts contained in the software repositories and (ii) the projects' contributors.

SOURCE 1: DIG INTO SOFTWARE ARTIFACTS AND DATA...

Software repositories offer us a great opportunity to complement quantitative studies with qualitative ones. For example, commit messages provide a (short) rationale of the performed changes, whereas information of what contributors discussed before an issue was fixed can be found in issue trackers. Similarly, other communication channels, such as mailing lists or chats, will help you discover the rationale of some project decisions.

...but be careful about noise and incompleteness!

Assuming that software repositories will tell you everything about a software project, and that information available there is fully reliable, the validity of your results can still be threatened. Previous studies have indicated that:

- *Not everything is recorded in software repositories*: as developers still discuss things via phone, unrecorded chats, or in face-to-face meetings [4]. Not to mention the need to trace heterogeneous repositories when, more often than not, links are incomplete or missing.
- *Software repositories contain noisy data*: this includes misclassification of artifacts, eg, issue reports classified as bug fixes when they are related to new features, or tangled changes in versioning systems (ie, multiple changes having different purposes committed together).

Last but not least, a manual analysis of developers' written discussions might be subject to a misleading interpretation when performed by outsiders. Therefore, every time one does not have sufficient elements to provide answers to research questions or explanation to given phenomena based solely on the manual or automated analysis of data from software repositories, the latter needs to be complemented with information obtained by interviewing/surveying developers.

SOURCE 2: GETTING FEEDBACK FROM DEVELOPERS...

Every time you obtain empirical results based on data from software projects, you should try to assess your findings with the help of developers involved in these projects. One possibility is to perform live/phone interviews. Using interviews has noticeable advantages, among others, the possibility of posing clarifying questions to participants, or using a semistructured or unstructured format, ie, adapting the questions to the context. A viable alternative is to conduct a survey (eg, through a web-based platform) using a predefined questionnaire. This is useful when (i) it is impossible to reach people live or physically, or, in general, (ii) participants prefer to answer the questionnaire at their own schedule. Moreover, by employing surveys you could engage people in more complex tasks that go beyond just answering a simple question. As an example, going back to our smell detector tool, we could imagine showing to participants some example of "smelly" code and asking them opinions or suggestions for refactoring. Truly, this can also be accomplished during a live interview, but as a matter of fact a web-based survey gives you an appropriate (and probably more relaxed) setting for that.

Interviewing developers in an industrial context is already challenging. When it comes to applying it to open source projects, things might become even more difficult, despite the fact that one has many projects, and potential respondents are available. A few suggestions:

- *Carefully target potential respondents*: random sampling over project email addresses might not always be the best solution. Do you need answers from core developers? Do you need people knowledgeable about specific artifacts?
- *Motivate respondents*: while you plan your interview/survey with your own research goal in mind, developers would be more willing to help if you are already providing them with findings of their interest.
- *Plan for relatively short questionnaires, with (if any) tasks that can be accomplished in a limited amount of time*: most the respondents are unlikely to spend more than 15–20 min on the task you are asking them to participate in.
- *Choose the most suitable interviewing protocol*: in most cases, the only way to gain information from software developers (especially in the open source) is to ask them to fill out a questionnaire. When a live or phone interview is possible, you will have many more degrees of freedom in terms of the interview structure (fully structured, semistructured, or totally unstructured). Also, different protocols are possible, such as think-aloud, or (focused) group interviews.

...and don't be afraid if you collect very little data!
Remember that here the quality of obtained feedback is more important than the statistical significance of our sample. Very few respondents could still be able to provide you with precious feedback to improve your approach/tool and make it applicable in the real world, or to provide you with an explanation of why your approach produced false positives or meaningless results in their project.

HOW MUCH TO ANALYZE, AND HOW?

In large studies on software repositories, exhaustive analysis is often unfeasible. One option is to perform a statistical (eg, random or stratified) sampling. However, this may or may not be what you need. In qualitative analysis, it is often useful a *purposeful* sampling, which focuses more on obtaining answers to your questions rather than achieving statistical representativeness and generalizability. Examples of purposeful sampling include [5]:

- *Extreme/deviant cases sampling*: analyze artifacts on which your tool worked very well, or did not work at all; talk with people that exhibited the highest (or lowest) productivity with your tool; in general, look at outliers.
- *Homogeneous sampling*: in some cases, you may want to focus on a specific class of artifacts/subjects. For example, you might want to understand how senior developers performed when using your recommender, or how well your smell detection tool worked on classes belonging to the graphical user interface of the analyzed system.
- *Snowball sampling*: this occurs when one sample suggests further ones. For example, while you are inspecting emails discussing licensing, you discover a pattern that allows you to sample further emails. Or, when interviewing a developer involved in a bug fix, you learn about other people involved in that activity.

BUILD A THEORY UPON YOUR DATA

Once data has been collected, the purpose of qualitative analysis is to provide an interpretation to it and, ideally, build a theory. To this aim, techniques inspired to grounded theory [6], such as open coding, are particularly suitable.

Open coding starts with the identification of keywords/regularities in the observed artifacts, and in the consequent creation of categories, that should be internally cohesive and consistent, and overall inclusive of the investigated reality. The open coding process should involve multiple and independent coders to limit subjectiveness, eg, one person performs the coding, the other replicates it, and then coding reliability is assessed through measures such as the *Krippendorff's Alpha* [7]. Multiple iterations of the process aim to merge, split, or remove categories. Such categories, their relationships, and the concepts abstracted from them allow you to answer questions such as:

- What do developers discuss before fixing a bug? How do discussions converge to a solution?
- What kinds of bugs occur in files affected by code smells?
- What are the typical problems developers encountered when using our new recommender system? What are the main suggestions for improvement?

CONCLUSION: THE TRUTH IS OUT THERE!

Studying a software process/product, or evaluating a novel approach/tool requires multiple, and different kinds of, evaluations. On one hand, quantitative studies have different scales, different levels of control, and different risks, eg, surveys, case studies, and controlled experiments, as well as their replication to increase statistical power and external validity of results. On the other hand, combining such quantitative studies with qualitative ones will help provide convincing arguments of *when* and *why* a prediction model or a recommender system works (or does not work).

In summary, information is there, but you need to look at it from different perspectives: quantitative (numbers) and qualitative (concepts).

SUGGESTED READINGS

Seaman [8] has discussed the application of qualitative methods in software engineering, and specifically about observing/interviewing developers, and complementing this with coding and theory building. Quinn Patton [5] provides a thorough overview of qualitative methods—mainly in the context of social science application. Last, but not least, a "must read" is the seminal work on grounded theory research [6].

Some chapters of this book specifically focus on certain qualitative analysis techniques. In their chapter *"Avoiding Survey Design Traps: A Successful Process for Sailing Past the Temptations of Persephone's Sirens"* Barik and Murphy-Hill provide hints on how to conduct survey research. In his chapter *"Card-sorting: From Text To Themes"* Zimmermann illustrates the card-sorting method that can be used to analyze open-text survey responses. Menzies's chapter *"Correlation is not Causation"* explains, through simple examples, the difference between claiming correlation and causation.

REFERENCES

[1] Kim M, Zimmermann T, DeLine R, Begel A. The emerging role of data scientists on software development teams. In: Proceedings of the 38th international conference on software engineering, ICSE 2016, May 14–22. Austin, TX: ACM; 2016.

[2] Bird C, Nagappan N, Devanbu PT, Gall HC, Murphy B. Does distributed development affect software quality? An empirical case study of Windows Vista. In: Proceedings of the 31st international conference on software engineering, ICSE 2009, May 16–24. Vancouver, Canada: ACM; 2009. p. 518–28.

[3] Quinn Patton M. Qualitative research & evaluation methods. 3rd ed. Sage Publications, Inc.; 2001.

[4] Aranda J, Venolia G. The secret life of bugs: going past the errors and omissions in software repositories. In: Proceedings of the 31st international conference on software engineering, ICSE 2009, May 16–24. Vancouver, Canada: ACM; 2009. p. 298–308.

[5] Quinn Patton M. Qualitative research & evaluation methods. Integrating theory and practice. 4th ed. Thousand Oaks, CA: SAGE Publications; 2014.

[6] Corbin J, Strauss A. Grounded theory research: procedures, canons, and evaluative criteria. Qual Sociol 1990;13(1):3–21.

[7] Krippendorff K. Content analysis: an introduction to its methodology. 3rd ed. Thousand Oaks, CA: SAGE Publications; 2013.

[8] Seaman CB. Qualitative methods in empirical studies of software engineering. IEEE Trans Softw Eng 1999;25(4):557–72.

A process for surviving survey design and sailing through survey deployment

T. Barik, E. Murphy-Hill
North Carolina State University

CHAPTER OUTLINE

In the Odyssey, Odysseus and his crew must confront Persephone's Sirens, creatures that sang in irresistible voices and lured sailors to their deaths. Still, adventurers risked the journey for the promise of knowledge, for through the Sirens' song, "[o]ver all the generous earth [the adventurers] know everything that happens." With guidance from Circe, the goddess of magic, Odysseus instructed his crew to plug their ears to deafen them from the song. He then had his crew tie him to the mast and commanded them not to release him under any circumstances. And so Odysseus and his crew navigated safely past the Sirens. Odysseus, having heard the Sirens' song, sailed away a wiser man (Fig. 1).

Surveys, as with Persephone's Sirens, are an attractive instrument that offer a similar lure of knowledge. Like Circe, we offer guidance, grounded in our own experiences, on a successful process for understanding the practice of software engineering through surveys.

THE LURE OF THE SIRENS: THE ATTRACTION OF SURVEYS

Surveys are an attractive option for several reasons. The first reason is easy scalability. After an initial sunk cost to develop the survey, our perception is that can we simply scale up by sending the survey to more participants. The second reason is that

FIG. 1

Ulysses and the Sirens, by Herbert James Draper, c.1900.

Source: https://commons.wikimedia.org/wiki/File:Ulysses_and_the_Sirens_by_H.J._Draper.jpg.

surveys are easy to deploy. Today, the preferred format is predominantly electronic survey distribution, not print, and many user-friendly, online services exist to help practitioners and researchers design and deploy surveys. A final reason is that surveys give us a certain sense of quantitative comfort because the survey responses can be downloaded into a spreadsheet or other statistical analysis software. A popular form of question-style, *Likert* statements (strongly disagree to strongly agree), can then be quantitatively analyzed through various descriptive and statistical techniques that are already familiar to us.

But as with Odysseus, these lures are only surface benefits. Our experiences have taught us the harsh lesson that, without caution, lurking beneath the waters are several traps that lead to shipwreck. Let's figure out how to avoid that fate.

NAVIGATING THE OPEN SEAS: A SUCCESSFUL SURVEY PROCESS IN SOFTWARE ENGINEERING

Homer's cautionary story warns us of the perils of early exploration without sufficient preparation. Odysseus succeeded where others before him had failed because of his careful planning.

Surveys in software engineering are frequently used as a way to obtain multiple viewpoints, or to *triangulate*. Surveys are also used to draw inferences about a larger population, or to *generalize*.

This six-stage process we present here is tailored for practitioners and researchers who want to better understand how software engineering is practiced in one organization or across many. In developing this process, we have learned from our own mistakes, from the feedback of peers, and from interviews with others who use surveys as an empirical method.

STAGE 1: INITIAL RECRUITMENT

It's tempting to jump right in and begin writing survey questions, and today's software packages almost entice you to do so. But as we learned with the Sirens, adventurers who dashed off on their journey without appropriate preparation ultimately met with tragedy. Consequently, it's essential to first consider the questions you want to ask and how you intend to use the answers to the questions. This is not simply a matter of taking your intuitions and translating them into survey question form. We've found, for example, that the phrasing of the question itself is highly contextually sensitive and that the survey-takers often do not have the same interpretation of questions as the survey-makers.

One way to mitigate this risk is to create a very short survey and cast a wide net to recruit participants with familiarity on the topic. For example, one survey on data science practices randomly sampled employees and asked them three simple questions: (a) "Do you perform data science activities?"; (b) "What's your biggest frustration when performing data science?"; and (c) "May we follow-up with you?"

Leave the survey open for at least a week to give participants adequate time to respond to the short survey. As responses come in, you'll want to recruit diverse participants to get a variety of stories from different backgrounds. For example, to learn how professionals in an organization use log and telemetry data, we recruited not only developers, but also project managers, operations engineers, data scientists, and even content developers. Next, follow up with several of these participants and conduct interviews with them.

STAGE 2: INTERVIEWS

The interview is one process through which we can gain information about software engineering. We've found a successful approach is to ask participants to share specific stories that relate to a particular topic. Often, participants will tell these in the form of "war stories," which describe particularly challenging situations and how they overcame them.

Think of these interviews as incredible sources of knowledge. Like the songs of the Sirens, these 30–45 min interview sessions provide us with rich stories, told directly through the voices of those who experienced them.

Nonetheless, these isolated anecdotes are difficult to generalize because they are highly contextualized. Also, because interviews are expensive and time-consuming to conduct, only a limited number of stories are practical to obtain. But by translating these stories into survey response questions, we can both generalize and scale these stories.

STAGE 3: SURVEY DESIGN

It's now time to design the survey. Just as Odysseus realized early on that he would not be able obtain the Sirens' knowledge through force, a similar principle holds for survey design. Since online surveys are self-administered, be careful about wording. Instead of inventing terms, use language that you encountered in the interviews conducted earlier. Otherwise, your questions might not connect with the survey participants.

There are two broad categories of questions you can ask: closed and open response. Closed response, such as multiple choice or Likert scales, are easy to statistically analyze, but fix the set of possible responses. Open response, such as short answer text fields, can provide new and unexpected insights. However, it's laborious to analyze these unstructured, free-text responses. Our preference is to use open responses sparsely and instead rely on the interview content for these types of questions.

The key to successful survey design, then, is to ensure that the majority of your questions are grounded in and derived from the experiences of the interviews. As an example, in our survey about game development and traditional software development, we asked a set of Likert statements on coding, process, and team. The statements were of the form "My software has high technical debt." (Coding), "My team uses a waterfall process, rather than an agile process." (Process), and "Creativity is highly valued on the team" (Team).

How did we know which statements to ask? Our statements came directly from the stories told by participants during our semistructured interviews. By doing so, we can triangulate stories we heard in the interviews and generalize those experiences quantitatively.

At the same time, your interviewees told you a lot of stories, so you'll have to be selective about what you ask survey participants about. Time permitting, you may also want to refine your interview statements through a review of existing literature. If a topic is already well-understood, it's probably not worth wasting the participants' time asking about it. Consider your goals carefully and only ask survey questions that help you reach those goals.

STAGE 4: SURVEY PILOTING

Don't count on your initial survey design to be perfect. In an extreme case, a collaborator spent nearly a year in preparation while his team argued about question wording. By the time they "finished," the survey had become obsolete and ultimately proved to be useless.

Instead, consider a more agile approach by *piloting* the survey: ask a few friends to take the survey and then analyze the results the way you normally would. With as few as five participants, you can often catch the most egregious mistakes. Piloting with people who are representative of your target population will help you find more mistakes.

During piloting, a useful perspective is to test your survey like you'd test software. Survey bugs can appear in the most unlikely of places. For example, one "bug" we found through this process was in our consent form. A participant could choose "I don't consent to participate," but still filled out the survey! This would have been disastrous, because we wouldn't know who consented and who didn't. We'd have to throw out all the data.

Here are some observations during piloting:

- Length matters, and you should pay attention to how long it takes to complete the survey. Based on our experiences as survey designers, we recommend that the survey not take more than 15 min.
- Cut, cut, cut! This is a good opportunity to identify questions that are redundant, confusingly worded, or overly difficult.
- Identify drop points where participants may give up on the survey.
- Pay attention to open response questions and don't expect rich answers. In general, people don't like typing stuff—that's what interviews are for.

Finally, providing a strong *initial recruitment letter* is perhaps just as important as the survey, but it is often overlooked or done as an afterthought. Participants are busy people, and it's easy for them to ignore your letter if they don't see why it's relevant to them. To improve participate rates, you should respect their time and explain how the participant benefits from the survey. Why should they take it? What do they get out of it? They always want to know, "Why'd you pick me?"

Though Odysseus had only one chance to face the Sirens, piloting offers you multiple opportunities to quickly practice your survey before embarking on the real journey.

STAGE 5: SURVEY DEPLOYMENT

It's time to send out the survey! If you've done everything right so far, this is where you, like Odysseus, will sail past the Sirens and obtain insight and knowledge from the journey. During deployment, there are still a few items to keep in mind:

- Have a finite close date. We usually give our participants two weeks to complete the survey.
- Responses come in a bathtub model. You get a lot of responses early, then nothing or a trickle, followed by a final burst. Send a reminder to those that didn't respond the first time around, but you should consider preliminary analysis after the first set of responses so that you're not blocked on survey completion.
- Be respectful and avoid oversampling the same participants or communities. Aim for diversity. Certain open source communities, such as Eclipse, Mozilla, and Apache, tend to be swamped with surveys from researchers all over the world.

There's no hard and fast rule for the number of survey responses to target, but for quantitative data, *power analysis* is a useful technique for estimating the number of responses you'll need.

STAGE 6: SURVEY ANALYSIS AND WRITE-UP

You've made it past the Sirens, but there's still some work to do. Expect to do a certain amount of data cleaning, since you've generated the survey in a way that benefits the survey taker, not you. For example, Likert responses are easier to analyze when converted to an ordinal 1–5 scale. Other questions, such as "number of hours worked on a task," are easier to ask in terms of hours and minutes, but simpler to analyze as fractions of hours (1 h 30 min to 1.5 h).

Even short surveys tend to generate large amounts of data for potential analysis, but not all of this information will be useful in your eventual write-up. That's okay, but consider it a learning experience—was it worth participants' time in asking a question (or asking it in a particular way) if you're not going to analyze the results?

During this process, try to triangulate and form a coherent narrative about the work using the interviews and the survey responses. Do the survey responses match the experiences of the interviews? Are there cases where they don't? Connecting your survey results back to the interviews enables you to generalize your interview results. This approach, for example, allowed us to say with some statistical certainty that "Creativity is valued more in game development teams," a statement that we heard in our interviews on games development and software engineering.

IN SUMMARY

Our take-away is that the survey itself is only a small part of the picture. In large part, the upfront work you invest before the survey will go a long way toward deciding if you succeed or if you shipwreck. In short:

- Pay special attention to ensure that the participants' time and effort is respected.
- Piloting is a good way to identify breakages early in the design process.
- What seems reasonable for a designer is not reasonable for the participant. Use language familiar to the participants.
- Surveys shouldn't be a standalone instrument; use them as a triangulation method and combine them with other techniques, such as interviews. This gives you both the breadth and depth to report your findings in a compelling way.

Certainly, surveys aren't always easy to design or deploy. But like the journey of Odysseus and his crew, the voyage is filled with uncharted experiences and undiscovered insights that make the adventure worthwhile.

ACKNOWLEDGMENTS

This material is based in part upon work supported by the National Science Foundation under grant number 1217700.

REFERENCES

[1] Barik T, DeLine R, Drucker S, Fisher D. The bones of the system: a study of logging and telemetry at Microsoft. In: Proceedings of the 38th international conference on software engineering. ACM; 2016.

[2] Murphy-Hill E, Zimmermann T, Nagappan N. Cowboys, ankle sprains, and keepers of quality: how is video game development different from software development? In: Proceedings of the 36th international conference on software engineering. ACM; 2014. p. 1–11.

[3] Lutters WG, Seaman CB. Revealing actual documentation usage in software maintenance through war stories. Inf Softw Technol 2007;49(6):576–87.

[4] Smith E, Loftin R, Murphy-Hill E, Bird C, Zimmermann T. Improving developer participation rates in surveys. In: 6th international workshop on cooperative and human aspects of software engineering (CHASE). IEEE; 2013. p. 89–92.

[5] Strauss A, Corbin J. Grounded theory methodology. Handbook of qualitative research. Thousand Oaks, CA, US: Sage Publications; 1994. p. 273–85.

[6] Witschey J, Zielinska O, Welk A, Murphy-Hill E, Mayhorn C, Zimmermann T. Quantifying developers' adoption of security tools. In: Proceedings of the 10th joint meeting on foundations of software engineering. 2015. p. 260–71.

Wisdom

Log it all?

G.C. Murphy

University of British Columbia, Vancouver, BC, Canada

CHAPTER OUTLINE

A PARABLE: THE BLIND WOMAN AND AN ELEPHANT

Imagine a group of blind women are asked to describe what an elephant looks like by touching different parts of the elephant [1]. One blind woman touches the trunk and says it is like a tree branch. Another blind woman touches the leg and says it is like a column. The third and fourth blind women touch the ear and tail, saying the elephant is like a fan and a rope, respectively.

Each of these women believes she is right, and, from her own perspective, each is right. But, each decision is being made on only partial data and tells only part of the entire story.

MISINTERPRETING PHENOMENON IN SOFTWARE ENGINEERING

When we collect data to investigate a software engineering phenomenon, we have to take care not to fall into the trap of taking a single perspective. Let's consider that we want to know more about the phenomenon of how software developers learn commands available in an integrated development environment (IDE). Understanding what commands are being used, and how and when new commands are learned, might help to develop tools to suggest other useful commands developers are not already using as a means of improving the developer's productivity (eg, Ref. [2]).

To investigate this phenomenon, we decide to monitor each and every command the developer executes as she works. As part of the logged information, we capture the time at which the command was executed, the command itself, and how the command was invoked. We try out the monitoring tool with those close to us and the data all seems to make sense. We then deploy a monitoring tool and start gathering the information from as many developers as we can convince to install the monitor.

As we gather the logged command data from (hopefully thousands of) developers and begin the analysis, we realize that there are many different subsequences of command usage we did not initially anticipate. For example, we may be surprised to see searches for references to uses of methods interspersed with debugging commands, such as step forward.

It is only at this point in our analysis when we realize that we are missing data about the context in which commands are executed, such as which windows were visible on the screen in the IDE when the command was executed. Had we captured this information, we could infer from the visible windows whether a command is likely being executed while debugging or while writing code. Understanding more about this context could enable us to build better recommender tools.

We had inadvertently fallen into the trap of looking at the phenomenon from only one perspective.

USING DATA TO EXPAND PERSPECTIVES

As the example demonstrates, capturing more data and making it available for analysis can help us expand our perspective on a software engineering phenomenon.

Imagine if we were now able to not just capture the windows visible when a command is executed, but we also knew which task on which the developer was working, such as the particular feature being developed. With this data, we might be able to start understanding which commands are most applicable for different kinds of tasks. And what if we could capture the developer's face as the tasks were performed? This data might help identify which commands require more concentration than others to execute and might change the sequence or situations in which a tool recommends particular commands to learn.

Although we might want to capture many kinds of data to understand a phenomenon, is more data always better? In determining what data to capture, we must consider a number of issues:

- Can the data be captured practically? Although we might want to capture video of a developer's face using an IDE, and although cameras for web conferencing are becoming more readily available, it is not practical to capture this data for a large number of developers working in a variety of environments.
- Will the developers accept the capture and use of the data? Not every developer is likely to feel comfortable with video of their face being captured as it raises many privacy concerns.

- What are the constraints on transmission and sharing of the data? Some data that might be captured might need to be protected because transmission or sharing of that data with the researchers might comprise intellectual property. In some cases, it may be possible to transform the data in such a way that alleviates the concerns about transmission and sharing. In other cases, there may not be a meaningful transform. Researchers must carefully consider how to ensure the data meets any constraints of the environment in which it is collected.
- Can the data be captured at a cost proportional to its likely value? Not all data can be captured at a reasonable cost to either the developer, or the user, or both. The potential benefits of how the data might influence the study of the software engineering phenomenon must be weighed against its collection costs.

RECOMMENDATIONS

We have described that collecting more data can help lead to a more accurate interpretation of a phenomenon of interest. We have also described that there are constraints on simply gathering data about everything happening in a situation of interest.

How can a researcher decide what data to collect, when? Here are some recommendations:

1. Decide on the minimal data you need to make progress on the problem of interest. Make sure you can collect at least this data.
2. Consider what other data it is feasible to collect and try to collect any and all data that is practical and cost-effective to collect and that will not violate privacy or security concerns of those in the environment in which the data will be collected.
3. Think through the analysis and/or techniques and tools driving the collection of the data. Ask questions about how whether the data intended to be collected is sufficient for the analysis or technique and tool creation.
4. Think about the threats to any analysis and/or techniques and tools driving the collection of the data. How might the data mislead?
5. Iterate across each step until you are certain that you have the right balance between data collection concerns and ensuring as accurate a view of a phenomenon as possible.

Above all, make sure your data doesn't lead you to miss the elephant for one of its parts.

REFERENCES

[1] Wikipedia. Blind men and an elephant. https://en.wikipedia.org/wiki/Blind_men_and_an_elephant.
[2] Murphy-Hill ER, Jiresal R, Murphy GC. Improving software developers' fluency by recommending development environment commands. In: SIGSOFT FSE; 2012. p. 42.

Why provenance matters

M.W. Godfrey

University of Waterloo, Waterloo, ON, Canada

CHAPTER OUTLINE

Here's a problem: You're a lead developer for a company that produces a web content management system, and you get email from an open source project leader who claims that your closed source project probably contains some of their open source code, in violation of their license. She lists three features of your product that she suspects are built around code copied from her system, and she asks you to investigate and respond. Can you determine if her claim has merit? How do you investigate it?

Here's another problem: Your company uses a commercial Java application that ships with embedded third-party libraries. One of these libraries is known to have had a major security flaw in version 2.1 that was fixed in version 2.1.1. Are you vulnerable? How can you tell?

Here's one more: You've recently agreed to take on the role of bug triage for a large open source project; that is, you are to examine each incoming bug report, decide if the report is legitimate and worth proceeding with, and, if so, assign a developer to investigate. However, often a single bug will manifest itself in different ways; obviously you don't want to assign multiple developers to fix the same underlying defect. So how can you tell if a given bug report is truly new, and not just a manifestation of something you've seen before? That is, how can you effectively "de-dup" a voluminous set of bug reports?

WHAT'S PROVENANCE?

What these problem scenarios have in common is that they depend on the *provenance* of software entities [1]; that is, we need to be able to analyze various kinds of evidence that pertain to the origin, history, and ownership of software entities to answer questions such as:

- What is the history of this entity? How did it come to be where it is currently?
- What other entities is it related to, and how?
- What is the evidence? How reliable is it?

Understanding the raw design artifacts that comprise our system—such as the source code, documentation, build recipes, etc.—gives us only a small part of the larger story. We need also to be able to reason about the relatedness of a wide variety of development artifacts, the processes that produce and manage them, their history and evolution, and the people involved and their roles.

WHAT ARE THE KEY ENTITIES?

To be able to address these issues, we need to able to identify which particular entities we are interested in, and how they relate to each other. There are several kinds of entities that we might want to consider:

- software artifacts that are managed by some tool as first-class entities, such as source code files, commits in a version control system (VCS), or bug reports in an issue tracking system;
- attributes of these artifacts, such as version identifiers, current status, comment histories, and timestamps;
- synthetic entities such as software features and maintenance tasks, which have strong meaning to developers but may not have crisp definitions or even independent existence; and
- relationships between any of the preceding items, which may be explicit, implicit, inferred, or even probabilistic.

WHAT ARE THE KEY TASKS?

Armed with a broad understanding of the kinds of entities in our project, we can then consider how we might use them to answer our questions. There are two key tasks that we need to be able to perform here:

- defining and scoping the entities that are of particular interest, and
- establishing artifact linkage and ground truth.

Additionally, we often need techniques to be able to explore the entity space, such as:

- scalable matching algorithms to query the large entity space, and
- various kinds of historical analyses to answer questions about the evolution of the system.

Depending on the task at hand, *defining and scoping the entities of interest* may be straightforward, or it may require tool support and/or manual intervention. For example, in the first problem scenario, we need to decide how to define and scope a feature. Then, we need to be able to map these features to sets of code fragments for both our system and the open source system. Finally, we need to examine the VCS commit history of the code that is related to these features within our system (and if the VCS history of the open source system is available to us, we can do the same for the open source system).

At this point we have a set of features, decomposed into code fragments across two systems, and a set of related VCS commits that touch these code fragments. *Establishing artifact linkage and ground truth* is the next problem we need to address. When the open source project leader mentioned three high level features she thought had been copied, we performed the mapping of the features to source code on both systems. Did we get it right? On the other hand, if we trust our decomposition, then the commit history gleaned from the VCS should be accurate, unless someone has rebased our git repository [2].

Now we probably want to compare code fragments of the two systems on a feature-by-feature basis using a comparison tool, such as diff, which compares raw text, or a code clone detector like CCFinder [3] or ConQAT [4], which has some understanding of the programming language. Because we've narrowed down our field of interest to a manageable set of code fragments, this step will probably be doable quickly.

But let's suppose that our company's lawyer now steps in with a bigger challenge: he wants us to make sure that nothing in our codebase closely matches any code in any of the five open source systems that are in our problem domain. Lucky for us, code clone detector tools are usually designed to be able to process large systems. In provenance analysis in general, we often have to compare complex structures such as source code against large datasets; *scalable matching algorithms* are required to make this feasible. This can often be achieved via a two-stage process:

1. Preprocessing of the artifacts reduces the dimensionality of the data, say by hashing each line of code; the preprocessed data can then be compared relatively quickly as sets or sequences of hash values.
2. When a quick comparison suggests a "hit," more complicated approaches can then be used on the original artifacts to prune away false positives.

Of course, in reducing the dimensionality of the data, we are losing information; for example, if I copy a method and then make a few changes, any line that is even slightly different from the original will result in a different hash value. But if we move to the granularity of tokens or characters, then the comparisons become much more time consuming. So we are always trading off accuracy against performance.

Finally, if we decide that some of the code in the two systems appears to be unusually similar, we can *perform a historical analysis* on the commit trails, to see when and how any "borrowed" code fragments might have made it into our codebase, and which developers might have been responsible. We may also wish to look for other historic trends, such as unusually large commits by inexperienced developers, since that might also indicate the incorporation of third-party code into the system.

ANOTHER EXAMPLE

Let's return to the second problem scenario now, since it's one we've explored in real life [5]. A company approached us with the problem of how to authoritatively ascertain the version identifier of a third-party Java library binary that has been packaged within a commercial application. This sounds like a simple problem, but it's surprisingly tricky to solve. Sometimes, the version identifier forms part of the name of the included jar file; however, this is merely developer convention, it is not always observed and isn't enforceable technically. Worse, in our investigations we found instances of where the version identifier had been edited to remove the "release candidate" designation, falsely implying that the included library was the final version.

Our first step was to decide on our entities of interest: versions of Java libraries that are in common use. Next, we needed to establish ground truth; that is, we decided to build a master database that effectively represented all recent versions of these libraries. We decided to use the Maven2 [6] repository as our data source, since it is very large and we found it to contain instances of almost all recent versions of almost all common Java libraries.

Our next problem was how to achieve scalable matching of our candidate library against the master repository. We couldn't just compare source code against source code because our candidate library might not contain any; similarly, we couldn't compare byte code against byte code because the binaries of two identical Java programs might differ if one used a different compiler or command line options. Instead, we extracted the signatures of the methods that the library contained; these would be extractable from both source code and byte code, and would not be affected by compiler choice. We then took the SHA1 hash of the library's API (declaration plus method signatures), and let that one hash value represent the library version in our database. So we downloaded all of Maven—no mean feat!—extracted the API information from every version of every library in it, and created the hashes using the provided version identifier as ground truth. This took some time and effort. However, once the master repository had been built, analyzing an application was very fast: we extracted the API from the candidate libraries, found the corresponding SHA1 hash value, and looked it up in the database to see if there was an authoritative version identifier.

Of course, there are a couple of problems with our approach: the library or the particular version we're looking for might not be in Maven at all. Worse, if the

API of a library remains stable across several versions, we may match multiple versions, requiring manual intervention to disambiguate. In practice, however, we found that these were rarely serious problems. New library histories could be added as needed to the master repository for next time, and manual intervention rarely required manually examining more than a small handful of possible matches.

LOOKING AHEAD

As a profession, we are getting better at instrumenting our processes and tracking our steps. As a profession, we are also increasingly concerned with questions of ownership, origin, evolution, and transparency of the various development artifacts we interact with on a daily basis. As more and more of our artifacts and processes are managed by tools, automatically logged, and annotated with metadata, so will the job of provenance analysis become simpler. And, of course, while we have examined the space of software development artifacts here, the issues and techniques of provenance are no less important for the broader field of data science [7].

REFERENCES

[1] Godfrey MW. Understanding software artifact provenance. Sci Comput Program 2015;97(1):86–90.
[2] Kalliamvakou E, Gousios G, Blincoe K, Singer L, German D, Damian D. An in-depth study of the promises and perils of mining GitHub. Empir Softw Eng [Online 05.09.15].
[3] http://www.ccfinder.net.
[4] http://www.conqat.org/.
[5] Davies J, German DM, Godfrey MW, Hindle A. Software Bertillonage determining the provenance of software development artifacts. Empir Softw Eng 2013;18(6):1195–237.
[6] http://maven.apache.org/.
[7] http://cacm.acm.org/blogs/blog-cacm/169199-data-science-workflow-overview-and-chal lenges/fulltext.

Open from the beginning

G. Gousios

Radboud University Nijmegen, Nijmegen, The Netherlands

CHAPTER OUTLINE

> *The problem in this business isn't to keep people from stealing your ideas; it is making them steal your ideas.*
> **Howard H. Aiken**

In research, we are obsessed with open access. We take extra steps to make our papers available to the public, we spend extra time for producing preprints, technical reports, and blog posts to make our research accessible and we lobby noncollaborating publishers to play along. We are not so zealous with the artifacts that comprise our research; source code, data, and documentation are treated as second class citizens that nobody either publishes or wants to have a look at.

I believe this is a grave mistake and leads to missed opportunities in increasing the impact of our research.

But why is open access to all research artifacts important for software data scientists? Let me share with you two stories.

ALITHEIA CORE

My involvement with empirical software engineering started in 2005. My PhD supervisor wanted to create a plot of the Maintainability Index metric for the whole lifetime of the FreeBSD project to include in his book. The initial version was a hacky shell and Perl script solution, similar to what most repository miners come up with at the time. After creating the plot, he thought that it would be interesting if we had a

233

tool to analyze the lifetime of projects based on repository mining and combine metrics at will. This gave birth to the Alitheia Core project, where a joint group of about 15 engineers and researchers set to write a software analysis platform that would allow anyone to submit a project repository for analysis.

What we came up with was a rather sophisticated repository mining tool, Alitheia Core, that was comprised of analysis plug-ins and offered a wealth of services, such as parsers, automatic parallelization, and even cluster operation. Alitheia Core was built in Java, using the latest and greatest technologies of the time, eg, object-relational mapping for database access and REST for its web APIs. It also featured no less than two web interfaces and an Eclipse plug-in. When it was announced, in mid-2008, it was probably the most technologically advanced repository mining tool. Along with Alitheia Core, we also delivered a curated dataset of about 750 OSS repositories, including some of the biggest available at the time. *After the end of the project*, we offered all source code and datasets to the software analytics community.

In numbers, the project looked like a resounding success; around 20 papers were published, four PhD students have written a dissertation based on it and more importantly, we could do studies with one or two orders of magnitude more data from the average study at the time. Unfortunately, though, outside of the project consortium, Alitheia Core had limited impact. From what we know, only one external user cared to install it and only two researchers managed to produce a publication using it. By any account, Alitheia Core was impressive technology, but not a successful project.

GHTorrent

Fast forward to mid-2011; GitHub's popularity had begun to skyrocket. They had just made available version 2 of their API and I thought that this was my chance to finally teach myself some Ruby and distributed systems programming. I went ahead and wrote scripts that monitored GitHub's event timeline and parsed them into two databases, MySQL and MongoDB. The whole process of monitoring the event timeline and parsing was decoupled through a queue server, and thus we could have multiple monitors and parsers working on a cluster. While all these might sound interesting from an architectural viewpoint, the initial implementation was rather uninteresting, technology-wise; just a couple of scripts that in a loop would poll a queue and then update two databases by recursively retrieving information from the web. The scripts where released as OSS software on GitHub in November 2011, while data dumps of both databases where offered through BitTorrent. This marked the birth of the GHTorrent project.

A paper describing the approach and initial implementation was sent to the 2012 Mining Software Repositories conference, but failed to impress the reviewers much: "The work is messy and often confuses the reader in terms of what have they done and how they have done [*sic*]" one reviewer wrote. "The experiment seems foley, results somewhat lacking [*sic*]" another reviewer added. The paper included some slightly embarrassing plots as well, eg, featuring holes in the data collection process, due to "a bug in the event mirroring script, which manifested in both event retrieval nodes." Nevertheless, the paper was accepted.

Shortly after the conference, something incredible happened; I witnessed a client connecting to our Bittorrent server. Not only did it connect, it also downloaded the full data dump of the MySQL dataset! This marked the first external user of GHTorrent, merely days after the end of the conference where we presented it. The paper that resulted from this download was published in early 2013, before even my second GHTorrent paper. This motivated me to take GHTorrent more seriously; I worked together with initial users to fix any issues they had and I was prompt in answering their questions. On the technical side, we (students, the community, and me) implemented services to access an almost live version of both databases, a dataset slicer and various interactive analyses and visualizations.

Since its public availability, GHTorrent grew a lot: As of this writing (January 2016), it hosts more than 9.5 TB of data. Vasilescu's paper marked the beginning of high speed (by academic standards) uptake of GHTorrent: more than 60 papers were written using it (one third of all GitHub studies, according to one paper), while at least 160 users have registered to the online query facilities. GitHub themselves proposed GHTorrent as a potential dataset for their third annual data challenge, while Microsoft funded it to run on Azure.

WHY THE DIFFERENCE?

The relative indifference that the research community reserved for Alitheia Core is in stark contrast with the fast uptake of GHTorrent. But why? Why did the community embrace a hacky, obviously incomplete and, in some cases, downright erroneous dataset while it almost ignored a polished, complete, and fully documented research platform? Let us consider some potential reasons:

- *GitHub is hot as a research target*: This is obviously true. But when Alitheia Core was done, SourceForge was also very hot as a research dataset, as evidenced by the number of projects that targeted it. Moreover, the unaffiliated Github Archive project offers a more easily accessible version of a subset of GHTorrent, so researchers could have just used this and ignored GHTorrent altogether.
- *The "not invented here" syndrome*: Researchers (and, to a lesser extent, practitioners) are very reluctant to use each other's code. This is not entirely unfounded: code, especially research code, is very prone to have issues that may be hard to debug. Researchers also know that dealing with inconsistencies in data is even worse; still, they flocked to GHTorrent.
- *Ad hoc solutions work best*: Data analytics is a trial and error approach; researchers need to iterate fast and an interactive environment coupled with a database makes them more productive than a rigid, all-encompassing platform.

Despite the fact that there is some truth in the preceding list, I believe that the main reason is **openness**.

Alitheia Core was developed using an opaque process that the project members certainly enjoyed, but was obviously not in touch with what the users wanted. On the other hand, GHTorrent grew *with* its users. As any entrepreneur or innovation expert can confess, it is very hard for an innovative product or service to be adopted by a community; adoption is much easier if it grows organically with it. Moreover, it is extremely difficult to dazzle users with feature lists (except perhaps if you are Apple): users, especially tech-savvy ones, put high value on construction transparency and compatibility with their work habits.

BE OPEN OR BE IRRELEVANT

To me, the difference is a clear win of the open source process and its application on research. Open access to all research artifacts from the very beginning can only be a good thing: collaboration attraction, spreading of research results, replication, and advancement of science in general are all things for which open access is a prerequisite. There is not much at risk, either: the only thing we risk with open access is that our research will be ignored; then, this already may mean something about the relevance of our research.

If I learned something from this experience, it would be the following three things:

- *Offer a minimum viable product*: Offer the least possible piece of functionality that makes sense and let people create by building on top of it. This can be data plus some code, or just data. Make sure that you make it easy for others to build on what you offer: make sure that your tools are easy to install and that your data is well documented. Be frank in the documentation; accurately state the limitations and the gotchas of your code/data.
- *Infrastructures are overrated*: The effort required to learn how infrastructure code works should not be overlooked. The invested effort must return some gains. Big effort must be followed by big gains in return, and there is always the risk of deprecation; this is why only very few infrastructure tools survive the test of openness. The Unix experience should be our guide; make tools and services that do one thing well, accepted text and return text.
- *Open now trumps open when it is done*: Finally and most importantly, no one is going to wait for you to perfect what you are doing. Opening your research up early on is not a sign of sloppiness; it is a sign of trusting in your work and acknowledging the fact that done is better than perfect. Don't be afraid that someone will steal your idea, for if someone invests time in stealing it, it is a great idea and you have a head start. Open access is an absolute must for the adoption and wide spreading of research results. This should happen as early as possible.

To cut the long story short: make your research open from the beginning!

REFERENCES

[1] Gousios G, Spinellis D. Conducting quantitative software engineering studies with Alitheia Core, Empir Softw Eng 2014;19(4):885–925.

[2] Gousios G. The GHTorrent dataset and tool suite. In: Proceedings of the 10th working conference on mining software repositories; 2013. p. 233–6.

[3] Vasilescu B, Filkov V, Serebrenik A. Stack overflow and GitHub: associations between software development and crowdsourced knowledge. In: 2013 ASE/IEEE international conference on social computing, social computing. IEEE; 2013. p. 188–95.

Reducing time to insight

T. Carnahan

Microsoft, Redmond, WA, United States

CHAPTER OUTLINE

WHAT IS INSIGHT ANYWAY?

Insight production, preferably with data (I jest), is a big part of my role at Microsoft. And if you're reading this chapter, I'll assert you are also an Insight Producer, or well on your way to becoming one.

Since insight is the product, let's start with a simple definition. The classical definition of insight is new understanding or human comprehension. That works well for the result of a science experiment and answering a research question. Industry, with its primordial goal of growing results, focuses my definition to new *actionable* comprehension for *improved results*. This constrains the questions of insight search to subjects and behaviors known to contribute business value.

Let's look at a more concrete example. As a purveyor and student of software engineering insights, I know large software organizations value code velocity, sometimes called speed or productivity and quality as a control. Organizations also value engineer satisfaction, if you're lucky. I seek to understand existing behaviors and their contribution to those areas. I am continuously hunting for new or different behaviors that can dramatically improve those results.

TIME TO INSIGHT

There is immeasurable distance between late and too late.
Og Mandino (American Essayist and Psychologist)

An insight's value can decay rapidly, and eventually expire altogether as unaction-able. History is full of war stories where intelligence arrived in time to change the outcome. Stock markets quickly sway and even crash based on insights. But an alert that my service is down, an hour after receiving a phone call from my best customer's lawyer to handle damages from the outage is both too late, and uninsightful! The key point here is that speeding up data processing and information production creates new opportunities for insight that was previously blocked, by giving time to take action on the new understanding. This also adds a competitive edge, in almost any human endeavor.

Let's start with a simple definition of time to insight (TTI): *Elapsed calendar time between a question being asked, and the answer understood, well enough for action to be taken.*

This seems pretty straightforward until you start peeling it apart. There are a couple big variables left:

1. *Who is the customer?* Who can ask the questions? For someone in Insight Production, this is often the person cutting the checks, and those responsible for making decisions and taking action. This matters immensely because they will need to be able to interface with you effectively to ask the questions, and comprehend the answers into insights to take appropriate action. If they don't know how to read a dendrogram, I recommend teaching them or giving them an alternative visualization.

2. *Which questions will deliver the most lifetime value?* With constrained resources to invest, it's worth prioritizing investment. A simple proxy I frequently use for this is how many times the question will be asked. Generally if you optimize for questions that have some value and are asked the most often, the results are good. It is more difficult to optimize for the highest value questions, which often only need to be answered once.

A great TTI experience to showcase is searching the internet with Google or Bing. Much of the world's population has been trained to ask their public domain questions in the little search box using keywords and seminatural language. And they all expect a fast, subsecond response! They may not get exactly the answer or insight they were looking for on their first try. But the cost of more attempts is so low that curiosity overcomes the friction and the result is an interactive Question and Answer session that often ends with some new or new-again knowledge (how many of you also forget the name of the actor in that movie and look it up on your phone?). If only my search engine was omniscient and I could ask it anything! An additional advantage of this search model is the feedback loop of what questions users are asking. Volumes and trends of what questions the world is asking turn out to be very valuable.

TTI is getting traction from Forbes and other similar companies [1,2], as the leading key performance indicator (KPI) for insight production and analytics teams. And I agree! In fact, I devote at least 50% of the insight production team I run at Microsoft to reducing the TTI. These engineers are experts at instrumenting, collecting, modelling, curating, indexing, and storing data for fast query into formats, schemas, indexes, and query engines that are the most familiar and accessible to those asking the questions. They can include a mixture of natural language and full-text search, CSV, Excel, SQL, OLAP cubes, and even visualizations in dashboards and scorecards. The goal is to deliver the customer's desired insight quickly, and in the most effective medium.

THE INSIGHT VALUE CHAIN

For industry and academia alike, the capability to produce insights fast is often a differentiated, competitive advantage. One pro tip is to think of insight production as a value chain [3,4]. Identify and evaluate the primary activities between a question asked, and an insightful response given. These often include, but are not limited to: collect data, analyze, transform, store, query, and visualize. And sometimes it also requires a person to help interpret the data for the customer, for them to have the ideal actionable insight.

Where is the time spent? Is data collection still manual? Perhaps there are expensive computations and transformations that add hours of lag. Evaluate each activity and identify the best systemic ways to reduce TTI. In other words, perform a value chain analysis [5].

WHAT TO DO

Here are a few tips from the trenches of insight production. This first set of tips helps you start with the end, or moment of insight, in mind. This is often a specific visualization, report, or scorecard with KPIs. It could also be a few fast *ad-hoc* queries to a well-modeled store to discover and validate the next big insight. But the result is valuable new understanding that is delivered in time to take that next positive action.

- Visualization matters! How long do people need to stare at the screen to have a "eureka" moment? A good example from industry is the simple key performance indicator, or KPI. There is little to no cognitive friction in a well-designed KPI.

It's red or green and a simple number. Learning to read candlestick charts takes a bit longer, but can still be the simplest way to communicate more complicated distributions and relationships.

- Assist human comprehension with the simplest models and easy access to experts and docs. The simplest model to explain typically yields the fastest comprehension. Simple statistical models are sometimes preferred over neural networks for this reason. And an insight may well require a subject matter expert to interpret and explain it, in addition to the visualization.
- The last mile on *fast* insights. Sometimes it is critical to get humans reacting to new information immediately. Consider firemen at the fire station responding to a call and alarms blaring and lights flashing. Sometimes a web page isn't going to reach recipients fast enough and you need to push the insight via information radiators, pagers, text messages, or even alarm bells to ensure the information is received with enough time to react.

Here are a few more technical tips.

- Automate everything! Data collection, cleansing, and curation. This might include saving or caching intermediary results that can take too long to re-compute. No manual step or computation is too small to automate when you need to scale.
- Use the right data store or index. Know when to use in-memory caches, relational stores, multidimensional stores, text search stores, graph stores, stream processing, or map reduce systems. Each is best for certain types of questions at different scales. At smaller scales, you might get away with one store. At cloud scales, you start specializing to get the incremental load and query latencies down to what you need for certain classes of questions. Fight the hype that one new store will rule them all.
- Push compute and quality upstream. Connect people who understand the insight desired with the people instrumenting the process. Well-designed instrumentation and collection coupled with standard or thoughtful data formats and schemas often yield data more fit for insights and require less transforms, joins, cleansing, and sampling throughout the pipeline. That produces speed and lower costs! Also, fewer distinct collection systems tend to reduce the join complications later by coalescing data formats, schemas and stores earlier.
- Shoot to deliver self-service [6,7]. Self-service means the person with the questions has access to all layers of data (raw to curated) and unfettered access to the instrumentation and transformation code. This builds transparency and trust in the insight, but it can also help the smart humans who can help themselves. Of course do this within the safety of your data policies.

A WARNING ON WASTE

Simply put, large data platform and analytical systems are usually expensive, in many dimensions: calendar, hardware, software, and data experts to build and run them. I have witnessed numerous projects invest too much and too early, to answer an interesting question exactly once. The advice I give is to always answer the first few questions, usually generated by a GQM (goal, question, metric) [8] exercise manually, as cheaply as possible. And then let usage, or the questions that keep getting asked repeatedly, guide and justify funding investments to automate and lower TTI on the questions your audience actually has *and* will act upon.

REFERENCES

[1] Upbin B. What's Your Time To Insight? http://www.forbes.com/sites/ciocentral/2012/08/10/whats-your-time-to-insight/; 2012.
[2] Howson C. Visual Data Discovery: More than a Pretty Face? http://insideanalysis.com/2012/08/visual-data-discovery/; 2012.
[3] Various. Value chain. Wikipedia.
[4] Porter ME. Competitive advantage: creating and sustaining superior performance. New York, NY: Simon and Schuster; 1985 [retrieved 2013].
[5] Jurevicius O. Value Chain Analysis. http://www.strategicmanagementinsight.com/tools/value-chain-analysis.html; 2013.
[6] Rockwell D. Speeding Time to Insight: Why Self-Service Data Prep is the Future of Big Data http://www.lavastorm.com/blog/post/speeding-time-to-insight-why-self-service-data-prep-is-the-future-of-big-data/; 2015.
[7] van der Meulen R, Rivera J. Gartner Says Power Shift in Business Intelligence and Analytics Will Fuel Disruption http://www.gartner.com/newsroom/id/2970917; 2015.
[8] Basili VR. Software modeling and measurement: the goal/question/metric paradigm. Technical report. College Park, MD: University of Maryland at College Park; 1992.

Five steps for success:
How to deploy data science
in your organizations

M. Kim

University of California, Los Angeles

CHAPTER OUTLINE

Data science has become popular over the past few years as companies have recognized the value of data, either in data products, or to optimize operations and to support decision making. Not only did Davenport and Patil proclaim that data scientist would be "the sexiest job of the twenty-first century," [1] many authors have published data science books based on their own experiences (see books by O'Neill and Schutt [2], Foreman [3], or May [4]). Patil summarized strategies to hire and build effective data science teams based on his experience in building the data science team at LinkedIn.

Software produces large quantities of data, such as user-oriented telemetry data, repository-based productivity and quality data, and business-oriented process data. Software development organizations are hiring data scientists to debug software, to estimate failure rates, to identify new features, and to assess software reliability.

Kim et al. [5] conducted interviews with 16 data scientists across several product groups at Microsoft. This chapter describes some lessons that we learned from the data scientists regarding how they increase the impact and actionability of their work and the strategies that they use to ensure that their results matter for the company.

Actionability is actually a big thing. If it's not actionable, the engineers then look at you, say, "I don't know what to do with this, so don't even bother me."

The strategies discussed in this chapter are from the study of data scientists at Microsoft. The complete details are in a technical report [5], which also includes other information, such as why data scientists are needed in software development teams, the education and training background of data scientists and their skillsets, the problems that data scientists work on and their daily activities, the organization structure of data scientist teams, how they interact with others in the teams, etc. The following paragraphs discuss the five steps for successfully employing data science in software development organizations.

STEP 1. CHOOSE THE RIGHT QUESTIONS FOR THE RIGHT TEAM

An important strategy for success is to choose the right questions for the right team. One data scientist described three conditions that must be met before his data science team engages in a project: priority, actionability, and commitment.

"(a) Is it a priority for the organization (b) is it actionable, if I get an answer to this, is this something someone can do something with? and, (c), are you, as the feature team—if you're coming to me or if I'm going to you, telling you this is a good opportunity—are you committing resources to deliver a change? If those things are not true, then it's not worth us talking anymore."

It is important to define actions in addition to generating insights from data.

You need to think about, "If you find this anomaly, then what?" Just finding an anomaly is not very actionable. What I do also involves thinking, "These are the anomalies I want them to detect. Based on these anomalies, I'm going to stop the build. I'm going to communicate to the customer and ask them to fix something on their side."

For data scientists, there are many more questions to pursue than they have time and resources for. So it is important for them to choose questions that enable their stakeholders to achieve their goals.

STEP 2. WORK CLOSELY WITH YOUR CONSUMERS

Another strategy that was mentioned in several interviews was to interact closely and engage with the stakeholders who plan to consume the results from the data analysis. Data scientists often set up channels such as weekly data meet-ups and brown bag lunches to regularly deliver project outcomes. It is important for stakeholders to define the questions and scenarios addressed by data analysis early and often. To make their data science work adopted by stakeholders, data scientists iterate with them to interpret the data and refine important questions and scenarios.

"You begin to find out, you begin to ask questions, you begin to see things. And so you need that interaction with the people that own the code, if you will, or the feature, to be able to learn together as you go and refine your questions and refine your answers to get to the ultimate insights that you need."

STEP 3. VALIDATE AND CALIBRATE YOUR DATA

The validation of quantitative data through qualitative channels was also mentioned as a criteria to ensure that measurements are meaningful and lead to correct actions.

"If you could survey everybody every ten minutes, you wouldn't need telemetry. The most accurate way to derive insights is to ask everybody all the time. The only reason we do telemetry is that (asking people all the time) it is slow, and by the time you get it, you're too late. So you can consider telemetry and data an optimization. So what we do typically, is 10% are surveyed and we get telemetry. And then we calibrate and infer what the other 90% have said."

It is important for data scientists to triangulate multiple data resources to increase the confidence in their analysis results.

STEP 4. SPEAK PLAINLY TO GIVE RESULTS BUSINESS VALUE

Many data scientists emphasize the need to explain findings in simple terms to non-experts. Talking to non-experts also requires the development of intuitive measurements. Data scientists need to "translate" findings into business values, such as dollars saved, customer calls prevented, and number of days that a product can be shipped early. Reporting precision, recall, and ROC curves, while convenient for the data scientists, are of less importance when presenting findings to analytics consumers.

Some data scientists argue that producing fancy results is bad, because fancy requires them to be there to explain in order for the person reading the results to figure out what's going on. So, it is better to produce easy-to-understand results than statistically valid, yet complex, results.

STEP 5. GO THE LAST MILE—OPERATIONALIZING PREDICTIVE MODELS

A strategy that we noticed in several interviews was the willingness to go the last mile to actively contribute to the operationalization of predictive models.

"They accepted (the model) and they understood all the results and they were very excited about it. Then, there's a phase that comes in where the actual model has to go into production… You really need to have somebody who is confident enough to take this from a dev side of things."

Many stakeholders want to deploy predictive models as a part of the product, so it is important to produce working software that leverages and integrates the predictive models. Producing accurate models that are not integrated or instantiated as new software features is not useful for the stakeholders. This implies that data scientists must be not only scientists who draw new findings, but also engineers who build systems based on their findings.

REFERENCES

[1] Davenport TH, Patil D. Data scientist: the sexiest job of the 21st century. Harv Bus Rev 2012;70–6.

[2] O'Neil C, Schutt R. Doing data science: straight talk from the frontline. Sebastopol, California: O'Reilly Media; 2013.

[3] Foreman JW. Data smart: using data science to transform information into insight. Wiley; 2013.

[4] May T. The new know: innovation powered by analytics. Wiley; 2009.

[5] Kim M, Zimmermann T, DeLine R, Begel A. The emerging role of data scientists on software development teams. In: ICSE' 16: proceedings of 38th IEEE/ACM international conference on software engineering. 12 pages. An earlier version of the paper appeared as a technical report, MSR-TR-2015-30.

How the release process impacts your software analytics

Bram Adams
Polytechnique Montréal, Canada

Transcript of a recent meeting with an anonymous grad student:

> *student: ... and then I built the oracles for our defect prediction models. I was able to find defects for 3 major releases of Mozilla Firefox!*
>
> *me: Nice, so how did you determine what release a defect belonged to?*
>
> *student: Easy, I compared the date on which the defect was reported, so all defects reported within 3 months after the release date are post-release defects of that release.*
>
> *me: Hmm, and how did you determine which code changes to use for training the prediction model?*
>
> *student: Similarly, I used all the code changes in the version control system within 6 months before the release date!*
>
> *me: 6 months, eh? Did you know that Firefox has a new release every 6 weeks?*
>
> *student: ...*

This student apparently did not make any real mistake, in fact he/she had done a great job reading the major papers on defect prediction and applying their evaluation methodology on our own research project. Basically, a file-level defect prediction model aims to relate characteristics of the source code files of a software release to the probability that those files would still contain a defect after the release. Testers could then use such a model for an upcoming release to focus only on those files predicted to be the most defect-prone.

Training and testing a defect prediction model requires at least two releases with known post-release defects. Since (by definition) no data is available about defects that have *not* been reported by users, only those defects recorded in the analyzed project's issue repository are considered. Given such defect reports, a prediction model can be trained and evaluated once it is known (1) for which release a defect has been reported and which source code files were involved and (2) which code changes are part of each release under study.

Unfortunately, steps (1) and (2) are not as straightforward as one might think, and require thorough knowledge of the release process used by the project being studied. While this chapter illustrates this impact of the release process in the context of file-based defect prediction, the underlying ideas and warnings can impact any form of defect prediction, or even software analytics in general!

LINKING DEFECT REPORTS AND CODE CHANGES TO A RELEASE

Ideally, each reported defect should specify what release it was found in. However, in many cases, only the date on which the defect was reported is available, and, even if a defect's release would have been recorded, one still needs to identify which files were affected by the defect. The most common way to achieve this is by linking each defect report to the code changes that fix the defect, for example by analyzing all code changes in a project's version control system (eg, git repository), or looking for changes whose change message mentions a defect report's identifier. The files changed by those defect fixes can then be considered as experiencing a defect upon release.

Unfortunately, as observed in the motivational example, the timestamp of such a defect fix is not a good indicator either of the release the defect was found in, since each project follows its own release process [1,2]. Roughly speaking, projects either use a feature-based release schedule (a release is made once all its intended features are ready), or a time-based schedule (a release is made periodically with all features that are ready at that time). Whereas, by definition, feature-based schedules do not have a fixed *cycle time* (time period between successive releases), even time-based schedules can have a cycle time anywhere from 12 h or less (Facebook web app) to 6 weeks (Mozilla Firefox) or even 6 months (OpenStack). In other words, the 3 months of defect reports considered by the student in the example would correspond to a timespan of two Firefox releases (2 times 6 weeks), but only half of an OpenStack release (0.5 times 6 months).

The problem here is not necessarily that 3 months is shorter or longer than a project's cycle time, since not every user switches immediately to a new release. For example, shortly after release 12 of Firefox appeared on the market, 37% of the users were still using older, unsupported Firefox releases. Hence, one could still expect defects to be reported for a given release well after the next release has been launched.

Instead, the real problem is that the timestamp of the code change fixing a defect is no longer sufficient to determine which release the defect is linked to (if this information is not recorded in the defect report). Indeed, defects fixed in weeks 7–12 following Firefox 11 could in fact be *post*-release defects of Firefox 12 (released at the end of week 6) instead of Firefox 11. Even worse, defects fixed in weeks 1–6 or 7–12 following Firefox 11 could also be *pre*-release defects of Firefox 12 or 13! Those are defects in new features developed for Firefox 12 or 13 rather than in code shipped in Firefox 11. To top things off, some time-based projects like

Firefox have special extended support releases (ESR) that are being supported much longer than regular releases, for example for 1 year (timespan of 8 or 9 regular releases). ESRs are targeted at companies who need stability and ongoing defect and security fixes.

Similar problems pop up when determining the code changes that went into a particular release, which is data that is essential for training a prediction model. At one given point in time, some developers could be working on features for the upcoming release, while others in parallel could be fixing defects or performing other maintenance tasks on one of the older releases. Hence, just by looking at the timestamp of a code change, it is impossible to know for sure to which release this code change belongs. In the case of the student, a training period of 6 months would span four Firefox releases. Given the adoption numbers of new releases, it is very likely that changes could have been made to any of these releases (especially if one of them would be an ESR).

To summarize, release process characteristics, such as cycle time and the degree of parallel development, can substantially impact the accuracy of time-based links between a release and code changes or defect reports.

HOW THE VERSION CONTROL SYSTEM CAN HELP

How to overcome these problems? Unless a project has explicit, detailed release roadmaps or wikis, the best recommendation is to analyze how releases are being recorded in the version control system. This is typically a Git or Subversion repository containing the entire code change history of a project.

The simplest case, which is how most people imagine software projects to work, would be a project working entirely on the master branch of their version control system (Fig. 1). The master branch is a chronological sequence of code changes where new features enter a project. When a release is pending, the master branch enters the stabilization phase, in which all feature development is paused ("frozen") and as many defects as possible are being ironed out for the upcoming release. Eventually, when deemed ready or when the scheduled cycle time is up, a release is made (and tagged in the master branch), after which changes for the next release start entering the master branch.

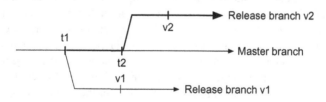

FIG. 1

Example branch architecture of a version control system, featuring one master branch and two release branches (releases v1 and v2). t1 and t2 are two different points in time.

In this fully sequential scenario, one is sure that all code changes made within one cycle time before a release belong to that release. However, it is impossible to know whether the defects fixed within one cycle time after a release are that release's post-release defects or the next release's pre-release defects. For many software analytics applications, this might not be a huge problem. However, if it does pose a problem, project documentation, project members, or other data sources (if available) would be needed to refine the data.

Fortunately, a more realistic scenario for projects is to use so-called release branches to indicate release-specific work, as shown in Fig. 1. Basically, as soon as regular development for release v1 is finished (time "t1"), stabilization does not start on the master branch, but on a release branch dedicated to the upcoming release. The master branch can then be used by developers already working on features for release v2.

Apart from harboring all code changes related to the stabilization of a release, the release branch will also contain any post-release maintenance code changes, including defect fixes! In other words, all code changes that went into release v2 and subsequent minor releases with defect fixes are highlighted by the bold "code lines" in the figure. They consist of all code changes on the master branch after the release branch for v1 was created on "t1" until the v2 release branch is created on "t2," plus any code changes on the latter release branch after "t2." These code changes can easily be obtained by asking a version control system for all code changes on the master branch between times "t1" and "t2" and on the release branch after time "t2." The code changes *after* time "v2" on the release branch then correspond to post-release defect fixes of release v2.

Focusing on defect fixes made after a release on the release's dedicated branch currently is the most reliable approach to identify a release's post-release defects. It is still not perfect, though. Of course, defects that were never reported will still be missed, but also post-release defects that are reported and/or fixed when the release has become obsolete due to newer releases. Such defects will be fixed in the later releases, but the fixes might not be "back-ported" (ie, copied) to the release branch of the original, defective release. For example, 98% of the reported defects in the projects with short, time-based releases studied by Alencar et al. took one or more releases before being fixed, compared to up to 60% for feature-based releases [3]. Hence, depending on a project's cycle time and development strategy, the impact of defect fixes that are not back-ported potentially could be large! The date on which the fixed defect was reported could give an indication that the defect is much older than expected, but (as discussed) would still not reveal the exact release.

Despite this issue with back-porting, release branches are popular in modern development, and chances are high that they exist as well in the projects that you will be analyzing, be it for building a defect prediction model or another software analytics task. It is interesting to realize that, whatever the size of a project in terms of developers or source code, release branches are common in practice and should be exploited to link code changes more accurately to their release than only time-based information allows us to do.

Hence, the take-home message of this chapter is to always consider the release process used by a software project, whichever software analytics task you are involved in. For other release process-related pitfalls for software analytics, please check our FoSE 2016 paper [4].

REFERENCES

[1] Humble J, Farley D. Continuous delivery: reliable software releases through build, test, and deployment automation, Addison-Wesley Professional; 2010. https://www.amazon.com/Continuous-Delivery-Reliable-Deployment-Automation/dp/0321601912.
[2] Bass L, Weber I, Zhu L. DevOps: a software architect's perspective, Addison-Wesley Professional; 2015. http://www.amazon.com/DevOps-Software-Architects-Perspective-Engineering/dp/0134049845/ref=sr_1_1?s=books&ie=UTF8&qid=1463082918&sr=1-1&keywords=devops+software+architect.
[3] Alencar da Costa D, Lemma Abebe S, McIntosh S, Kulesza U, Hassan AE. An empirical study of delays in the integration of addressed issues. In: Proceedings of the 30th IEEE international conference on software maintenance and evolution (ICSME), Victoria, Canada; 2014. p. 281–90.
[4] Adams B, McIntosh S. Modern release engineering in a nutshell—why researchers should care. Leaders of tomorrow: future of software engineering (FoSE). In: Proceedings of the 23rd IEEE international conference on software analysis, evolution, and reengineering (SANER), Osaka, Japan; 2016. p. 78–90.

Security cannot be measured

A. Meneely

Rochester Institute of Technology, Rochester, NY, United States

CHAPTER OUTLINE

Which of the following is more secure: Windows, Mac OS X, or the White House?

All of them have been broken into. They all have security features. A lot of money has been spent on making them secure (some of that money was better spent in some places than in others). They also serve different purposes and have different designs. So which is it? Which is more secure? Or is that a fair comparison at all?

In software security assessment, we cannot make empirically-sound statements about the overall security of a product. We can understand various properties of the system that can influence security, but we cannot make absolute claims. In particular, when analyzing security data, we need to be aware of a lot of practical and conceptual concerns. Consider the following inescapable truths ("Gotchas") that one must consider when assessing security empirically.

GOTCHA #1: SECURITY IS NEGATIVELY DEFINED

The security of a software system is typically defined as the combination of three properties: Confidentiality, Integrity, and Availability. Confidentiality is the ability of a system to keep sensitive information from leaking out. Integrity is the ability of the system to prevent unauthorized users from tampering with data or functionality. Availability is the ability of the system to continually be accessible to the user.

Each of those properties, however, is defined according to what people should *not* be able to do. An attacker should *not* be able to steal passwords. An attacker should *not* be able execute arbitrary code.

From a requirements engineering point of view, security is considered to be a *constraint* on the entire system that does not trace to any one feature. Instead, security applies to all features.

Security is not alone in being negatively defined, however. Other negatively defined non-functional requirements include safety and resilience as they are properties that the system must demonstrate in extreme circumstances.

Furthermore, security is an *emergent* property of software. An emergent property is one that builds upon many cooperating factors and can be brought down by a single flaw. Consider pitching a tent in the rain. The "staying dry" property is not a single feature of the tent, it's a combination of many different factors: the tent must be leak-free, deployed properly, the flap closed, and not be placed in a lake. Security must be achieved through a wide variety of means and can be compromised by one problem.

For all negatively defined properties, developers cannot simply execute a checklist to maintain those properties. Improving security does not mean "do A, B, and C," instead it means "nowhere should X, Y, Z or anything like them be allowed."

GOTCHA #2: HAVING VULNERABILITIES IS ACTUALLY NORMAL

You might be tempted to assume that admitting your precious software product has vulnerabilities is a liability to your everyday business. The company brand is at stake! Why let a few wrong lines of code be such a big deal?

However, companies have matured beyond the non-admitting approach to practice responsible disclosure, that is, disclosing the details about a vulnerability after it is has been fixed. Responsible disclosure has led to a variety of benefits, such as the current cultural shift to the assumption that having vulnerabilities is normal. In fact, the practice of responsible disclosure has been a significant driver in modern vulnerability research as developers can learn from each other's mistakes.

Thus, many products may have only a recent track record of having vulnerabilities. Does that mean they were secure before? No. Nobody was keeping track, and the fact that vulnerabilities are now being cataloged is actually a sign of maturity.

GOTCHA #3: "MORE VULNERABILITIES" DOES NOT ALWAYS MEAN "LESS SECURE"

In the age of Responsible Disclosure, vulnerabilities have become a common occurrence. The National Vulnerability Database has recorded thousands.

Given that, one may be tempted to claim that one product was more secure when it had fewer vulnerabilities reported. Even year-over-year, researchers and practitioners alike have reported that "this year we had fewer vulnerabilities."

At the very least, severity must be taken into account (although that measurement is also fraught with problems). Suppose we decided to catalog all security vulnerabilities on your house, and do a big security audit: we change to pick-resistant locks and add locks to two of the windows, totaling three "vulnerabilities" fixed. This month, we left the door open for a week. Which month was less secure?

As a case study, the US National Vulnerability Database has increased in size dramatically over the past several years. If one were to strictly adhere to the assumption of metrics such as "defect density," one might assume that this influx of vulnerabilities was due to a widespread security problem. On the contrary, many developers are becoming more aware of their security problems and are tracking the fixes.

Furthermore, vulnerability records are interesting data sets today for the following reasons:

- Record-keeping practices have improved with the evolution of distributed version control systems, code review systems, and collaboration tools that maintain artifact traceability.
- Discovery of a single vulnerability often leads to the discovery of other, similar vulnerabilities since developers are learning security principles as they fix vulnerabilities.
- Software projects are improving their responsible disclosure practices, leading to an increase in interest from the security enthusiast community.
- Due to the severe nature of vulnerabilities, prominent companies such as Google and Microsoft offer bounties in the thousands of US dollars for information leading to a vulnerability. Google currently pays out those bounties on a nearly monthly basis.
- The availability and quality of comprehensive vulnerability taxonomies, such as the Common Weakness Enumeration, have improved recently.
- Improved security awareness among developers has led to developers retroactively labeling traditional defects as vulnerabilities.

GOTCHA #4: DESIGN FLAWS ARE NOT USUALLY TRACKED

Vulnerabilities come in all sizes. A small, code-level mistake such as a format string vulnerability can be easily remedied in a single, one-line fix, for example. Lacking the ability to provide audit logs to mitigate repudiation threats, however, is a much bigger problem. Historically, most vulnerabilities reported today tend to be code-level vulnerabilities. Design flaws, security-related or not, are rarely tracked in any consistent way. These design flaws are often disguised as "new releases," "new features," or "refactoring," and are never really factored into vulnerability assessment.

Some code-level vulnerabilities are significantly mitigated in their severity by solid design. Distrustful decomposition is a security-inspired design pattern that takes privileged actions and places them in small subsystems that map to small, privileged processes (ie, executing programs). For example, Apache HTTPD uses distrustful decomposition to have two processes: one very simple process that listens to port 80 and then passes the data off to another, larger process that will do most of the work, but with limited operating system privileges. This design decision is protective in nature: any vulnerabilities in the large, complex part of the system (eg, processing

HTTP requests) would not get far into the operating system. Distrustful decomposition requires constant attention to inter-process communication, reducing coupling between the processes, and keeping the privileged processes simple enough that the lack of vulnerabilities remains obvious.

While using distrustful decomposition gains enormous security benefits in certain situations, the "lack of distrustful decomposition" is not necessarily a design flaw. This issue makes quantifying architectural design decisions nearly impossible.

Sadly, this problem is not unique to security. Most empirical software engineering research studies that quantify some form of "quality" will not delve into design problems because they are simply not tracked as part of software development practice. The definition of what a "single" design flaw actually looks like is much more abstract than what a single "bug" is anyway, so we're not likely to see improvement in this area any time soon.

As a result, we cannot make comprehensive statements about the security of a system based on code-level vulnerabilities alone. Any empirical analysis about the security of a system must have both qualitative and quantitative components.

GOTCHA #5: HACKERS ARE INNOVATIVE TOO

We could also state this as "there are always more gotchas." Hackers are very innovative, have tons of time of their hands, and only need to be lucky once. Every day, new types of attacks are being formed, new vulnerabilities are being discovered, and new information is being bought and sold on the dark web.

Thus, any measurement or analysis of security that relies on a "bag of tricks" approach is doomed to fail. "Tried SQL injection? Tried cross-site scripting? Then you must be secure." This is a reactive approach that does not take into account future innovation. Hackers start with the well-known vulnerabilities, yes, but security is defined by its lack of failures—including those that have not even been conceived of.

Too often, security assessment (even security research) focuses on preventing attacks that have already happened and focus less on preventing all attacks in the future. Most security measurement tools will fail when placed under the microscope of security's most unforgiving question: "how will this protect us from attacks we don't even know of yet?"

Instead, a more mature mindset is one that understand the trade-offs. "If we encrypt this traffic, it would prevent attackers from observing these events." This mentality requires an engineer to understand what security measure they're taking that go beyond the superstitious application of best practices.

AN UNFAIR QUESTION

How secure is Android? Sadly, questions like that are empirically unanswerable. The measurement of security is fraught with problems, ranging from the practical to the fundamental.

Instead of phrasing that question as an absolute, we should be discussing trust and economics. Consider these more specific questions facing software engineers and digital citizens alike:

- Should we adopt this third-party library given its track record of security?
- Should we add this feature knowing the potential security ramifications?
- Should I entrust my personal data to this device?

Each of those questions has a positive outcome and a negative outcome that can be better estimated on an individual basis. Benefits and drawbacks can be weighed, and more informed decisions can be made.

Gotchas from mining bug reports

S. Just* and K. Herzig[†]

Researcher, Software Engineering Chair & Center for IT-Security, Privacy and Accountability, Saarland University, Germany* Software Development Engineer, Microsoft Corporation, Redmond, United States[†]

Over the years, it has become common practice in empirical software engineering to mine data from version archives and bug databases to learn where bugs have been fixed in the past, or to build prediction models to find error-prone code in the future.

Simplistically, one counts the number of fixes per code entity by mapping closed reports about bugs to their corresponding *fixing* code changes—typically one scans for commit messages that mention a bug report identifier. This, however, relies on three fundamental assumptions:

- The location of the defect is the part of the code where the fix is applied.

    However, this is not always true, and bug fixes can have very different natures. Consider a method M that parses a string containing email addresses and returns the email alias without the domain. However, M crashes on strings containing no @ character at all. A simple fix is to check for @ characters before calling M. Although this resolves the issue, the method that was changed to apply this fix is not the one that is defective, and might also be located in a different source file.

- Issue reports that are flagged as BUGs describe real code defects.

We rely on the fact that work items marked as BUGs are really referring to bugs. If this is not the case, the work item and its associated code changes are considered bug fixes, although they might implement a new feature or perform a refactoring.

• The change to the source code is atomic, meaning it's the minimal patch that fixes the bug without performing any other tasks.

Similar to the previous assumption, we treat code changes associated to work items as a unit. Thus, we assume that all code changes applied in the same commit serve the same purpose defined by the associated work item. But what if a developer applies code changes serving multiple purposes together? Even if she stated the fact in the commit message, eg, "Fixing bug #123, implementing improvement #445 and refactoring module X for better maintainability," we do not know which code change belongs to which work item nor which code change implements the bug fix.

Violating the first assumption yields models that predict bug fixes rather than code defects—but there is very little we can do, as bugs themselves are not marked in the process, and as bug fixes can be assumed to be at least close to the actual defect. Therefore, we will focus on the remaining two assumptions.

Violating the two latter assumptions, however, would lead to noise and bias in our datasets. In fact, if we are unable to separate bug fixes from code changes, and if code changes are frequently tangled with other noncorrective code changes, then counting such tangled bug fixes effectively means counting changes, or churn, rather than code defects or bug fixes. A serious problem if we want to predict quality rather than churn. Thus, violating the latter two assumption imposes serious risks, and might lead to imprecise code quality models.

DO BUG REPORTS DESCRIBE CODE DEFECTS?

There is no general answer to this question. Fundamentally, the answer depends on the individual bug reports filed against a system and on the more fundamental question: what is a bug? If we would ask this question to five developers, we would probably get six different answers or most of them would answer: "this depends." Asking 10 people on the street, including people who are not software development engineers, would add even more diversity to the set of answers.

IT'S THE USER THAT DEFINES THE WORK ITEM TYPE

Although the question of a definition of a bug seems unrelated, we should bear in mind that bug trackers are communication tools between engineers and customers—potentially people from the street. And it is often the customer, the non-expert, who creates these "bug" reports. Even worse, it is the customer that is responsible for assigning an issue report type: typically something like BUG,

RFE (feature request), IMPR (improvement), REFAC (refactoring), etc. However, if the user is a customer with little software expertise, he might not know the difference between BUG and IMPR. And even if he does, his definition of BUG may not match the one of a developer.

Thus, the threat of violating our second assumption (bug reports describe real code defects) is high, depending on the data source and who is involved in creating bug reports.

AN EXAMPLE

We illustrate the conflict of definitions on a small example (real-world) between the three parties that are involved in creating and accessing bug report data, ie, users, engineers, and analysts: the *user* of a system complains about the fact that pressing buttons in the graphical user interface raises a bell tone. She files a BUG report complaining about the fact that she cannot disable the bell tone. She uses the BUG type either because users tend to mark all unexpected behavior as bugs or because BUG is the standard selection in most bug trackers. The *engineer* responsible for resolving the "bug" solves her issue by providing the ability to turn off the audio effect. However, he considers this to be a new feature as turning off the audio effect was not supported and lead to multiple changes in multiple layers of the program.

WHO CARES ABOUT THE REPORT CATEGORIES?

Studies have shown that fields of issue reports change very rarely, once an initial value is assigned. The reason is that engineers have very little benefit of changing these values. Once the engineer knows the actual report category, he is close to a solution of the issue. Going back to the report and changing the report type costs only time, in some bug tracking tools this is not even possible without deleting and creating a new report. The same is true for other issue report fields, such as severity or priority. Thus, it is the data analyst, the person with the least knowledge about the individual reports, who has to rely on the work item category.

As a consequence, data analysts should not blindly rely on user input data, especially if the data might stem from nonexperts or data sources that reflect different points of view. It is important keep in mind that the data to be analyzed is most likely created for purposes other than mining and analyzing the data. Going back to our assumption on bug reports and the types of work items, we should be careful about simply using the data without checking if our second assumption holds. If it does not hold, it is good practice to estimate the extend of the data noise and whether it will significantly impact our analyses.

HOW BIG IS THE PROBLEM OF "FALSE BUGS"?

In a study Herzig et al. [1] investigated 7000 bug reports from five open source projects (HTTPClient, Jackrabbit, Lucene-Java, Rhino, and Tomcat5) and manually classified their report categories to find out how much noise exists in these frequently used bug report data sets and what impact this noise has on quality models.

The authors found that *issue report types are unreliable*. In the five bug databases investigated, more than 40% of issue reports were categorized inaccurately. Similarly, the study showed that *every third bug report does not refer to code defects*. In consequence, the validity of studies regarding the distribution and prediction of bugs in code is threatened. Assigning the noisy original bug data to source files to count the number of defects per file, Herzig et al. [1] found that 39% of *files were wrongly marked as fixed* although *never* containing a single code defect.

DO DEVELOPERS APPLY ATOMIC CHANGES?

The third assumption commonly made when building quality models based on software repositories is that commits applied to version archives represent atomic code changes. However, this assumes that humans work sequentially and that individual work items are independent. Neither assumption is correct [1,2]. Developers do not work sequentially, but rather work on many different tasks in parallel, at least when using the version control perspective.

VERSION CONTROL SYSTEMS ARE NOT GRANULAR ENOUGH

Version control commits are snapshots in time. Their patches summarize code changes that have been applied since the previous commit. However, this perspective disregards the purpose of these changes and their fine-grained dependencies, eg, in which order they were performed.

A developer fixing a code defect by overwriting an entire method and replacing its content with a faster algorithm that also fixes the defect cannot be separated into a set of code changes fixing the defect and applying an improvement. And even if manual separation is possible, eg, fist fixing a code defect before renaming variables, there is little to no motivation and benefit for engineers to work this way, eg, an create local branches to fix simple bugs. This is very similar to the reasons of noisy bug report types. An engineer's focus lies on completing a task and to get work done— that is what she is paid for. And for the developer, there is no (imminent) benefit to working in such a way that data analysts and their models gain higher accuracy.

Thus, even if developers do work sequentially on work items and development tasks, we rely on them to group the applied changes in provide the appropriate snapshots (commits). At the same time, we provide little to no motivation for developers to perform this extra (and potentially time consuming) work.

HOW BIG IS THE PROBLEM OF "TANGLED CHANGES"?

Each *tangled change* threatens the validity of models relying on the assumption that code changes are atomic entities, eg, assigning the number of bugs by identifying bug references in commit messages and assigning the fixed bug to all files touched in the assumed atomic commit.

Among others, Herzig and Zeller [3] showed that the bias caused by tangled changes can be significant. In their study, the authors manually classified more than 7000 individual change sets and checked whether they addressed multiple (tangled) issue reports. Their results show that up to 12% of commits are tangled and cause false associations between bug reports and source files. Further, Herzig [4] showed that tangled changes usually combine two or three development tasks at a time. The same study showed that between 6% and 50% of the most defect-prone files do not belong in this category, because they were falsely associated with bug reports. Up to 38% of source files had a false number of bugs associated with them and up to 7% of files originally associated with bugs never were part of any bug fix.

IN SUMMARY

Mining bug reports and associating bug fixes to files to assess the quality of the code has become common practice. However, it is crucial to remember that this method relies on assumptions that need to be verified to ensure that resulting models are accurate and reflect the intended property. There has been outstanding research performed on automatically correcting some of the noise and bias commonly experienced in software repositories, eg, classifying issue reports using text-based approaches [5]. Using manual validation and automated cleanup methods is essential to ensure that the data matches our expectations. Otherwise users of our models will open bug reports complaining about the inaccuracy of our model. As an owner of the model, would you consider that a bug, or rather, as an improvement?

REFERENCES

[1] Herzig K, Just S, Zeller A. It's not a bug, it's a feature: how misclassification impacts bug prediction. In: Proceedings of the 2013 international conference on software engineering, Piscataway, NJ, USA; 2013. p. 392–401.

[2] Kawrykow D, Robillard MP. Non-essential changes in version histories. In: Proceedings of the 33rd international conference on software engineering (New York, NY, USA, 2011), ICSE'11. ACM; 2011. p. 351–60.

[3] Herzig K, Zeller A. The impact of tangled code changes. In: Proceedings of the 10th working conference on mining software repositories, Piscataway, NJ, USA; 2013. p. 121–30.

[4] Herzig K. Mining and untangling change genealogies. PhD Thesis; 2012.

[5] Antoniol G, Ayari K, Di Penta M, Khomh F, Guéhéneuc Y. Is it a bug or an enhancement? A text-based approach to classify change requests. In: Proceedings of the 2008 conference of the center for advanced studies on collaborative research: meeting of minds (New York, NY, USA, 2008), CASCON'08. ACM; 2008. p. 23:304–18.

Make visualization part of your analysis process

S. Diehl

University of Trier, Trier, Germany

CHAPTER OUTLINE

Visualization is a powerful tool. It can play a crucial role when it comes to generating hypotheses or presenting results. Visualization should become an integral part of your analysis process. You can use it to clean the data before the actual analysis. During the analysis, it can help you to see the unexpected and to generate hypotheses for further analysis. Finally, you can combine different kinds of visualizations to tell a story about your data and present your findings to others.

LEVERAGING VISUALIZATIONS: AN EXAMPLE WITH SOFTWARE REPOSITORY HISTORIES

Software repositories, or in more technical terms, source control management systems, such as CVS, SVN, Git, or TFS, contain historical information in terms of different versions, or revisions, of a software system. Data extracted from software repositories may be problematic for various reasons. For example, there may be developers who regularly access most of the code, or there may be overly large transactions. These developers may turn out to be bots, and the large transactions results of merging branches. These problems show up as outliers in simple visualizations like histograms or matrix visualizations of the raw data, here, the transactions. Depending on what your goals are, the corresponding transactions could be removed or handled separately.

Once you have the data cleaned, you can proceed with more advanced analyses. For example, you could apply sequence rule mining. Unfortunately, you might get thousands of rules, and might ask yourself if there are common patterns or outliers among these rules. To detect these, you can exploit that rules often have common prefixes and visualize the rules as a decision tree. Very likely, you will detect that the tree is extremely flat, and, depending on how you draw it, that it will not fit

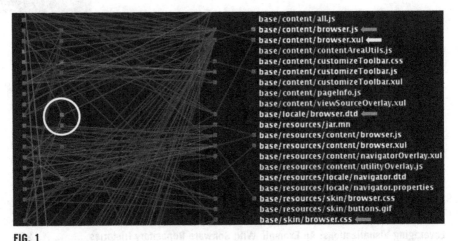

FIG. 1

Parallel Coordinates visualization of Mozilla Firefox.

on the screen. So you try another standard visualization technique: Parallel Coordinates. Now the data fits on the screen, and based on my experience, chances are good that you might actually detect patterns and outliers. Assume that you found the pattern that files in directory A are typically changed before files in directory B. As I said before, Parallel Coordinates can fit all, or at least many rules on the screen. Fig. 1 shows a Parallel Coordinates visualization of sequence rules mined for the /*base* directory of Mozilla Firefox. In this figure the file *browser.dtd* is highlighted as an interesting case. Typically, after a change to *browser.js* or *browser.css* the file *browser.dtd* is changed, and then the file *brother.xul*.

HOW TO JUMP THE PITFALLS

Seeing should not be believing. Your eyes easily trick your mind. For example, in graph visualizations, aliasing effects may suggest relations where there are none. Here, aliasing means that different visual elements become indistinguishable because of lack of resolution.

   When we try to make sense of data, we have to combine various techniques. Visualization is just one of them. If we try to understand what we see, we have to understand how the visualization was produced, ie, the extraction, analysis, statistics, and visualization of the data. Without this knowledge, it is hard to trace visual phenomena back to the underlying phenomena in the data. Even worse, the extraction, or analysis steps may pollute the data, eg, discretization of continuous data or aggregation of data with different scales. To minimize the risk of drawing wrong conclusions, you should check the data after each step. Simple visualizations may help here as well. Consider our previous example. In the Parallel Coordinates view, we should not only look at each rule that contributes to a pattern, but also for each rule look at least at some transactions that are instances of these rules.

In the past, I have often heard practitioners complaining about visualizing all kinds of graphs related to software. What often happens is that they use an off-the-shelf graph-drawing tool and are disappointed by its results, or use it to show off how complex their data is. Thus, choosing the right visualization technique and preparing the data in advance is important. To select the right technique, you have to characterize your data. Is it categorial, numerical, relational, or multivariate? Do you have small, large, or big data? Is it densely or sparsely distributed? Cognitive factors, computational, or sociological factors may be important as well. If you are not sure, ask a visualization expert. If no expert is available, you can find many resources in the InfoVis-Wiki.

Scalability is often an issue. Graphs are typically drawn as node-link diagrams. While many graph drawing approaches yield just hairballs for large graphs, some approaches, such as parallel edge splatting, may produce meaningful patterns. In any case, if the visualization does not scale, you can try to reduce the amount of data produced in the previous steps by aggregation, filtering, or other methods.

Donald Knuth once warned his readers "Beware of bugs in the above code; I have only proved it correct, not tried it." I think that many papers in software engineering have similar disclaimers: "Beware of wrong claims in the above analysis; I have only mined the data, but not visualized it." Or vice versa, "Beware of misinterpretations of the above visualization; I have only explored the data, but not done a proper analysis." Making visualization an integral part of your analysis process and using it end-to-end will make your analysis more effective and more robust.

Don't forget the developers! (and be careful with your assumptions)

A. Orso

Georgia Institute of Technology, Atlanta, GA, United States

CHAPTER OUTLINE

DISCLAIMER

This chapter is not about data science for software engineering specifically; it is rather a general reflection about the broad set of techniques whose goal is to help developers perform software engineering tasks more efficiently and/or effectively. As a representative of these techniques, we studied spectra-based fault localization (SBFL), an approach that has received a great deal of attention in the last decade. We believe that studying SBFL, how it evolved over the years, and the way in which it has been evaluated, can teach us some general lessons that apply to other research areas that aim to help developers, including software analytics.

BACKGROUND

Spectra-based (or statistical) fault localization is a family of debugging techniques whose goal is to identify potentially faulty code by mining both passing and failing executions of a faulty program, inferring their statistical properties, and presenting developers with a ranked list of potentially faulty statements to inspect. Fig. 1 shows the typical scenario of usage for these techniques: given a faulty program and a set of test cases for the program, an automated debugging tool based on SBFL would produce a ranked list of potentially faulty statements. The developers would then inspect these statements one at a time until they find the bug. It is worth noting that, in this

FIG. 1

An abstract view of the typical SBFL usage scenario.

context, being able to look at only about 5–10% of the code in a majority of cases is typically considered a good result.

The first instances of these techniques (eg, [1,2]) were clever, disruptive, and promising. Case in point, the work by Jones and colleagues [1] was awarded an ACM SIGSOFT Outstanding Research Award, and Liblit's dissertation, which was based on [2], received an ACM Doctoral Dissertation Award. Unfortunately, however, SBFL somehow became too popular for its own good; a few years after these first and a few other innovative techniques were presented, researchers started to propose all sorts of variations on the initial idea. In most cases, these variations simply consisted of using a different formula for the ranking and showing slight improvements in the effectiveness of the approach. This trend is still in effect today, to some extent.

ARE WE ACTUALLY HELPING DEVELOPERS?

One of the main reasons for this flooding of alternative, fairly incremental SBFL techniques, we believe, is that researchers got too excited about (1) the presence of readily available data (test execution and outcome data), (2) the possibility of easily analyzing/mining this data, and (3) the presence of a clear baseline of comparison (the ranking results of existing techniques). These factors and excitement made researchers lose sight not only of the actual goal of the techniques they were developing, which was to help developers, but also of the many potential issues with their data analysis, such as bias, wrong assumptions, confounding factors, and spurious correlations.

To support our point, we performed a user study in which we assigned two debugging tasks to a pool of developers with different levels of expertise and studied their performance as they completed these tasks with, and without, the help of a representative SBFL technique. The results of our study clearly showed that SBFL techniques, at least as currently formulated, could not actually help developers: the developers who used SBFL did not locate bugs faster than the developers who performed debugging in a traditional way. This result was further confirmed by the fact that the performance of developers who used SBFL was not affected by the position of the faulty statements in the ranked lists produced by the technique (ie, having the fault ranked considerably higher or lower in the list did not make a difference in the developers' performance).

A more in-depth look at our results also revealed some additional issues with the (implicit) assumptions made by SBFL techniques. A first assumption is that *locating a bug in 5–10% of the code is a good result*. Although restricting the amount of code in which to locate a bug to a tenth of the software may sound much better than inspecting the whole program, in practice, this may still mean going through a list of thousands of statements, even for a relatively small program, which is clearly unrealistic. A second assumption is that *programmers exhibit perfect bug understanding* (ie, they can look at a line of code and immediately assess whether it is faulty). Unfortunately, developers cannot typically see a fault in a line of code by simply looking at that line without any context. On the contrary, we observed that the amount of context necessary to decide whether a statement is faulty could be considerable, and developers could take a long time to decide whether a statement reported as potentially faulty was actually faulty. A final assumption is that *programmers would inspect a list of potentially faulty statements linearly and exhaustively*. The assumption that developers would be willing to go through a list of potentially faulty statements one at a time, until they find the actual fault, is also unrealistic. In fact, we observed that developers stopped following the provided list and started "jumping" from one statement to the other (or completely gave up on the tool) after only a few entries. (Developers in general have a very low tolerance for false positives.)

SOME OBSERVATIONS AND RECOMMENDATIONS

The results we just discussed provide evidence that SBFL, a technique that appears to work well on paper, may not actually work that well or be helpful to developers in practice. As we mentioned at the beginning of this chapter, our goal is to use the example of SBFL to point out some common pitfalls for research that aim to help developers. We therefore conclude the chapter with a set of observations and recommendations derived from our results with SBFL that we believe can be of general value for at least some of the research performed in the area of data science for software engineering.

- The first, obvious observation that we can make based on our results is that *techniques that are supposed to help developers should at some point be put into the hands of developers to be evaluated*. We have to be especially careful when assuming that surrogate and easy to compute measures of success (eg, the percentage of statements in the code to be inspected for SBFL) are sensible and reasonable indicators of actual usefulness without any actual evidence of that.

- An additional, less obvious, observation is that it is easy to make several (often implicit) assumptions about the developers' behavior when defining a technique. If these assumptions, or even just some of them, are unrealistic, the practical usefulness of the technique will necessarily be negatively affected. To make the situation worse, sometimes it is difficult to even realize that these assumptions are there, so subsequent work may simply take them for granted and perpetuate the issue (as it has happened for years in the context of SBFL). In other words, *we should be careful with our assumptions*. Strong assumptions may be fine in the initial stages of research and in new areas. Such assumptions should, however, be made explicit and tested when the research becomes more mature.
- Based on these observations, we strongly believe that *we should perform user studies whenever possible*. The best, and maybe only way to understand whether an approach is effective, its assumptions are reasonable, and its results are actually useful is to perform user studies in settings that are as realistic as possible. Again, this is particularly true for mature approaches, for which analytical evaluations tend to fall short and provide limited information.
- Researchers should also avoid going for the low-hanging fruits that can only result in incremental work and add little to the state of the art. There are several egregious examples of this in the SBFL area, with dozens of papers whose main contribution is the improvement of success indicators (eg, rank of the faulty statements) that have been shown to be misleading. We see a similar risk for the area of software analytics, where the abundance of data, and of well-known data analysis techniques, makes it far too easy to produce results that may be publishable, but are not particularly useful or actionable.

In summary, when trying to help developers, we have to be careful about making sure that the approaches we develop are not just a nice technical exercise, but are actually useful. Doing so entails questioning our assumptions, looking for novel, rather than incremental results, and, ultimately, evaluating our techniques with real developers and in realistic settings.

ACKNOWLEDGMENTS

This chapter is based mainly on work [3] performed jointly with Chris Parnin (now a faculty member at North Carolina State University).

REFERENCES

[1] Jones JA, Harrold MJ, Stasko JT. Visualization of test information to assist fault localization. In: Proceedings of the international conference on software engineering (ICSE 2002); 2002. p. 467–77.

[2] Liblit B, Aiken A, Zheng AX, Jordan MI. Bug isolation via remote program sampling. In: Proceedings of the conference on programming language design and implementation (PLDI 2003); 2003. p. 141–54.

[3] Parnin C, Orso A. Are automated debugging techniques actually helping programmers. In: Proceedings of the international symposium on software testing and analysis (ISSTA 2011); 2011. p. 199–209.

Limitations and context of research

B. Murphy

Microsoft Research, Cambridge, United Kingdom

CHAPTER OUTLINE

The software industry has existed for over 60 years and is now a massive multinational, multi-billion dollar industry. Software controls a vast amount of our daily lives, from providing entertainment, controlling household goods, controlling transport systems, and providing worldwide services such as internet searching. The objectives and attributes of software range from small game applications that focus on fast-feature deployment, to software controlling planes whose focus is fault and safety tolerance. The products range in scale from software that runs on individual mobile phones all the way to a search engine running across tens of thousands of machines distributed across multiple server farms distributed around the world. During this time, the number of people working in the software industry has expanded significantly, as has the number of software engineering researchers. In theory, these software engineering researchers should be driving the future of software development, but even the most optimistic software engineering researcher would not make this claim. The increase in the number of people developing software should have resulted in an increase in the numbers attending research conferences to learn what is happening in the field of research. In reality, there is concern within the research community over the lack of practitioners attending software engineering conferences.

This section examines research limitations that may explain its apparent disconnect with the software engineering industry. A number of these issues are interrelated and are detailed herein.

SMALL RESEARCH PROJECTS

As discussed previously, there are great variations in the types of software being developed, and many factors that can influence development. The accuracy of any study is dependent on the ability of the researchers to interpret results, and a major factor influencing this is how clean the data is. Data cleaning can take significant domain knowledge, enabling researchers to interpret whether exceptions are valid or invalid. Often, research will be performed on small projects due to the lack of available data from the larger projects. These small projects can be controlled by the researchers, but are often contrived projects using students as developers. In these projects, researchers focus on a small number of development attributes on a single or small number of products. The results of these studies are unique to the data set and product and are rarely reproducible on any other data set for any other product. Open Source and repositories like GitHub have helped researchers access software project developments, but as discussed later in the chapter, these repositories have issues of data quality. Additionally, with the exception of Eclipse, little data from large software developments is available for research.

Although, due to necessity, papers often make claims that results are generic, which often undermines the research in the eyes of practitioners. The potential consumers of research are commercial developers who would like to see results in their own context, often large proprietary software developments. Often, they struggle to understand how to apply research to their projects. This differs from research disciplines such as systems, where the Symposium on Operating Systems Principles (SOSP) conference offers papers on large projects based on the work of many researchers.

THE IMPORTANCE OF BEING THE FIRST AUTHOR ON A PUBLICATION

A significant driver of researchers wishing to publish in conferences is the need for publication requirements to allow students to graduate. For the students, it is very important that they are the first author of any paper so they can claim ownership of their work, another factor is the importance of conferences that publish their work. This inevitably results in two limiting factors:

- The research projects are small, as there are limited resources that can be applied to the projects as other students in the group would rather focus on their own projects than that of their colleagues.
- Each student, and tenure-seeking faculty member is supposed to be carving their own unique research area, which is shown through being the first author on the paper, but also detracts from the work of the collaborators on the paper.

Other research disciplines that try to promote larger research projects will place authors in alphabetic order, and credit the work to all authors.

REQUIREMENTS FOR NOVEL RESEARCH TECHNIQUES

One of the major criteria for a paper's publication in both journals and at conferences is the novelty of the technique. As discussed herein, there are great variations in the types of software products, their attributes, and the development methods applied. Additionally, software development is a human activity, and as such, has great variations between different development teams, even if they are applying the same development techniques. To fully understand the universality of a specific finding, the same research experiment should be applied to numerous products developed by different development groups. But replicated studies are implicitly discouraged in software engineering because top software engineering venues reject papers that are not considered to be novel research areas.

Most other engineering disciplines welcome the publication of papers that reflect the application of the same engineering techniques within different environments. For instance, medical journals encourage replicated trials, applied to different sets of patients, which often result in different results. The medical journals value the ability of the researchers to interpret the differences between the two trials; this enhances the general knowledge of the discipline. The lack of replicated studies in software engineering research results in the limitations of any proposed technique not being fully understood, and more importantly, its limitations will be unknown. As practitioners understand that most techniques have limitations, then they will not apply any new techniques whose limitations are unknown.

The quality of papers within the research community is measured by the number of citations in other research papers. Conferences (Foundations of Software Engineering (FSE), International Conference on Software Engineering (ICSE)) define influential papers over time based on the "novelty" of the idea and the number of citations. Other engineering disciplines, logically, measure a paper's influence based on its impact on the industry.

DATA QUALITY OF OPEN SOURCE REPOSITORIES

Over recent years there has been a significant increase in the amount of data available to system engineering researchers due to the increase in developers using open repositories such as GitHub. This has opened up a vast resource of software development activity for research. But there are various data quality issues that hinder interpretation of its results, specifically;

1. GIT provides tremendous flexibility in how code can be moved between branches, but that flexibility can result in a lot of data attributes, such as on which branch a change was made and the time order it occurred, being lost.
2. Triaging of bug data: A bug submitted to a repository may not be reproducible due to lack of data, or insufficient description of the defect. Additionally, a submitted bug may be a replica of an already existing bug in the repository.

In theory, engineers, when correcting or discarding a bug, will properly document the reasons for their actions, in practice, they rarely do as it is far too time consuming. As such, it is difficult to relate the bugs in the repository to defects in the software.

3. Definition of the complete product: Often the code repository will contain a master branch, with the natural assumption is that all code in that branch forms the released product. In reality, the code in the master branch will be a mixture of product, test, and process code, often developed using different criteria, complicating the interpretation of any results.

4. Source code from industry is often limited to post-release information (eg, Android): A much richer data set would be the development period, but that is rarely made available.

5. Limited access to, and identification of, developers: A major issue with the analysis of software engineering data is the management of exceptions. The simplest way of interpreting data is to talk to the engineers responsible for the development; without access to the developers, the researchers manage outliers using statistical techniques that may not necessarily be accurate.

LACK OF INDUSTRIAL REPRESENTATIVES AT CONFERENCES

The steering committees, chairs, and program committees (PCs) are dominated by academics, with few industrial representatives, with most of these being from research departments within the industry. While academics personally benefit from working at conferences, industrial practitioners get little recognition within their companies for working at conferences, and may even need to perform the work on their own time. Additionally, as these conferences grow, the amount of work required from people on the committee grows: the recent ICSE conference required each PC member to review 18 papers, to respond to authors' comments, and to discuss the papers with other reviewers. As the number of industrial representatives at conferences drops, it is inevitable that these engineering conferences will increasingly focus on academics' interests, without any reference on whether those interests are relevant to the software industry.

RESEARCH FROM INDUSTRY

As previously noted, industry involvement in software engineering conferences is limited. A factor in this is the decrease in the number of research labs in industry, with companies closing down or limiting their research departments, and newer companies not creating new labs; although a number of these companies do employ researchers who do submit research material for publications. A major source of publications from industry are those written by interns, studying at universities, but working in industry for a short period of time.

Industrial researchers have access to a much richer data set than academic researchers, using open source data. This is due to product teams often triaging bug data to identify replicated bugs and to discard bugs that are non-reproducible. Additionally, industrial bug data will often contain a reference to any resulting code changes. Industrial researchers often have full access to developers and product information, allowing them to better interpret their results. They also have the flexibility to apply the same techniques to different data sets for the same or equivalent products developed by different product groups within the same company, resulting in much larger experiments, and a greater ability to identify limitations in any technique.

A major issue is industrial research limiting access to the raw, or interpreted, data. They also rarely provide absolute values in their papers, leaving the y-axis values in graphs blank. There are many reason for this, as firms may fear for their reputation if the absolute values of bug reports are published. Another frequent reason is that data may contain information on products from other companies, which they do not have the right to release. For instance, Windows crash data contains a large amount of non-Microsoft failure data, including the names of third party drivers and applications. This can produce negative reactions by academic reviewers of papers written by industry practitioners.

There are also practical issues regarding getting industry people to contribute to conferences or journals. The most important factor is that the majority of industry practitioners will not personally benefit from getting work published, as that is not their primary job. To attend a conference, they will need permission, so their company will have to view attending a conference as beneficial. Ironically, the greater the amount of industrial participation at a conference, the more attractive the conference is to industry. Industrial practitioners are also at a disadvantage as the structure of academic papers are different to those in industry, so practitioners often struggle to ensure the paper will meet all the required criteria.

SUMMARY

There has been a growing disconnect between software engineering research and software practitioners, and based on the underlying factors driving academia discussed in this chapter, this disconnect is only going to increase. There are numerous people within academia who work closely with industry, but perversely, publishing the results of these joint collaborations is more difficult than focusing on purely theoretical areas. Improving the impact of software engineering research, in terms of its applicability in the software industry, will require universities to change the way they measure the contribution of their students, decreasing the focus on published papers and increasing how they value their contributions to the field. Conferences should actively recruit people from industry to help drive their direction, which requires the conferences to lower the burden on participating in the conference. Additionally, conferences, and technical journals, need to focus less on the quality of the paper, in terms of its structure and technical content, and rather, they should focus on how much the paper adds to the general knowledge of software engineering.

Actionable metrics are better metrics

A. Meneely

Rochester Institute of Technology, Rochester, NY, United States

CHAPTER OUTLINE

- "Frank, I'm sorry, we're letting you go."
- "Why? What did I do wrong? I've been your best developer for 30 years!"
- "We ran some metrics and found that your code used the letter 'm' 10 times more than anyone else."
- "What does that matter?"
- "We've found that code using the letter 'm' is more likely to have memory leaks, and you use it all the time, don't you?"
- "You mean malloc? But, you asked me to rewrite our memory manager!"
- "Not our problem. Data never lie."

True, data is just data. But humans use data to lie all the time... with metrics. Metrics are a huge part of our evidence-based society. Metrics drive what data we collect, determine the exact phrasing of our conclusions, and shape our perspectives. One wrong step with a metric, and we can grossly misunderstand the world around us.

In software development, a common data misinterpretation is to always assume that a metric is *actionable*. That is, are we using this metric to directly drive decisions? Does the metric actually tell us what to do next? Or is it more of an indication of a condition?

WHAT WOULD YOU SAY... I SHOULD DO?

An actionable metric is one that inspires us to improve. Consider these metrics in our everyday lives:

- Hours spent in the gym
- Speed of your car in relation to the speed limit
- Number of dollars spent on movies

In each of those situations, a specific property is being measured—and that property is something that the person being measured has direct control over. What happens when "Number of hours spent in the gym" decreases? Improving upon that metric is easy: go to the gym!

Now consider these metrics:

- Number of home runs hit this season
- Number of hackers who attacked this operating system
- Body temperature
- Exam grade

A general manager would be unfair to approach his players and say "hit more home runs," or a CIO telling her system administrators: "get hacked less." That's not useful. Everybody wants those metrics to improve, but *how* improvement is to be made is not a directly controllable action for the people involved. The preceding metrics, rather, are *emergent* properties: they are the result of many good forces cooperating at once.

Consider body temperature as another example. In medicine, a high body temperature is a *symptom* of an illness, not the *cause*. Note that body temperature is still useful as a metric because it indicates problems and can guide treatment, but it does not provide an obvious direction to doctors on a cure.

The distance between actionable metrics and emergent properties can be a wide chasm. Notice how "Hours spent in the gym" is not necessarily a direct measure of your overall physical fitness: perhaps you get exercise in other ways. Gym attendance metrics in general would be meaningless if you lacked a gym membership to begin with. Thus, actionable metrics are typically tied to a *process* in which they are intended to be used. In software development, a developer who is slow at responding to pull requests could be a large problem, or a small one depending on how pull requests are used. Bridging the gap between actionable metrics and emergent properties is a regular part of good project management.

THE OFFENDERS

Unactionable metrics are commonplace in software engineering. Two metrics stand out as being particularly frustrating to developers: number of bugs and code churn.

NUMBER OF BUGS

The "number of bugs" metric is ubiquitous in software quality discussions. Defect density, failure rate, fault occurrences, and many other variations all try to show the same picture: how many problems have we had with this system? Ideally, software quality is much more nuanced than simply the number of bug reports, but managers count what they have, and the number of bugs is easy to count.

Unfortunately, the existence of a bug is not the result of one simple action. A single bug can be a combination of all kinds of software engineering failures: requirements mistakes, design flaws, coding errors, lack of testing, miscommunication, or poor process. To aggregate all of these complex scenarios into a single metric and then ask developers to reduce them is simply not helpful to developers. To behave as if it were actionable is indicative of a get-it-right-the-first-time mentality instead of continuous improvement. Number of bugs, therefore, is *emergent*, not actionable.

CODE CHURN

Code churn is a metric that describes the amount of change a module has undergone. As a software project evolves, source code is added and deleted constantly. By mining the source code management system (such as the Git or Subversion repository), researchers can collect the number of lines of code that have changed for a given file over time. Historically, churn is a predictor of quality problems, such as bugs and vulnerabilities: files that change a lot overall are more likely to have big problems later. In the empirical software engineering research world, code churn has become a staple in bug prediction models.

But, code churn is difficult to act upon. What should developers do... not change code? No bugfixes? No new features? No compatibility upgrades? Of course not! That code churn works in a bug prediction model means that we have a good indication of where problems will be, but we don't understand why. Code can churn for all sorts of reasons, most of which are unavoidable.

While code churn by itself is unavoidable, specific variations of code churn can be more actionable. For example, suppose we define a metric called "un-reviewed churn" that counts the number of changes that did not undergo a code inspection. A high un-reviewed churn has a clear recommendation. If we have empirical support that the metric is also correlated with bugs (and we do from some recent studies), then the recommendation is clear: do more code reviews on those changes.

ACTIONABLE HEROES

After seeing the worst, let's take a look at some metrics that are actionable in interesting ways.

NUMBER OF DEVELOPERS

Source code management is not just a record of what code changed, it can also be a record of how developers are working together. When two developers make changes to the same source code file, they have a common cause. One useful metric that comes out of this is the "number of different developers who changed this file." The metric typically defined over a period of time, such as 1 year or the most recent release. Historically, this metric is correlated with later having bugs and vulnerabilities—the more developers who work on a file, the higher the probability of bugs later on.

"Number of developers" is important because it can indicate organizational problems in your team. If a file has 200 developers committing to a single source code file, then chances are they are not all coordinating with each other to make joint decisions. Unintended effects of many changes at once can plausibly introduce bugs. A high number of developers might also indicate design problems that force developers to maintain a monolithic file. Build files, for example, might need to be touched by many developers if not properly broken down according to a subsystem.

NUMBER OF CALLEES (COUPLING) AND NUMBER OF PARAMETERS

When examining the source code itself, metrics such as "number of method callees" and "number of parameters" can indicate actionable problems in your product. If a method makes many external calls, or accepts many different parameters, perhaps that method has too much responsibility. A well-designed method should have a single responsibility that is clearly understood. Reducing the number of callees and number of parameters through refactoring can directly help this responsibility problem.

CYCLOMATIC COMPLEXITY: AN INTERESTING CASE

Metrics can be actionable, but not empirically useful at the same time. McCabe's cyclomatic complexity is one such metric. Broadly speaking, cyclomatic complexity is derived by counting the number of potential paths through the system (typically at the method level). Originally designed to estimate the number of unit tests a method needs, cyclomatic complexity is built into a lot of metric tools and static analysis tools. Developers can and often do use it to measure their notion of "cognitive" complexity, and use it to target their refactoring efforts. Lower the cyclomatic complexity, and improve the testability of your code. However, many empirical studies have shown that, historically, cyclomatic complexity is strongly correlated with the number of lines of code [1]. In fact, cyclomatic complexity provides no new information in predicting bugs than the size of the method (or file or other unit of measure). Well-designed code will be both more concise and have fewer conditionals. Therefore, in comparison to the easier-to-collect "number of lines of code," cyclomatic complexity provides very little new information: it is actionable, but typically not useful.

ARE UNACTIONABLE METRICS USELESS?

Of course not! Unactionable metrics (aka emergent metrics) can be quite useful in telling us about the symptoms of a problems. Like "number of bugs," we can get an overall assessment of how the product is doing. Emergent metrics are most useful when they are a surprise, for example, when a student's grade comes back lower than expected. We simply cannot rely upon emergent metrics to diagnose the problem for us.

Thus, an *actionable* software development metric is one that measures a property directly under a developer's control. An *emergent* metric is one that aggregates a variety of potential problems into a single measurement without an obvious diagnosis. Actionable metrics tell us how to improve, whereas emergent metrics tell us where we are. Both are useful in their own right, but our expectations and applications of these metrics must be consistent with the information they provide.

REFERENCE

[1] Shin Y, Meneely A, Williams L, Osborne JA. Evaluating complexity, code churn, and developer activity metrics as indicators of software vulnerabilities. IEEE Trans Softw Eng 2011;37(6):772–87.

Replicated results are more trustworthy

M. Shepperd

Brunel University London, Uxbridge, United Kingdom

CHAPTER OUTLINE

THE REPLICATION CRISIS

The need to replicate results is a central tenet throughout science, and empirical software engineering is no exception. The reasons are threefold.

First, it's a means of testing for errors, perhaps in the experimental set up or instrumentation. The Fleischmann-Pons cold fusion experiment is a famous example where other teams were unable to replicate the initial findings, which then cast doubt over the initial experimental results and analysis.

Second, it helps the scientific community better understand how general the findings are, throughout time, and through different settings. For example, an intervention may work well for small agile projects, and be unhelpful for large safety-critical systems.

Third, it helps us better approximate the confidence limits on a reported effect size. Note that even for well-conducted studies undertaken by the most scrupulous researchers, we can still find Type I (ie, false positives) or Type II (ie, false negatives) errors at a frequency approximately determined by the α and β settings, so for example, we would typically expect 1 in 20 studies to wrongly reject the no-effect hypothesis, and perhaps as many as 2 in 10 to studies fail to reject the null hypothesis (of no effect) when there actually is an effect. This means relying upon a single study has an appreciable degree of risk. For a more detailed, but accessible, account see Ellis [14].

So it's quite surprising to observe that there is no single agreed-upon set of terminology for replication of research. Schmidt [1], writing for an audience of psychologists, observed the paucity of clear-cut guidance or a single set of definitions. He differentiates between *narrow* replication, which entails replication of the experimental procedure, and *wider*, or conceptual replication, which entails testing of the same hypothesis or research question, but via different means.

Both narrow and wide replications are carried out in software engineering. An example of the former is Basili et al.'s [2] idea of families of experiments and materials being explicitly shared. Clearly, in such circumstances, it's essential to ensure that you have confidence in the validity of such materials. Wide, or conceptual, replications are more commonplace, but frequently appear in a less structured fashion, which can lead to considerable difficulties in making meaningful comparisons. This has been highlighted by various meta-analyses such as the Hannay et al. [3] study on pair programming and the Shepperd et al. [4] analysis of software defect classifiers.

In a mapping study de Magalhães et al. [5] report that whilst there has been some growth in the number of replication studies in recent years for empirical software engineering, the numbers remain a very small proportion of the total number of studies conducted. They found a total of 135 papers reporting replications, published between 1994 and 2012. Miller [6] comments that one reason for the poor uptake of replication as an important research technique is that it's perceived as "*only* [my emphasis] about proving robustness of pre-existing results," in other words, a narrow view of replication with potentially negative connotations. This needs to be changed.

In fact, the problem is even more serious, and came forcibly to my attention when attempting a meta-analysis of results from the field of software defect prediction. For some time I and other researchers were concerned about the lack of agreement between individual studies; informally it seemed that for every study by Team A that reported strong evidence for X, the next study by Team B reported strong evidence for NOT(X) Menzies and Shepperd [7].

Lack of agreement between studies triggered a formal meta-analysis of defect classifiers all derived from competing statistical and machine-learning approaches conducted with co-authors Bowes and Hall. Despite locating over 200 primary studies, we had to *reject more than 75%* due to incompatible experimental designs, lack of reported details, and inconsistent or inappropriate response variables [4]. This is an dispiriting waste of research energy and effort. Nevertheless, we were still able to meta-analyze 600 individual experimental results. Our conclusions were quite stark. The choice of machine learning algorithm had almost no bearing upon the results of the study. We modeled this using a random effects linear model using ANalysis Of VAriance (ANOVA), and then added moderators to characterize aspects of the experimental design such as training data, input metrics, and research group (the latter being determined through a single linkage clustering algorithm based upon co-authorship). To our astonishment, we found that research group is many times (of the order 25×) more strongly associated with the actual results than the choice of prediction algorithm. We believe the causes of this researcher bias include:

- differing levels of expertise
- incomplete reporting of experimental details
- the preference for some results over others; scientists are human after all!

In this setting it is no surprise that there is presently little agreement, that is, reliability between research results.

Note that replication for nonexperimental investigations is an interesting and complex question that is not covered by this chapter (see, for instance, Eisenhardt [8] on replication logic for case studies).

REPRODUCIBLE STUDIES

In order for a study to be repeated naturally it must be reproducible, by this I mean there must be sufficient information available to enable this to happen. Schmidt [1] quotes Popper who states "Any empirical scientific statement can be presented (by describing experimental arrangements, etc.) in such a way, that anyone who has learned the relevant technique can test it." However, this begs the question of what characteristics should a study report? There are four areas that must be considered, although their relative importance may vary from study to study:

1. Explicit research question: this needs to be carefully articulated, as exploratory trawls through data sets are difficult to replicate.
2. Data and pre-processing procedures: this militates against studies that use data not in the public domain, and such authors need to find persuasive arguments as to why using such data are necessary.
3. Experimental design: differences in design can significantly impact reliability. Note that for example in machine learning the impact of using a Leave-one-out cross-validation (LOOCV) as opposed to $m \times n$ cross-validation is not well understood.
4. Details of algorithms employed—most machine learners are complex, with large free spaces for their parameter settings. Choices are often governed by experience or trial and error.

Much of the preceding list could be simplified once specific research communities are able to define and agree upon standard reporting protocols. This would be particularly beneficial for new entrants to the field and for meta-analysts.

RELIABILITY AND VALIDITY IN STUDIES

We need studies that are reliable, that is, if repeated will tend to produce the same result. They also need to be valid since reliably invalid is, to put it mildly, unhelpful! Hannay et al. [3] in their meta-analysis report that "the relatively small overall effects and large between-study variance (heterogeneity) indicate that one or more moderator variables might play a significant role." This is a similar finding to the Shepperd et al. [4] meta-analysis in that experimental results are typically confounded by differences in experimental design and conduct. This harms reliability. Likewise, Jørgensen et al. [9] randomly sampled 150 software engineering experiments from their systematic review. Again, they found significant problems with the validity. Two particular problems appear to be researcher bias and low experimental power.

SO WHAT SHOULD RESEARCHERS DO?

There is much consensus from researchers both within software engineering, for example, Jørgensen et al. [9] and beyond, for example, the psychologist Schooler [10] for more replications and meta-studies. In order to accomplish this I believe we need:

- Blind analysis: this is a technique to reduce researcher bias, whereby the experimental treatments are blinded by means of re-labeling so that the statistician or analyst is unaware which is the new "pet" treatment and which are the benchmarks. This makes fishing for a particular result more difficult [11].
- Agreed-upon reporting protocols: so that replications are more easily possible without having to guess as to the original researchers' implementation.
- To place more value on replications and nonsignificant results: Ioannidis [12] demonstrates—as a somewhat hypothetical exercise—how a game-theoretic analysis of the different goals of the different stakeholders in the research community can lead to problematic outcomes and that we need to therefore address the "currency" or payoff matrix. I see no easy shortcuts to achieving this but, minimally, awareness may lead to better understanding and more fruitful discussions.

SO WHAT SHOULD PRACTITIONERS DO?

Clearly the (long-term) purpose of software engineering research is to influence its practice. Hence, practitioners are concerned with research that generates "actionable" results. This implies:

- Practitioners should be wary of implementing the results of a single study. The findings should not simply be extrapolated to all settings because there are likely to be many sources of potentially important variation between different contexts.
- Given the importance of context, "one size fits all" types of result should be treated with caution.
- More generally, we need to promote evidence-based practice [13], which in turn requires that all relevant evidence be collated, combined, and made available.

REFERENCES

[1] Schmidt S. Shall we really do it again? The powerful concept of replication is neglected in the social sciences. Rev Gen Psychol 2009;13(2):90–100.

[2] Basili V, et al. Building knowledge through families of experiments. IEEE Trans Softw Eng 1999;25(4):456–73.

[3] Hannay J, et al. The effectiveness of pair programming: a meta-analysis. Inf Softw Technol 2009;51(7):1110–22.

[4] Shepperd M, et al. Researcher bias: the use of machine learning in software defect prediction. IEEE Trans Softw Eng 2014;40(6):603–16.

[5] de Magalhães C, et al. Investigations about replication of empirical studies in software engineering: a systematic mapping study. Inf Softw Technol 2015;64:76–101.

[6] Miller J. Replicating software engineering experiments: a poisoned chalice or the Holy Grail? Inf Softw Technol 2005;47(4):233–44.

[7] Menzies T, Shepperd M. Special issue on repeatable results in software engineering prediction. Empir Softw Eng 2012;17(1–2):1–17.

[8] Eisenhardt K. Building theories from case study research. Acad Manag Rev 1989; 14(4):532–50.

[9] Jørgensen M, et al. Incorrect results in software engineering experiments: how to improve research practices. J Syst Softw 2015; Available online http://dx.doi.org/10.1016/j.jss.2015.03.065.

[10] Schooler J. Metascience could rescue the 'replication crisis'. Nature 2014;515(7525):9.

[11] Sigweni B, Shepperd M. Using blind analysis for software engineering experiments. In: Proceedings of the 19th ACM international conference on evaluation and assessment in software engineering (EASE'15); 2015. http://dx.doi.org/10.1145/2745802.2745832.

[12] Ioannidis J. How to make more published research true. PLoS Med 2014;11(10) e1001747.

[13] Kitchenham B, et al. Evidence-based software engineering. In: Proceedings of the 27th IEEE international conference on software engineering (ICSE 2004), Edinburgh; 2004.

[14] Ellis P. The essential guide to effect sizes: statistical power, meta-analysis, and the interpretation of research results. Cambridge University Press; 2010.

Diversity in software engineering research

H. Valdivia-Garcia, M. Nagappan

Rochester Institute of Technology, Rochester, NY, United States

CHAPTER OUTLINE

INTRODUCTION

With the popularity and availability of Open Source Software (OSS) projects, Software Engineering (SE) researchers have made many advances in understanding how software is developed. However, in SE Research, like in any other scientific field, it is always desirable to produce results, techniques, and tools that can apply to a large (or all if possible) number of software projects. The ideal case would be to randomly select a statistically significant sample of software projects. However, past SE studies evaluate hypotheses on a small sample of deliberately chosen OSS projects that are out there in the world. More recently, an increasing number of SE researchers have started examining their hypotheses on larger datasets, which are deliberately chosen as well. The aim of the large-scale studies is to increase the generality of the research studies. However, generality of results may not be achieved if the sample of projects chosen for evaluation are homogeneous in nature and not diverse with respect to the entire population of SE projects.

To better understand the challenge of sampling, consider a researcher who wants to study distributed development in a large number of projects in an effort to increase generality. Now, consider two possible strategies to get the sample of projects:

- The researcher goes to json.org and selects 20 projects (all of the JSON parsers) that cover a wide variety of programming languages (Java, C#, Python, Ruby, Perl, etc.). Then, any findings will not be representative because of the narrow range of functionality of the projects in the sample.
- The researcher goes to gnu.org and selects 20 projects (all of them written in C) that cover a wide range of domains (eg, compilers, DBMS, editors, games, web browsers, etc.). Then, any findings will not be representative because of the narrow range of languages of the projects in the sample.

These two situations are extreme cases, but help illustrate the importance of systematically selecting the sample of appropriate projects for an empirical study. In this chapter, we present the initial work done on diversity and representativeness in SE research. We first define what we mean by diversity and representativeness in SE research. Then, we present: (a) a way to assess the quality of a given sample of projects with respect to diversity and representativeness and (b) a selection technique that allows one to tailor a sample with high diversity and representativeness.

WHAT IS DIVERSITY AND REPRESENTATIVENESS?

Diversity and representativeness are two complementary aspects of the quality of a sample selected from a population. A *diverse sample* contains members of every subgroup in the population, and within the sample, the subgroups have roughly equal size. In a *representative sample,* the size of each subgroup in the sample is proportional to the size of that subgroup in the population. For example, if the population is comprised of two subgroups: 400 members of type X and 100 members of type Y, then 25X and 25Y would be considered a diverse sample, and 40X and 10Y a representative sample. Following are definitions of the terms needed to formally define diversity and representativeness.

- A large set of projects in a domain are defined as the universe. Examples of SE universes are: all open-source projects, all web applications, all mobile phone applications, all Java applications, etc.
- Each project within a universe is characterized by one or more dimensions. Examples of dimensions are: size in lines of code (LOC), main programming language, number of developers, rating, price, etc. The subset of dimensions that are relevant for research topics are referred to as the space of the research topic.
- For each dimension d in the space of the research topic, a similarity function is defined: $similar_d(p1, p2) \rightarrow \{0, 1\}$ that decides whether projects $p1$ and $p2$ are similar at dimension d. The collection of similarity functions in the space are referred to as the configuration of the space. Now, two projects $p1$ and $p2$ are similar, if all their dimensions are similar or $similar(p1, p2) = \prod_d similar_d(p1, p2)$.
- The subgroup of projects (within the universe) that are similar to one another, are in the same neighborhood.

Based on the preceding definitions, the sample coverage (the numerical representation of the amount of the universe covered by the given sample of projects) of the set of projects P for a given universe of projects U is computed as follows: $\text{coverage}(P) = \left| U_{p \in P} \{ q | \text{similar}(p, q) \} \right| / |U|$.

Depending on the research studies, the universe, space, and similarity function can vary. In fact, it is up to the researcher to define the most suitable similarity function for their research topic (space) and target population (universe). In addition, it is also important to discuss the context in which the coverage was computed. The researcher should always keep in mind these questions: What projects is the research intending to be relevant for (universe)? What criteria matter for findings to hold for other projects (space, configuration)?

WHAT CAN WE DO ABOUT IT?

Now that we know how to assess the coverage of a given sample, the next step is to learn how to systematically tailor a sample with maximum coverage. The selection technique is a hybrid strategy that combines ideas from Diversity and Representativeness. The main parts of the technique can be summarized as follows:

- Taking ideas from diversity, identify the neighborhoods (subgroups) of all projects in the population. Here, it is important to note that: if two projects are similar, their neighborhoods will overlap.
- Taking ideas from representativeness, select the project based on the size of their neighborhood not yet covered by the sample. With the "not yet covered" condition, the projects in the sample are ensured to not share neighborhoods.
- For selecting a sample of K projects with high coverage, the previous step is repeated, at most, K times.

A detailed description of the algorithms to compute the sample-selection and the sample-coverage can be found in prior work [1]. Additionally, an R implementation of the technique is provided in the online repository. This way, the interested reader can easily use them either in her/his research or to complement the reading of the present chapter.

EVALUATION
EVALUATING THE SAMPLE SELECTION TECHNIQUE

All the active projects monitored by the OpenHub platform (formerly Ohloh) were considered the universe. The universe consisted of a total of 20,028 projects. For the purpose of the demonstration, the "comparison features" in OpenHub were used as the dimensions of the space. More precisely, the data for seven dimensions: language, size in LOC, # contributors, churn, # commits, project-age, and project-activity was extracted.

The experiment shows that the best sample with 100% of coverage has 5030 projects. A deeper analysis of the top 15 projects with the highest coverage in the sample show that they are very small projects (<1000 LOC) written mostly in scripting languages. This result illustrates the importance of including smaller projects in our case studies (contrary to popular belief that research always has to scale to large software and pay less attention to smaller projects).

EVALUATING THE SAMPLE COVERAGE SCORE

For our second experiment, the sample coverage of projects from papers in over 2 years of two SE conferences was computed. Although 635 unique projects were found in the papers, only 207 projects could be mapped to the universe of OpenHub projects.

The experiment showed that these 207 projects studied in papers at the two SE conferences covered 9.15% of the OpenHub population. At first glance, this score seems low, but one has to keep in mind that (a) it is based on a strict notion of coverage; and (b) the relevant target universe may be different for each paper and therefore different from OpenHub.

RECOMMENDATIONS

So far, based on the results from past work, the reader may be tempted to think that studies with low coverage do not contribute much to the body of knowledge in SE. On the contrary, we think that coverage scores do not increase or decrease the importance of research, but rather, enhance our ability to reason about it and understand the context under which the results are applicable.

In SE research it is a common practice to have a section that summarizes the characteristics of the studied projects. We think that this section is the appropriate place to report the coverage of such projects and discuss the target population to be researched (universe) as well as the dimensions relevant for the research (space).

FUTURE WORK

In the future we need to examine how and when the preceding approach does not actually generalize results. We also need to examine if choosing projects randomly is better than choosing projects that cover a certain neighborhood of projects in the universe, or a possible hybrid between the approach described herein and random sampling.

REFERENCE

[1] Nagappan M, Zimmermann T, Bird C. Diversity in software engineering research. In: Proceedings of the 2013 9th Joint Meeting on Foundations of Software Engineering—ESEC/FSE 2013. Saint Petersburg, Russia: ACM Press; 2013. p. 466–76.

Once is not enough: Why we need replication

N. Juristo

Universidad Politécnica de Madrid, Spain

CHAPTER OUTLINE

MOTIVATING EXAMPLE AND TIPS

Imagine you land on an uncharted planet where no human has been before. For one reason or another, you are unable to leave the spaceship to explore the unknown, and you can only gather information about the planet through the spaceship windows. You look out and see a strange being: an alien of a shape, size, and color that you could have never imagined. You are extremely surprised, and you carry on looking at it in order to unlock the mystery and form an idea of what sort of thing you have in your sights. Are you sure that what your eyes are seeing (and your brain is perceiving) through the window really is a true likeness of the outside world? What if the food you had to eat last night had gone off? What if you are seeing things, and there really is nothing out there? What would you do to make sure?

- **Tip:** *Empirical studies results should not be blindly trusted. Empirical data can also lie. How to be sure that what you observe exists?*

For ruling out the possibility that you are seeing things, you ask one of your traveling companions to look out of the window as well. You will not tell her anything about what you have seen. You lead her to the window and ask her what she can see, taking care not to manipulate her in any way. She looks out of the window next to yours and cannot see anything at all. Is that so? You go round to the window where she is stationed and find that you cannot see the alien from there either, while she takes her place at your window. Aha! There is a light of some kind shining into this window, and it makes the alien invisible from here. Your traveling companion confirms that she, too, can see the alien from your window. It does exist then; it's out there!

- **Tip:** *Site and researchers are variables that might induce different results of the same identical empirical study. Different researchers being able to reproduce your results in their labs increase confidence in your empirical results. Is that all we need?*

"There is a red living being out there," she says. Are you two sure enough that the alien is really red? Could it be that the glass in the window is so thick that it is deforming the alien's profile? What if the glass is not perfectly transparent and is altering his color? "Al is watching us!" your colleague shouts, astonished (by this time you have given the creature a pet name). "Watching us?" you ask with surprise, "I can't see any eyes." You and she each take turns looking out of the window, and you discuss and compare what you see. What she referred to as an eye looks to you like a blotch on its skin (if you can call the alien's outer covering skin…). She decides to climb up to the observatory on top of the spaceship to study Al using the onboard telescope. Great! Thanks to this new instrument, she can distinguish details that were unappreciable by just looking through the windows. The information that she proffers from the telescope is crucial in making out the eye-blotch controversy, as well as some particulars that were unclear from the window.

- **Tip:** *Instruments matter. Even the best-designed empirical study interferes with the phenomenon at hand. It is of utmost importance that the same phenomenon is studied with different instruments in order to guarantee that the observation is independent of the instrument.*

EXPLORING THE UNKNOWN

This imaginary scenario has a lot in common with empirical research work. We empirical software engineering researchers are every inch the spaceship's crew on our way to an unexplored planet. We are on a voyage into the unknown: software development. Unfortunately, we cannot *penetrate* the unknown. We cannot travel to the place where the strings of software development are pulled; the place where the development variables causing the external behavior that we observe in software projects are cooked up. The software *backstage*, where hidden variables are ruling development behavior, is equally as impenetrable to our senses as gravity is. We human beings cannot perceive the gravitational forces that are at work behind the behaviors that we observe (for example, when we spill our coffee or when the Earth obediently moves in its orbit around the Sun). Likewise, we cannot directly observe the relationships between the variables causing the behaviors that we observe in software development. The only option open to us is to gather information about software development indirectly through empirical studies.

Any empirical study is a window onto the software development backstage. But the prospect from such a window gives us only one view of the reality that we are scrutinizing. Unfortunately, the window is not open; it contains a piece of glass that has a bearing on what we see. Thus, we have to take the same precautions as our friends on the spaceship that just landed on the unexplored planet.

TYPES OF EMPIRICAL RESULTS

If an experiment is not replicated, there is no way to distinguish whether results were produced by chance (the observed event occurred accidentally), results are artifactual (the event occurred because of the experimental configuration but does not exist in reality), or results conform to a pattern existing in reality. Different replication types help to clarify which of these three types of results an experiment yields.

When you see something shocking, striking, and unexpected, what do you do to be sure? You look twice. To build a piece of reliable knowledge from an empirical study, you need to be sure that the observed results did not happen accidentally. So, do it twice! Repeat the study: same experimenters, same lab, same instrumentation, and same protocol. To rule out chance results and get an estimation of the natural variation of the observation, we need identical repetitions.

Still, if the results are repeated in your lab, we need to know if they can be generalized to other sites and researchers. The way to get such a level of certainty in empirical findings is for other researchers in their labs to replicate your study. To rule out local and researcher-dependent results, we need identical replications.

One empirical study, no matter how well designed it is, might produce artifactual results. There exists a relationship between reality and the observation instrument; no one individual empirical study can yield definitive results, as the observation instrument itself (the study setting) may be affecting some aspects of the findings. Other designs, other protocols, and other instrumentations will be able to confirm if results hold. To rule out artifactual results, we need conceptual replications.

One type of empirical study offers one view of the phenomenon under observation. In order to make our evidence more reliable, we have to go a step further and observe the phenomenon using another type of instrument. Other types of empirical studies observing the same phenomenon provide new perspectives. Different types of empirical studies (experiments, observational studies, historical studies, case studies, surveys...) and empirical paradigms (qualitative and quantitative approaches) provide complementary views of the reality that we are studying, and we can piece together a more accurate picture of the development phenomenon under study by synthesizing their results.

DO'S AND DON'T'S

What is the moral of this story? Results from one single empirical study are just a preliminary piece of information; we should even consider it just an anecdote. Our studies have to be repeated, replicated, and triangulated in order to form a reliable idea of any SE phenomenon that we investigate. Building a reliable piece of knowledge out of empirical studies requires:

- Do the same study
  - by the same researchers in the same site. This type of repetition is needed to get away from fortuity and start walking toward evidence.
  - by other researchers in a different site. Other researchers replicate the study with the same protocol as the baseline study. This strategy confirms that the results are independent of the researcher, site, and sample.
  - with a different protocol. Studies (of the same type) should be performed using different settings or protocols (operationalize the variables differently, use other study designs, other measurement processes, etc.). This strategy guarantees that the results are independent of the instrument used.
- Do a different study with same goals. Alternative studies should be conducted. Observing the same reality through different types of studies provides new information that cannot be gathered from the baseline empirical study type.

Notice that leaving out steps might lead to uncertain situations. If you move directly to step three and the results you get are different (of which there is a high probability), you will be unable to trace back the source of variations since there are so many. The new information, and the old information will not fit together and nothing new can be learnt. Through baby steps, each study will contribute, with pieces fitting together like parts of a puzzle, and the bigger picture will emerge.

Just because it once happened that you observed something emerging from a set of data (being either produced by your study or borrowed from a repository) *don't* trust it. Replication is the tool science has for being sure that something observed really exists. Do it again!

FURTHER READING

[1] Gómez O, Juristo N, Vegas S. Understanding replication of experiments in software engineering: a classification. Inf Softw Technol 2014;56(8):1033–48.

[2] Juristo N, Vegas S. The role of non-exact replications in software engineering experiments. Empir Softw Eng 2011;16(3):295–324.

Mere numbers aren't enough: A plea for visualization

P. Runeson
Lund University, Lund, Sweden

CHAPTER OUTLINE

NUMBERS ARE GOOD, BUT...

Quantitative data comes with enormous possibilities for presenting key characteristics of the data in a very compressed form. Basic descriptive statistics, like mean and standard deviation, comprise thousands or millions of data points into single numbers. This is a very powerful tool when communicating quantitative data analyses. In contrast, qualitative data, with its focus on descriptions, words, and phrases does not come with such powerful tools, leading to wordy descriptions of the analysis. However, mean and standard deviation do not bring the full understanding of the underlying phenomenon, and not even the underlying distribution.

In data science for software engineering, we cannot trust numbers only, but need additional tools to analyze the data and communicate the findings and conclusions of the analysis. Visualization, or visual analytics, provides such a tool. Visualization combines the exactness and compactness of quantitative data with the richness and communication of qualitative communication. Thereby, both the analysis and interpretation of data can be improved.

CASE STUDIES ON VISUALIZATION

As examples of the use of visualization in data science for software engineering, we show two case studies on product scoping [1] and test selection [2], respectively.

PRODUCT SCOPING

Selecting which features to spend development resources on is a key task for product managers, referred to as product scoping. The product manager must decide which features to invest development effort in and which to exclude from the project. In order to analyze how well a company was able to identify the feasible set of features at an early stage for later development and release, researchers collected data on which features were selected for development. Further, they analyzed which features made it into the final release, and which were excluded during later stages of development, for example, due to changing market situations or competing products. Excluding features late in the process implies that development effort is wasted.

The researchers defined several relevant metrics. Basic ones include the average share of excluded features, and the time to birth and time to removal of a feature. However, the overall view was hard to communicate until they presented the feature survival chart, visualizing features and their status change in an x-y–diagram, see Fig. 1. The features are listed on the y axis—one row for each feature—and time and milestones are marked on the x axis. Feature status is color coded: red/dark

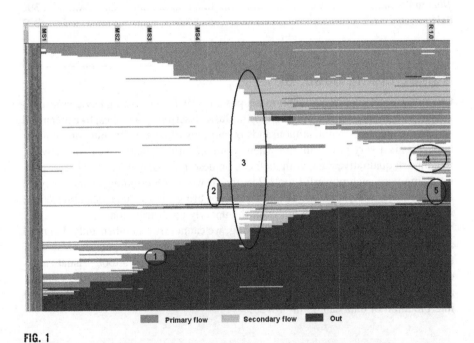

FIG. 1

Product scoping chart.

From Wnuk K, Regnell B, Karlsson L. What happened to our features? Visualization and understanding of scope change dynamics in a large-scale industrial setting. In Proceedings of the 17th IEEE international requirements engineering conference, 2009. p. 89–98.

for excluded features, and two shades of green/grey for inserted features, depending on the source of the feature request.

Through the visualization chart, managers got an overview of the scoping of features and were able to connect major decisions in the project to the scope, marked with numbers in Fig. 1, and further explained by Wnuk et al. [1]. For example, number 1 in Fig. 1 represents a significant scope reduction (features turning from green to red), related to a cancellation of the products from the product line. At number 3, new features were included, while others were excluded in parallel. This was the desired behavior at the company, since development resources were limited. On the contrary, at number 4, new features were included late in the project, which is related to significant risks. This analysis helped them rethink the scoping process to make it more efficient.

REGRESSION TEST SELECTION

Selecting test cases for regression testing of a new software version is the second case study on visualization. In a product-line project, there are several dimensions that are relevant to analyze to support the choice of regression tests, for example (1) levels of abstraction (unit, integration, system, etc.), (2) regression testing as the system evolves over time with new versions, and (3) testing over different product variants, sharing a common code base [3]. We collected data on a number of test cases, test case executions, failed tests, etc. However, for test designers and managers, none of these metrics were sufficient to support their regression test selection. The many dimensions made it hard to understand which test cases were run at which level, version, and variant.

We prototyped a visualization tool that enables the users to see multiple views of the data, and to combine several dimensions, see Fig. 2 for an example of a subset of an industrial software system [2]. Each dot represents one test coverage item, and the color coding signals the frequency of the metric under analysis, for example, the number of executed test cases. In this case, red means an insufficient number of test cases for the item under test, green means a sufficient number of test cases, and blue indicates the range in between. The example shows that version 3.0 was well tested in the system test, but insufficiently in the unit test. More unit testing and less system testing was conducted in versions 3.2 and 3.3, while integration testing remains the same across the releases.

We evaluated the tool in three industrial focus groups with experienced test managers and consultants. The users were generally in favor of the visualization prototype, while they provided detailed feedback on which data to visualize, and how. They wanted the x–y position to represent a meaning, and requested more dynamic interaction in the views than our prototype could manage.

These case studies clearly show the power of visualization. Graphs may help stakeholders get an overview of data, which is tailored to support their decisions. In the feature scoping case, some managers interpreted all descoped features as a waste, which might not be the case. The organization may have learned something

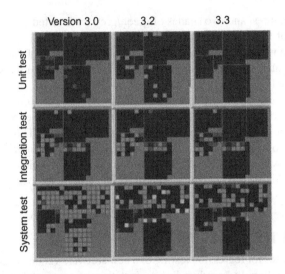

FIG. 2

Test coverage item overviews for test levels and software versions.

From Engström E, Mäntylä M, Runeson P, Borg M. Supporting regression test scoping with visual analytics. In Proceedings of the international conference on software testing, verification and validation, 2014. p. 283–92.

during the work with the feature, although the visualization clearly signals it as a waste. This message has to be brought together with the visualization, so the graphs are not over-interpreted.

WHAT TO DO

Based on the experience from our case studies, we conclude that visualizations help with analysis and interpretation of software engineering data. Thus, we recommend that practitioners:

1. *Create visualizations from data.* Visual representation of data helps interpret and communicate the collected data in software engineering data science. There is no standard visualization model that fits every purpose; it has to be adapted to the type of data, the audience, and the purpose of the visualization.

2. *Allow interactions in the graphs.* Once the visualizations are produced, the users start realizing the opportunities to interact with the graphs. In our cases, users asked for the ability to change views and select data subsets dynamically, in order to understand the situation. Thus, visualization should be considered a dynamic, not a static, view of collected data.

3. *Beware of the power of visualization.* Visualizations may give a stronger impression than is actually supported by the data. Thus, the visualization has to be discussed with the users to understand how they interpreted it, to enable any necessary adjustments.

These recommendations align with Shneiderman's classical visualization mantra: *Overview first, zoom and filter, then details-on-demand* [4].

REFERENCES

[1] Wnuk K, Regnell B, Karlsson L. What happened to our features? Visualization and understanding of scope change dynamics in a large-scale industrial setting. In: Proceedings of the 17th IEEE international requirements engineering conference; 2009. p. 89–98.

[2] Engström E, Mäntylä M, Runeson P, Borg M. Supporting regression test scoping with visual analytics. In: Proceedings of the international conference on software testing, verification and validation; 2014. p. 283–92.

[3] Runeson P, Engström E. Software product line testing—a 3D regression testing problem. In: Proceedings of 2nd international workshop on regression testing; 2012.

[4] Shneiderman B. The eyes have it: a task by data type taxonomy for information visualizations. In: Proceedings IEEE symposium on visual languages; 1996. p. 336–43.

Don't embarrass yourself: Beware of bias in your data

C. Bird

Microsoft Research, Redmond, WA, United States

CHAPTER OUTLINE

DEWEY DEFEATS TRUMAN

The 1948 U.S. presidential election proved to be one of the greatest blunders in applied statistics history.

As is often the case, many polls were conducted in the run up to the election. Gallup, still one of the most trusted polling organizations today, predicted that republican Thomas Dewey would handily defeat democrat Harry Truman. In fact, the press was so convinced by the "empirical evidence" that the Chicago Daily Tribune had already printed the first edition of the paper with the headline "Dewey Defeats Truman" before final election results were in (see Fig. 1). Unfortunately for them, the election results the next morning were anything but expected, as Truman had won the electoral vote with 303 votes to Dewey's 189. This was a landslide, of course, but in the opposite direction.

In the modern era of data collection and statistics, how could such a thing have happened? The answer lies not in the analysis of the data, but in the hidden biases it contained. Consider just one of many errors in the polling methodology. Like today, polling was conducted by selecting people randomly and contacting people via telephone. However, in 1948, telephones were mostly owned by individuals who were more financially well-off. At that time, those with higher income levels tended to lean republican. While the polling was indeed random, the population sampled (people that had telephones) was biased with respect to the entire voting population. Thus, any results drawn from the polling data were similarly biased. The problem

FIG. 1

The press was so sure that Dewey would win based on telephone polling that they printed results in the newspaper before official vote counts were completed!

has not completely been solved even today as certain demographics may be more likely to answer the phone or less likely to vote.

This is an interesting cautionary tale, but surely such a mistake couldn't happen in the 21st century on data drawn from software engineering…

IMPACT OF BIAS IN SOFTWARE ENGINEERING

A *biased* sample is a sample that is collected in such a way that some members of the intended population are less likely to be included than others. In layman's terms, a sample of data has bias if some characteristic in the population being sampled is significantly over or under-represented. Bias is usually a result of how the data is created, collected, manipulated, analyzed, or presented. As a trivial example, if you were measuring the height of students at a university and used the basketball team as your sample, the data would be biased and inaccurate because short students are much less likely to make the team. Any analysis and results arising from this data would also be biased, and most likely invalid. If bias is not recognized and accounted for, results can be erroneously attributed to the phenomenon under study rather than to the method of sampling.

Unfortunately, bias exists in software engineering data as well. If left unchecked and undetected, such bias in data can lead to misleading conclusions and incorrect predictions.

A few years ago [1], we examined defect data sets to determine if there was bias in the "links" between a defect in the defect database and the corresponding defect correcting change in the source code repository. Knowing which code changes fix which defects can be quite valuable because this can provide much more context about a code change, and also allows us to determine which prior code changes actually introduced a bug. It also allows us to see who is introducing the defects, who is correcting the defects, and what types of defects are corrected in different parts of the code base. Research has shown that this information can be used to learn characteristics of code changes that lead to defects or to teach machine learning methods to accurately predict where in the source code a defect is based only on the bug report. Because of the value of these "links," a long line of research exists on techniques to infer these links. See Sliwerski et al. for one of the most well-known examples [2]. In our study of these links in five software projects, we found that there was bias in the severity level of defects that could be linked to defects in four of the projects. That is, the lower the severity level for a fixed bug, the higher the likelihood that there was a link between the defect and the commit. As an extreme example, out of all defects labeled "minor" in the Apache Webserver that were indicated in the defect database to have been fixed, we were able to identify the corresponding fixing commit for 65% of them. In contrast, for those bugs in the category of "blocker" that were fixes, we were only able to find the fixing commit 15% of the time.

Fig. 2 shows the proportions for all projects. Note that AspectJ appears to suffer far less from bias in bug severity for links between defects and commits.

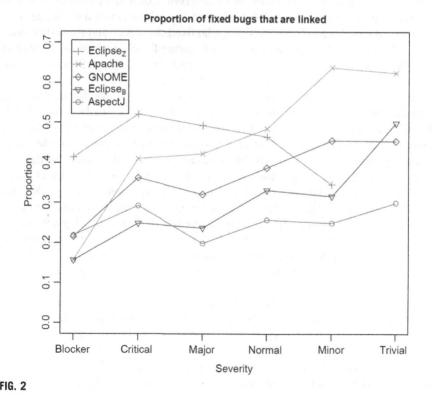

FIG. 2

Proportion of fixed bugs that are linked to corresponding source code changes ordered by severity for five bug data sets.

While we identified bias in the data, what's worse is that this bias appeared to affect the results of research that used the data. We used the linked defects and fixing commits to train a defect prediction model (a statistical model that would predict what parts of the code were most likely to contain defects). When we evaluated our prediction model, it was much better at predicting those defects that had lower severity than those that had higher severity. In practice, one would likely prefer a machine learning method that points to likely defective areas in the code to either be agnostic of the severity of the defects, or favor indicating locations with higher severity defects. We were getting the opposite due to bias in the data. Inadvertently using biased data can impact the quality of tools or models and the validity of empirical findings.

IDENTIFYING BIAS

The first step in avoiding the use of biased data is in determining if bias exists in the first place. This can be done via visualization or statistics, but often requires some a priori knowledge or expectations about the data as well. To do this, you first decide what *feature* you are interested in examining. A feature is any individual measurable property of the data or phenomenon being observed. Concretely, features of defects in a defect tracking system can include (but are certainly not limited to) the severity, how long it took for a defect to be fixed, who fixed the defect, and the textual summary of the defect. Features of a source code commit could include the number of lines in a change, the person that made the change, the type of file or files being changed, and whether a comment was added to the code.

In the best case scenario, you may have information about the distribution of an important feature in the population. In the study of defects, we had the severity levels for all fixed defects in a project. This forms our *population* distribution. We then compared that to the severity levels for fixed defects that we could find the corresponding commits for, our *sample* distribution. Generating histograms for the population and sample severity distributions is relatively easy to do in R or Excel, and if there is bias, it is often easy to spot them visually using such visualizations. One nice aspect of using histograms is that they work for both categorical *and* numerical data.

Statistically, one can compare distributions of categorical data using a Pearson's chi-squared test or a Fisher's exact test. Both are readily available in any statistical environment such as R, SPSS, or SAS. For numerical data, the Kolmogorov-Smirnov test (also called the K-S test) can tell you if there is a statistically significant difference between the two populations. Note that in all of these cases, the result of the test is a likelihood that the two distributions come from the same population (a so-called *p*-value). The tests *do not* indicate how the distributions differ (eg, which way a sample is biased or which category is over-represented). It is up to you to investigate further and determine what exactly the bias is and how extreme it is.

While statistics can help, it is important that you understand the data being collected and that you know what you expect to see in the data and why. In our study, we examined the way the development happened and that defects were fixed, and based on our knowledge of the projects, we believed that each defect that was fixed should have the same likelihood of being linked to a commit as any other. However, consider a software project where minor bugs are assigned to junior developers and their fixes must be reviewed by senior developers. In this case, it may make more sense that minor bugs would be explicitly linked to their commits (for review), and so our expectations would be that lower severity defects have a higher link rate. Understanding your data and the processes that it came from can aid greatly when examining your data visually or statistically for bias.

Unfortunately, you may not always have in-depth knowledge about some characteristic of your data. In the absence of information about the population, distributions from samples expected to be similar could be used. For instance, if you are examining the number of developers actively contributing to Python over the past year, you could compare the distribution of active developers this year to previous years for Python. You might also compare it to other projects that you consider to be similar to Python in some way, such as Perl or Ruby. For these types of comparisons, statistical tests are unlikely to provide much value, as the distributions will likely be different to some degree, and that may not indicate real bias. A visual inspection will help you determine if they are different enough to warrant further investigation.

If you lack any other distribution for comparison, the best approach is to calculate descriptive statistics from your sample, visualize the sample via histograms, PDFs, or boxplots, and make a judgement as to how well the distribution of a feature matches your expectations. If they differ widely, then either the data or your expectations are incorrect. In both cases, you should likely "dig in" and do some more manual investigation into where the data came from, how it was produced, and anything that may be out of the ordinary.

As a concrete example, consider an investigation into the impact of years of experience on the time to complete tasks in a software company. As part of this study, one would need to select one or more projects to investigate. Suppose that after selecting a project and gathering data, such as the experience of developers and the time taken to complete various tasks, the investigator wants to determine if there is any bias (and if so how much) in his data. One step would be to collect the years of experience from developers in the entire company (or from a purely random sample of developers). Putting the data into R and drawing a simple boxplot (shown in Fig. 3) will quickly show that the project selected is highly biased with respect to age of developers, and thus the findings may not generalize to the entire company. A Kolmogorov-Smirnov test in R also indicates that the sample is statistically different from the population of developers in the company.

ASSESSING IMPACT

Just because bias exists in a data set does not mean that the bias will have an impact on the results of using the data. In our study, we found that when defects used to train a model were biased with respect to severity, the predictions from the model were

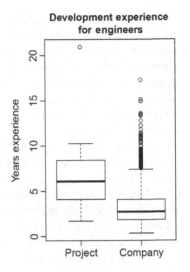

FIG. 3

Years of experience for all developers in the company compared to developers just in the project selected for a study.

also biased in a similar way. However, consider a defect model trained on defects that were fixed mostly (though not completely) on even days of the month (eg, Jan. 2, Oct. 24, etc.). While the data is biased with regard to the parity of the fix day, it is unlikely that such a model would do much better when evaluated on defects fixed on even days than on defects fixed on odd days.

How can we assess the impact of bias?

If we had access to all defects for all days, that would help. We could train one model on the biased sample and another on the larger, less-biased sample and look at the difference to assess the impact of the bias. However, usually if we have a biased sample, we don't have access to a larger, less-biased sample. In the absence of this less-biased sample, one approach is to select subsets of your sample such that they are biased in different ways. In the preceding example, we could remove all of the odd days so that the model is *only* trained on defects fixed on even days. Does the performance of this second model differ from the original model? What about training the model only on days that are multiples of four or ten? These are "super-biased" data sets. We could go the other way and create a subset from our sample that has the same number of defects fixed on odd and even days. Does a model trained on this data set perform differently? If we see (as I suspect we would), that the amount of "day parity" bias does not affect model results, then we may not need to worry about the bias. If in your investigations, you find that there *is* a feature (such as age of a developer, size of a commit, or date of a defect report) that is biased and that does effect the results of a study, accuracy of a model, or utility of a technique, you are not completely out of luck. This just means that the bias needs to be reported so that others consuming your research have all the salient facts they need.

WHICH FEATURES SHOULD I LOOK AT?

Having said all of this, an additional key question to ask is what features to examine for bias. Data collected from software repositories have nearly endless dimensions (features). A developer working on a project has an associated age, gender, experience level, education, location, employment history, marital status, etc. A code review has an author, a date, the contents of the changed code, the phase of the development cycle it occurs in, the files that are modified, and the number of lines changed. These are just a few of the features that exist for just a few of the artifacts that may be examined as part of a research endeavor. Exhaustively investigating bias for all possible features will take an inordinate amount of time and most of that time will be wasted.

A better approach is to start by reading related research and brainstorming those features that you hypothesize may be related to the outcome of interest. That is, if you are conducting a study related to collaboration of developers, identify those features whose bias you believe is most likely to impact results and validity. Next, identify those features that you can actually measure in your data (sadly, this often a much shorter list). Then rank these features and investigate them as outlined in this chapter. Whether or not you do find bias, be sure to report your investigation and the outcome in any publication, most often in a "Threats to Validity" or "Evaluation" section.

REFERENCES

[1] Bird C, Bachmann A, Aune E, Duffy J, Bernstein A, Filkov V, Devanbu D. Fair and balanced? Bias in bug-fix datasets. In: Proceedings of the ACM SIGSOFT foundations of software engineering. New York: ACM; 2009.
[2] Sliwerski J, Zimmermann T, Zeller A. When do changes induce fixes? On Fridays. In: Proceedings of the international workshop on mining software repositories; 2005.
[3] Friedenson B. Dewey defeats Truman and cancer statistics. J Natl Cancer Inst 2009; 101(16):1157.

Operational data are missing, incorrect, and decontextualized

A. Mockus

The University Of Tennessee, Knoxville, TN, United States

CHAPTER OUTLINE

BACKGROUND

Big data is upon us and the data scientist is the hottest profession. In software engineering, analyzing software development data from social networks, issue trackers, or version control systems is proliferating.

Data science is defined as generalizable extraction of knowledge from data [1]. While this definition sounds quite profound, how exactly does data science differ from traditional science? Traditional science extracts knowledge[1] [2]: data left as traces from operational support tools and then integrated with more traditional data. With many human activities increasingly transacted partially or entirely within the digital domain, voluminous traces of OD wait to be explored, understood, and used.

---

[1]By knowledge here we mean a useful model from experimental data. Data science, on the other hand, claims to be able to extract knowledge from all data and, in fact, many of the success stories of data science rely on operational data (OD).

It is quite tempting to apply a variety of statistical and machine learning techniques that have been refined on experimental data to OD, but pitfalls await as OD is not experimental data. The following three examples illustrate the principal drawbacks of OD: missing observations, incorrect data, and unidentified context.

EXAMPLES
MISSING DATA

During World War II, to minimize bomber losses to enemy fire, researchers from the Center for Naval Analyses conducted a study of the damage done to aircraft that had returned from missions, and recommended that armor be added to the areas that showed the most damage. Statistician Wald pointed out that only aircraft that had survived were observed and proposed to reinforce the areas with no damage, since planes hit in such areas would be lost. We will revisit this example later, but the key lesson is that many of the events observed in software development, such as defects, are contingent on numerous factors, such as the extent of software use and the ability of users to report issues, that are typically not observed. More defects reported by users, consequently, yet counter-intuitively, tend to indicate better quality software.

HOW TO AUGMENT?

The simplest way to measure the defectiveness of software as perceived by end users is to normalize the number of user reported defects by the extent of use as, for example, described in [3]. The extent of use may be more easily and readily available for common software delivered as a service. Other types of events may need similar normalization. For example, a code commit, or a joining of a new participant, should be considered in the context of what is not observed, such as commits that could have been made and the pool of potentially interested and capable participants who chose not to join. A discussion as follows suggests techniques that could be used to augment the OD with critical missing pieces.

INCORRECT DATA

In a large telecommunication equipment company with a large customer support business, the reliability of systems is critical because technicians need to be dispatched at great expense to repair the broken parts. When flash memory cards began to be used instead of CDs for system installation and operation, it was noticed that service technicians tended to replace a large number of flash cards: a number tens of times larger than would have been expected based on the flash card manufacturer specifications. A natural reaction would have been to confront the manufacturer and demand compensation for not meeting the specs. However, the reliability obtained based on the number of flash cards replaced is obviously wrong for someone understanding how service technicians work. Many of the problems in complex systems are transient or hard to reproduce, and replacing the flash card is the simplest step a technician can do. If the system operates normally after the replacement, technicians do not have time or tools to prove that the culprit was indeed a failed flash card. While the services OD clearly indicates how many flash cards were replaced because of failure, this data is incorrect if used to assess the reliability of the flash card. Virtually all of OD in software engineering is similarly incorrect. For example, a developer may fix a bug and declare it to be so, but often they fix another bug or cause the symptom of the bug to disappear under certain conditions. It is not unusual to see the same bug being fixed many times over for many years until, if ever, the ultimate fix is implemented.

HOW TO CORRECT?

The OD record cannot be taken at face value. It can only get meaning from the understanding of what the actor thought (and did not think), knew (and did not know), and did (and did not do) at the time the event was recorded. Fortunately, the behavior of individuals and groups have regularities. Identifying such regularities and using them to fix problematic data can be done as described in, for example [4].

DECONTEXTUALIZED DATA

Some interesting metabolic theories, for example, allometric scaling [5], postulate a relationship between the body size and the heart rate. Measures of heart rate and sizes of animals are observed from tiny mice to huge elephants and a relationship is found to be $\frac{3}{4}$ power law. Obviously, comparing animals of such diverse sizes is certainly an interesting intellectual activity and, in this particular case, it may reveal some fundamental aspects of animal metabolism. Similarly, in software development, people's productivity, source code files, and software projects vary greatly in size with scales that differ by much more than the size of mice versus elephant. These artifacts of disparate sizes are recorded the same in the operational support tools: a file with 10 million lines is treated the same as a file with one line or as a binary file where the lines of code are not even meaningful. Unlike in the example of a grand unifying metabolism theory noted herein, it often makes absolutely no sense to treat these disparate files, defects, projects, and other artifacts as being of the same nature. The only aspect that unifies them is that they are recorded the same way by operational support tools, but otherwise have no inherent relationship that is worth theorizing about.

HOW TO IDENTIFY CONTEXT

A basic understanding on the types of activities (fixing, branching) and roles (developer, tester, and builder) in conjunction with how these activities and roles may be reflected in the specific event patterns can provide a way to contextualize events. More generally, the example illustrates that stratifying OD into different groups is a problem-specific exercise.

A LIFE OF A DEFECT

Software defects are of concern to developers and users. The next few paragraphs will draw attention to identifying missing data and adjusting the analysis accordingly, identifying inaccurate values and correcting them, and in segmenting the events into "mice" and "elephants" in the context of software defects.

If we observe a defect fixed in a file, it is instructive to think what had to happen for this to occur. First, the event is predicated on someone running, testing, or building the software. For vast majority of FLOSS project repositories hosted on major forges such as GitHub, that premise is not likely. We should not be surprised that most projects do not have any fixes or, even more extremely, claim that these projects are more error-free than projects with bug fixes. Even when this premise is satisfied, the user has to be motivated and capable enough to report the issue and do it in a way that allows developers to reproduce and fix it [6]. Once the issue is reported, the fix is predicated on developers' willingness to pay attention to it and having the spare time to do it, as well as the issue being important enough to be worth the effort needed to fix it. This reasoning suggests that fixed issues depend on existence of an experienced user base and active development community. For example, the issues that end up being fixed may not be the ones that inexperienced users encounter, or the chances of them being fixed may depend on how busy the developer community may be at a particular point in time.

In addition to the factors noted herein, the issues would not "get fixed" if the developer does not note the issue in a commit message [7]. Different developers and different types of issues are likely to result in different chances of the issue ID being noted. Unfortunately, these are just a small list of problems related to missing data in a single domain: the count of fixed issues.

For the same domain, let's see how issues may be "incorrect." For example, an important part of the issue is the affected component of the system: it is often very difficult for issue reporters to get it right [8,9]. The fix date for an issue may not accurately represent its actual fix date [4]. Finally, the issue description may be often incorrect. An extreme example involved highly reliable software where, under mysterious conditions, a certain table was filling up too fast, causing the system to restart. Via simple search of past fixes, I found a fix describing exactly the same problem that was delivered to a major customer six months earlier. Celebration? Alas, even though the fix mentioned the right table, it was actually a fix for a different table, and was unrelated to the problem at hand. Why was the description incorrect? It was written by the issue reporter and, even though the developer fixed it, there was no compelling reason to change the description. Analysis of serious defects related to a synchronization issue revealed fixes spanning seven years [10] all claiming to have fixed the issues for the problem to reappear again. Basic techniques to use natural constraints to identify and correct some errors in issue data are described in [4].

As noted herein, an issue reported by one person may not be an issue for another person. This maxim holds even stronger when comparing distinct projects. It is therefore surprising to think that a defect discovered and fixed for, for example, flight control software, would be in any way similar to a layout issue for a specific Java-Script framework. Similarly, an issue in Bugzilla used to track code inspection results is probably quite unlike any issues used to report a security vulnerability. In both of these cases, the same or similar operational support tool (issue tracker) is used, but the fact that all trackable items in an issue tracker are "issues," does not provide a mandate to put them into the same category and analyze deep relationships, as in the case of the metabolic theory.

WHAT TO DO?

The three examples point out key differences between OD and experimental data. In order to apply the wealth of techniques developed for experimental data, we first need to bring OD to the quality standards associated with experimental data. It is helpful to think about OD as precise but tricky-to-use measurement apparatus. As with any precise instruments that need extensive tuning and calibration, opportunities for misuse abound. Having a clear understanding of how OD came to be and developing practices on how to use it effectively are essential. Unlike instruments measuring natural phenomena, this apparatus works on traces left by operational support tools, and, as the activities involving these tools change and the tools evolve, the measurement apparatus will have to be updated or the measurements will lose accuracy.

The examples justify "the 98% of the effort spent that goes into data preparation and data cleaning activities that precede data analysis." While it is impossible to describe all possible traps that await an eager explorer of the OD, there are a number of steps that can (and should) be taken to address some of the issues noted in various publications, for example [11,12].

Typically, the first step is to understand how the OD get recorded. The best approach is to select a sample of actors to observe them doing their work and then compare to what has been recorded. If it is not possible to observe the action directly, the actors can be identified from the OD and asked about the recorded events and our interpretations of what they mean. OD that cannot be subject to validation cannot be trusted for any downstream analysis.

Fortunately, narrowing the domain to software engineering in general and focusing on common developer actions such as code commits and issue handling can bring the necessary understanding on how to interpret the recorded events, how to model behavior in order to identify and correct inaccuracies, and how to separate events by context. Unfortunately, none of these tasks is trivial, for example, separating defects by priority inferred from the number of users affected [13] or a data-driven way to add context as done in, for example [14]. This is what makes OD such an interesting area to play with and in which to make discoveries.

REFERENCES

[1] Dhar V. Data science and prediction. Commun ACM 2013;56(12):64–73.

[2] Mockus A. Engineering big data solutions. In: ICSE'14 FOSE; 2014.

[3] Hackbarth R, Mockus A, Palframan J, Sethi R. Customer quality improvement of software systems. IEEE Softw 2015;99:1.

[4] Zheng Q, Mockus A, Zhou M. A method to identify and correct problematic software-activity data: exploiting capacity constraints and data redundancies. In: ESEC/FSE'15. Bergamo: ACM; 2015.

[5] West GB, Brown JH, Enquist BJ. A general model for the origin of allometric scaling laws in biology. Science 1997;276(5309):122–6.

[6] Zhou M, Mockus A. What make valuable contributors: willingness and opportunity in OSS community. IEEE Trans Softw Eng 2015;41(1):82–99.

[7] Bachmann A, Bird C, Rahman F, Devanbu P, Bernstein A. The missing links: bugs and bug-fix commits. In: Proceedings of the eighteenth ACM SIGSOFT international symposium on foundations of software engineering. New York: ACM; 2010. p. 97–106.

[8] Xie J, Zhengand Q, Zhou M, Mockus A. Product assignment recommender. In: ICSE'14 demonstrations; 2014.

[9] Xie J, Zhou M, Mockus A. Impact of triage: a study of Mozilla and Gnome. In: ESEM'13; 2013.

[10] Shihab E, Mockus A, Kamei Y, Adams B, Hassan AE. High-impact defects: a study of breakage and surprise defects. In: Proceedings of the nineteenth ACM SIGSOFT symposium and the thirteenth European conference on foundations of software engineering, ESEC/FSE'11. New York: ACM; 2011. p. 300–10.

[11] Mockus A. Software support tools and experimental work. In: Basili V, et al., editors. Empirical software engineering issues: critical assessments and future directions. LNCS 4336. New York: Springer; 2007. p. 91–9.

[12] Mockus A. Missing data in software engineering. In: Singer J, et al., editors. Guide to advanced empirical software engineering. New York: Springer; 2008. p. 185–200.

[13] Mockus A, Fielding RT, Herbsleb J. Two case studies of open source software development: Apache and Mozilla. ACM Trans Softw Eng Methodol 2002;11(3):1–38.

[14] Zhang F, Mockus A, Keivanloo I, Zou Y. Towards building a universal defect prediction model with rank transformed predictors. Empir Software Eng 2015;1–39.

Data science revolution in process improvement and assessment?

M. Oivo

University of Oulu, Oulu, Finland

In God we trust, all others bring data. This legendary statement from quality guru W. Edwards Deming has been used and quoted countless times in motivating and justifying the role of data in software process improvement (SPI). It is now more relevant than ever, but data science has the potential to revolutionize the collection and analysis of data in SPI.

Deming was promoting statistical process control. His thinking in the famous plan-do-check-act (PDCA) cycle is based on planning improvement actions, implementing them, measuring the effect, and then acting accordingly. In PDCA, we predefine actions, and consequently we predefine what we want to measure. This predefined data is used to guide improvement actions. The fundamental change that data science can bring about is that we are now able to analyze large amounts of data and draw conclusions based on that data without having preplanned the data collection specifically for predefined actions or items.

There have been SPI methods and solutions since the 1980s. Assessment-based SPI approaches collect and analyze data with predefined methods. They have been popular since the introduction of the SEI's capability maturity model (CMM) in the late 1980s, and its successor, the capability maturity model integration (CMMI), since 2000. An international standard for process assessment and improvement (ISO/IEC 15504) is another key approach. The automobile industry has been an active user of ISO/IEC 15504 and has its own version called Automotive SPICE.

The assessment process is based on a predefined data collection, which occurs mainly in the form of document analysis and interviews. The basic idea behind assessment methods is using a reference model to which the processes of an organization can be compared. Process capability or organizational maturity is determined based on an assessment of the processes of the organization. Improvement recommendations are made based on the assessment results, aiming at higher capability and maturity levels as defined in the model. The data collection is predefined by the process model and practices of the assessment method.

There were some research efforts as early as in the 1990s attempting to integrate assessments with measurements in order to automate at least part of the data collection process and to enable a continuous assessment that could replace or complement regular assessments that are done only after relatively long intervals. One of the key problems of automatic data gathering is that there is a lot of data, and it is unstructured, incomplete, and often hard to get. Assessments require precise and complete data. Strikingly—does this sound familiar to data scientists who are used to working with large amounts of data that is unstructured, not perfect and not precise? They are, however, still able to analyze the big data and draw useful conclusions.

So why not use data science in assessments? Would it be sufficient for process improvement to have the big picture in an assessment that is based on the analysis of unstructured big data to complement the traditional assessment that digs into all the nitty-gritty details of every project that happens to be in the focus of the assessment? Would it be better if all the projects were in the focus of an assessment using data science rather than thoroughly analyzing a sample of only a few projects? Could we replace the traditional aim for accuracy that uses a (small) sample in the assessment with company-wide coverage of all projects with big data approaches? Would the results actually be more accurate this way?

The traditional problem with SPI is the lack of evidence of the effect of improvement actions. It is very difficult, if not impossible, to show with hard evidence what the benefits of certain SPI actions are. Real life is complicated, and the effects of SPI are mixed with a myriad of other events in companies. Proving the causality of SPI actions and quantitative improvements is extremely tough. Finding correlations is often the only thing we can do. But wait a minute! Isn't this exactly what data science is doing? Could SPI learn something from data science? Would it be okay sometimes to find good enough correlations rather than attempting to find evasive but accurate causations of SPI actions? Would it be enough to know "what" is happening or to predict what will happen after improvement actions, rather than trying to accurately know "why" it is happening?

There is already a wealth of experience in using data science in business intelligence. Big data may even be considered as a "hype term." Data science has also been used in business process improvement. SPI has many similarities with business process improvement and can benefit from the experiences in business processes.

Software development produces a lot of data from tools like issue tracking systems, version control systems, test data, code, documents, and so on. The amount of data available explodes with recording keyboards, voice recording, and video recording. This kind of data may not have any structure and can include just about anything, but it is potentially useful for big data analytics. Surely we will face similar privacy issues as with most big data applications that use personal data. Despite these challenges, the payback may be considerably high.

Another area in which data science has not yet reached its potential is the use of customer data to guide and improve the products and software development processes. The game industry and Internet companies are pioneering these approaches. By launching games or services in limited customer segments, they quickly collect usage data and user experiences to improve their products and software processes.

Traditional SPI tries to define processes in order to optimize them. However, it is often challenging to distinguish between official defined processes and actual processes used in practice. An alternative is to deduce the software processes from the data gathered from actual software development, resulting in a description of the actual process, not just the official or desired process. This data can also be used to analyze the workflows and identify bottlenecks.

Many of the SPI methods are based mainly on analyzing the past and making an assessment and improvement recommendations based on that analysis. However, what we really need is to know the future. We would like to predict what will happen in our future endeavors or estimate the effort required for software development. This is where predictive analytics and estimation methods come into play. We already have a growing community of researchers who work on analyzing large amounts of software engineering data to learn from it and to predict what will happen in software development if we take certain actions. These analysis methods go far beyond the simple postmortem analysis.

An interesting trend is the use of large cross-project and open source repositories for analyzing software engineering data and drawing conclusions from that data. Several such repositories have emerged. One example of the promising repositories is the PROMISE dataset (http://openscience.us/repo/), which includes data from hundreds of projects. It aims to serve as a long-term repository for software engineering data that researchers worldwide can use. Good examples of the use of such data include defect and cost modeling, which are used for prediction and estimation.

Correlation is not causation (or, when not to scream "Eureka!")

T. Menzies

North Carolina State University, Raleigh, NC, United States

CHAPTER OUTLINE

WHAT NOT TO DO

Legend has it that Archimedes once solved a problem sitting in his bathtub. Crying *Eureka!* ("I have it!"), Archimedes leapt out of the bath and ran to tell the king about the solution. Legend does not say if he stopped to get dressed first.

When we stumble onto some pattern in the data, it is so tempting to send a *Eureka!* text to the business users. This is a natural response that stems from the excitement of doing science and discovering an effect that no one has ever seen before.

Here's my warning: don't do it. At least, don't do it straight away.

I say this because I have often fallen into the trap of *correlation is not causation*. Which is to say, just because some connection pattern has been observed between variables does not necessarily imply that a real-world causal mechanism has been discovered. In fact, that "pattern" may actually just be an accident—a mere quirk of cosmic randomness.

EXAMPLE

For an example of nature tricking us and offering a "pattern" where, in fact, no such pattern exists, consider the following two squares (see Fig. 1). (This example comes from Norvig.) One of these was generated by people pretending to be a coin toss

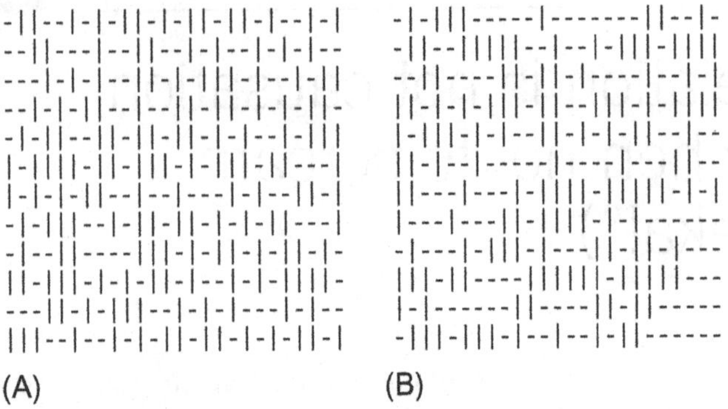

```
-||--|-|-||-|-||-||-|--|-|      -|-|||-----|--------||--|-
--||---|--||--|-|--|-|-|--      -||--||||||--|---|-|||-||||
---|-|-|--||-|-|||-|--|-||      --||----||-||-|-----|--|-|
--|-|-||--|--||-||-|-|-||-      ||-|-|-|||-||--|||-|-||||
-|-||--||-||-||-|-|--|-|||      |-|||-|-|--||-|-|-||-|--
|-||||-||-|||-|-|||-||---|      ||-|--|-----|----|---||--
|-|-|-||--|--|---|-|--||-|      ||---|---|-||||-|||||-|-|
-|-|||--|-||-||-|-|-||---|      |---|---||-||||-|-|-----
-|-||-----|||-|-||-|-||-|-      -|---|-|||-|---||-||-|---
||-|||-|-|-||-|--|-|-||||      |||-||----|||||-|||||---
---||-|-|||--|-|-|---|-|--      |-|-----||-----||-|-----
|||--|--|-|-||-||-|-|-||-|      -|||-|||-|-|--|--|-||-----
```

(A)   (B)

FIG. 1

Coin toss patterns (which one is truly random?)

while the others were generated by actually tossing a coin, then writing vertical and horizontal marks for heads or tails.

Can you tell which one is really random? Clearly, not (B) since it has too many long runs of horizontal and vertical marks. But hang on—is that true? If we toss a coin 300 times, then at probability 1/4, 1/8, 1/16, 1/32 we will get a run of the same mark that is three, four, five, or six ticks long (respectively). Now $1/32 \times 300 = 9$ so in (B), we might expect several runs that are at least six ticks long. That is, these "patterns" of long ticks in (B) are actually just random noise.

EXAMPLES FROM SOFTWARE ENGINEERING

Sadly, there are many examples in SE of data scientists uncovering "patterns" which, in retrospect, were more "jumping at shadows" than discovering some underlying causal mechanism. For example, Shull et al. reported one study at NASA's Software Engineering Laboratory that "discovered" a category of software that seemed inherently most bug prone. The problem with that conclusion was that, while certainly true, it missed an important factor. It turns out that particular subsystem was the one deemed least critical by NASA. Hence, it was standard policy to let newcomers work on that subsystem in order to learn the domain. Since such beginners make more mistakes, then it is hardly surprising that this particular subsystem saw the most errors.

For another example, Kocaguneli et al. had to determine which code files were created by a distributed or centralized development process. This, in turn, meant mapping files to their authors, and then situating some author in a particular building in a particular city and country. After weeks of work they "discovered" that a very small number of people seemed to have produced most of the core changes to certain Microsoft products. Note that if this was the reality of work at Microsoft, it would mean that product quality would be most assured by focusing more on this small core group of programmers.

However, that conclusion was completely wrong. Microsoft is a highly optimized organization that takes full advantage of the benefits of auto-generated code. That generation occurs when software binaries are being built and, at Microsoft, that build process is controlled by a small number of skilled engineers. As a result, most of the files appeared to be "owned" by these build engineers even though these files are built from code provided by a very large number of programmers working across the Microsoft organization. Hence, Kocaguneli had to look elsewhere for methods to improve productivity at Microsoft.

WHAT TO DO

Much has been written on how to avoid spurious and misleading correlations to lead to bogus "discoveries." Basili and Easterbrook and colleagues advocate a "top-down" approach to data analysis where the collection process is controlled by research questions, and where those questions are defined *before* data collection.

The advantage of "top-down" is that you never ask data "what have you got?"—a question that can lead to the "discovery" of bogus patterns. Instead, you only ask "have you got X?" where "X" was defined before the data was collected.

In practice, there are many issues with top-down, not the least of which is that in SE data analytics, we are often processing data that was collected for some other purpose than our current investigation. And when we cannot control data collection, we often have to ask the open-ended question "what is there?" rather than the top-down question of "is X there?"

In practice, it may be best to mix up top-down with some "look around" inquires:

- Normally, before we look at the data, there are questions we think are important and issues we want to explore.
- After contact with the data, we might find that other issues are actually more important and that other questions might be more relevant and answerable.

In defense of a little less top-down analysis, I note that many important accidental discoveries might have been overlooked if researchers restricted themselves to just the questions defined before data collection. Here is a list of discoveries, all made by researchers pursuing other goals:

- North America (by Columbus)
- Penicillin
- Radiation from the big bang
- Cardiac pacemakers (the first pacemaker was a badly built cardiac monitor)
- X-ray photography
- Insulin
- Microwave ovens
- Velcro
- Teflon
- Vulcanized rubber
- Viagra

IN SUMMARY: WAIT AND REFLECT BEFORE YOU REPORT

My message is *not* that data miners are useless algorithms that torture data until they surrender some spurious conclusion. By asking open-ended "what can you see?" questions, our data miners can find unexpected novel patterns that are actually true and useful—even if those patterns fly in the face of accepted wisdom. For example, Schmidt and Lipson's Eureqa machine can learn models that make no sense (with respect to current theories of biology), yet can make accurate predictions on complex phenomena (eg, ion exchanges between living cells).

But, while data miners can actually produce useful models, sometimes they make mistakes. So, my advice is:

- Always, always, always, wait a few days.
- Most definitely, *do not* confuse business users with such recent raw results.

In summary, do not rush to report the conclusions that you just uncovered, just this morning. For example, in the case of the Kocaguneli et al. study, if a little more time had been taken reading the raw data, then they would have found the files written by the core group all had funny auto-generated names (eg, "S0001.h"). This would have been a big clue that something funny was happening here.

And while you wait, critically and carefully review how you reached that result. See if you can reproduce it using other tools and techniques or, at the very least, implement your analysis a second time using the same tools (just to check if the first result came from some one-letter typo in your scripts).

REFERENCES

[1] Basili VR. Software modeling and measurement: the goal/question/metric paradigm: Technical report. College Park, MD: University of Maryland; 1992.

[2] Easterbrook S, Singer J, Storey M-A, Damian D. Selecting empirical methods for software engineering research. In: Guide to advanced empirical software engineering. London: Springer; 2008. p. 285–311.

[3] Kocaguneli E, Zimmermann T, Bird C, Nagappan N, Menzies T. Distributed development considered harmful? In: Proceedings of the 2013 international conference on software engineering (ICSE '13). Piscataway, NJ: IEEE Press; 2013. p. 882–90.

[4] Norving P. Warning signs in experimental design and interpretation, http://goo.gl/x0rI2.

[5] Schmidt M, Lipson H. Distilling free-form natural laws from experimental data. Science 2009;324(5923):81–5.

[6] Shull F, Mendoncaa MG, Basili V, Carver J, Maldonado JC, Fabbri S, et al. Knowledge-sharing issues in experimental software engineering. Empir Softw Eng 2004;9 (1–2):111–37.

Software analytics for small software companies: More questions than answers

R. Robbes

University of Chile, Santiago, Chile

CHAPTER OUTLINE

Software analytics have been shown to be useful for many use cases. Examples are numerous, and many of these are mentioned in this book. Software analytics have also been successfully applied in the industry. Again, the examples are numerous. But these examples share one characteristic: they come mostly from large software companies. For instance, Microsoft has a dedicated research group studying its software engineering practice [1], so does Google, or ABB. However, most software companies are small: Richardson and Wangenheim estimated that 85% of software companies had fewer than 50 employees, as of 2007 [2].

These small companies face a different reality than large software companies. They do not have so many resources to allocate to long-term projects, being instead more focused on the short-term. Should software analytics also attempt to address these cases? Should practitioners in these companies take an interest in the topic? If the answers to these questions are far from clear, we bring some elements to the discussion, taking examples from the Chilean software industry as a basis. We particularly focus on the example of Amisoft, a small Chilean software company that successfully used software analytics [3].

THE REALITY FOR SMALL SOFTWARE COMPANIES

Small software companies have different factors that must be taken into account in order to successfully apply software analytics. We identified the following main factors:

- Software projects taken by small software companies may be smaller and shorter than the ones taken by larger companies, limiting the amount of data available.
- The goals and needs of small software companies may be different than the ones in large software companies.
- Resources in small companies are always very tight.

Despite these factors, software analytics could be very important for these companies. Taking the example of Chile, we know that small software companies suffer from a high mortality. Certainly, analytics could be helpful there.

SMALL SOFTWARE COMPANIES PROJECTS: SMALLER AND SHORTER

The Diagnostic Report of the Chilean Software and Services Industry mandated by the GECHS (the Chilean Association of Software and Services Companies) reports on the reality faced by 40 software companies in Chile [4]. Among other findings, companies that were working on projects for clients had project durations of 6 months or less. Service contracts were of similar lengths. Companies developing products did so, in a large majority of cases, in less than a year. A recent survey by the GEMS project found similar results.

The consequences of this is that shorter projects have necessarily much less data to provide for software analytics approaches. If an approach needs at least two years of data to be effective, it will not be applicable in the context of many software companies. Unfortunately, this evaluation criteria is often not present in the evaluation of many Software Analytics or Mining Software Repositories' approaches. Evaluations are generally seen as much more convincing if they involve large-scale projects.

While a few mining software repositories (MSR) approaches (such as the work of Zimmermann et al. [5]) did some evaluation of the technique's performance over time as part of a comprehensive evaluation, it is very uncommon to see this. Further, these approaches did show that a certain amount of time (either measured by amount of time or amount of commits) was necessary for the approaches to reach good performance, telling us that performance with a low amount of data should not be taken for granted, and should definitely be evaluated explicitly. This leads us to formulate this requirement for the design and evaluation of software analytics approaches:

Software Analytics approaches should consider the cases where little data is available, and be evaluated in these cases, so that practitioners in these situations have an idea of the performance they can expect.

DIFFERENT GOALS AND NEEDS

We know of one Chilean small company, Amisoft, that made use of software analytics [3]. Our interview with them was insightful on the differences in priorities between what a large company such as Microsoft needs, and what a small company such as Amisoft needed. We found the overlap between information needs at Amisoft, and the ones at Microsoft [6], to be narrow: of the 17 indicators found to be of interest at Microsoft by Buse and Zimmermann, only three were similar to indicators in use at Amisoft.

Amisoft keeps track of a variety of indicators (for more detail, see [3]), most important of which are how closely the progress follows its expected schedule. Amisoft tracks metrics such as requirement volatility, adherence to its specified process, percentage of time spent on various types of tasks, functional tests and crashes, and client satisfaction. Of note, a significant portion of the data is collected manually (based on employee time sheets) and consolidated manually by project managers and a dedicated data analyst. Amisoft does not collect detailed metrics about the usage of the version control system and the bug tracker (although these tools are in use).

Of course, we cannot answer for all companies based on one datapoint. However, we found that project-level indicators were much more interesting for the CEO than low-level indicators, as could be found in the software repositories that are often mined. To paraphrase the CEO: "I don't really have a need for an approach that tells me where the bugs are. I know that the database access component is the most risky already, hence I personally review changes to it already." Needless to say, actually deploying a defect prediction approach may still have an impact, particularly to reveal other defect-prone modules that are not as prevalent.

However, the CEO particularly appreciated that the approach that Amisoft implemented, based on following higher-level tasks described in the process that they were using, gave him and his project managers far better visibility into their progress. This helped them react much more quickly to delays, and avoid the "heroic" rushes before deadlines that can lead to developer burnout. It also helped them negotiate much more comfortable schedules with their clients, "building in" the estimate for the most likely delays, avoiding that the delay be shown to clients.

As such: *Software analytics for small companies may need to reassess what the most optimal data sources and insights needed are.*

Perhaps a systematic treatment of the issue is needed. The work on information needs of Buse and Zimmermann came a long way toward documenting the needs and perceptions of actual software engineers at Microsoft. A similar study in the context of small software companies could lead to a much more accurate view of what practitioners in small companies need.

WHAT TO DO ABOUT THE DEARTH OF DATA?

We can think of two approaches to address the lack of data for short-term projects. The first is to use finer-grained data: while a single commit in a version control repository gives a single data point, developer interaction data recorded while people use their development tools record hundreds. This can be helpful to paint a higher quality picture of the development sooner, and hence make recommender systems helpful earlier (one of our studies provides evidence of this [7]). Fine-grained interaction data also allows developer to focus on self-improvement via personal feedback. Codealike [8] is a commercial tool geared towards practitioners that collects interaction data from the IDE and the web to provide actionable information to individual developers, and small teams. Codealike uses this data to provide developers dashboards with a variety of information, including analyzing in which activities time was spent, technical debt analysis, and, at the team level, predicting whether an interruption to a given developer will be okay or too disruptive.

The other approach is to use data from other projects, instead of the current project where data might be lacking. Cross-project defect prediction is, for instance, an active area of research, where significant progress has been made to predict defects on projects that have little or no history [9]. Work has been performed in effort estimation as well (which is a topic probably closer to small companies' interests than defect prediction). It remains to be seen how practical these approaches are, and whether other tasks highly relevant to small software companies can be solved in the same way.

WHAT TO DO ON A TIGHT BUDGET?

We'll close this chapter by briefly considering the resources needed to use analytics. Again, as little is known so far, we'll focus on the example of Amisoft. Amisoft's CEO found that the cost of implementing the program was worthwhile in his experience. The upfront cost was relatively high, since a full-time employee (out of 43 at the time) was focused on the project for 3 months, with the CEO himself dedicating significant time (3.5% of the workforce). Once the program was set up, the impact on individual employees was estimated to be 1 h a week of manual data gathering (which could be reduced with more automation), with the full-time employee staying on to consolidate and analyze the data. We also note that this was possible due to the previous effort in the company to formalize the development process: there would not have been anything to measure before that.

In case this appears too high, a lighter-weight entry in analytics would be the individual feedback offered by tools such as Codealike: data collection is entirely automatic, the only thing needed is the discipline to regularly check the dashboards produced by the tool. The only uncertainty is whether insights provided by the tool would align with the insights needed in a small company (they certainly seem to be useful at the developer level).

REFERENCES

[1] Bird C, Murphy B, Nagappan N, Zimmermann T. Empirical software engineering at Microsoft Research. In: Proceedings of CSCW 2010; 2011. p. 143–50.

[2] Richardson I, Von Wangenheim CG. Guest editors' introduction: why are small software organizations different? IEEE Softw 2007;24(1):18–22.

[3] Robbes R, Vidal R, Cecilia Bastarrica M. Are software analytics efforts worthwhile for small companies? The case of Amisoft. IEEE Softw 2013;30(5):46–53, http://users. dcc.uchile.cl/~rrobbes/p/SOFTWARE-analytics.pdf. Also available online.

[4] Sexto Diagnóstico de la Industria Nacional de Software y Servicios, http://bligoo.com/media/users/0/32814/files/GECHS-6o_informe_diagnostico.pdf; 2008.

[5] Zimmermann T, Weißgerber P, Diehl S, Zeller A. Mining version histories to guide software changes. IEEE Trans Software Eng 2005;31(6):429–45.

[6] Buse RPL, Zimmermann T. Information needs for software development analytics. In: Proceedings of ICSE 2012; 2012. p. 987–96.

[7] Robbes R, Pollet D, Lanza M. Logical coupling based on fine-grained change information. In: Proceedings of WCRE 2008; 2008. p. 42–6.

[8] Codealike. https://codealike.com.

[9] Zhang F, Mockus A, Keivanloo I, Zou Y. Towards building a universal defect prediction model. In: Proceedings of MSR 2014; 2014. p. 182–91.

Software analytics under the lamp post (or what star trek teaches us about the importance of asking the right questions)

N. Medvidovic*, A. Orso[†]

University of Southern California, Los Angeles, CA, United States* Georgia Institute of Technology, Atlanta, GA, United States[†]

CHAPTER OUTLINE

PROLOGUE

In "Remember Me," an episode of *Star Trek: The Next Generation*, Dr. Beverly Crusher does not realize that, due to a science experiment gone awry, she has ended up inside a space-time disturbance. After a series of unexpected and, to her, unexplainable events, she tries to calm herself and assess her situation so that she can find a way out of it. Thinking back over what has transpired, Dr. Crusher states: "If there's nothing wrong with me, maybe there's something wrong with the universe!"

This was an easy conclusion to make in that it did not require Dr. Crusher to question her assumptions. However, it was an extreme conclusion, and in this instance, obviously the wrong one. Yet, as a scientist, frustrated by her inability to understand the observations she has made inside the space-time disturbance (ie, the data she collected "with her own eyes and ears," with her handheld tricorder, and via the countless sensors on the starship enterprise), she actually considered this possibility. Fortunately, the episode had to be concluded in 45 min and, as always, one of the main characters had to be saved. Otherwise, Dr. Crusher might still be trying to resolve her predicament based on incomplete data, lack of awareness of the precipitating event, and analysis of the available data from the wrong perspective—she was unaware that she got pulled into the space-time disturbance and that, in the world of Star Trek at least, the usual laws of physics did not apply there.

How does this relate to software analytics? Very closely, actually! First, we are practitioners of one of Herb Simon's "sciences of the artificial," meaning that we cannot rely on laws of physics or their analogs to help us understand the phenomena we are studying. Second, very often, we do not understand the precipitating events for the phenomena in which we are interested, either because that data was never recorded or because nobody actually realized at the time that they had encountered something important. Third, despite the seemingly huge amounts of data we can now collect about a system (the humans who built it, the bugs that were in it, and so on), by definition that data is incomplete; we are often looking for "second-order events" because the actual phenomena in which we are interested have not been recorded or are altogether unobservable (eg, we routinely try to assess code quality by measuring the number of bug reports for that code). Finally, we bring our biases to the processes of data collection and analysis. In other words, we often (consciously or otherwise) select the perspectives from which we collect and analyze the data, and those perspectives may end up coloring our conclusions.

LEARNING FROM DATA

In the remainder of this chapter, we describe our view, as informed outsiders, of the landscape of the research in and applications of data science for software engineering. To do so, we introduce seven categories of results that we have observed in this field, which we order by quality (and ultimately usefulness) of the corresponding research, from low to high. In other words, the first category is to avoid at all costs, whereas the last category is the one for which one should strive.

Note that, while the discussion herein may be generally applicable to any Big Data endeavor, our particular interest is in the role and potential impact of conclusions drawn specifically within data science for software engineering. We urge the reader to approach the following discussion in that vein.

We also want to point out that, although our objective is to provide a general overview that can be used to categorize existing work in this area, we do not engage in such a categorization. Put another way, we deliberately refrain from focusing on specific projects or publications even though our discussion is informed by our (and, as it turns out, many other colleagues') impressions of the work that has appeared in various software engineering venues over the past decade.

1. Incorrect conclusions

    Incorrect conclusions can be drawn because of reliance on incomplete, tainted, and/or noisy data, poor statistical analysis, wrong inferences, and overgeneralization. Some of these pitfalls (eg, bad statistics) can be remedied through appropriate training. Others (eg, bad data) cannot be remedied as readily. Acting on incorrectly drawn conclusions can clearly have serious consequences.

2. Partially correct conclusions

    Conclusions regarding complex phenomena may be correct in certain respects, while being wrong in others. Unfortunately, basing important decisions on them may be as detrimental as acting on completely incorrect conclusions. Especially in software engineering, the extent of our current understanding of the factors that yield such (partially) incorrect conclusions is limited at best. This is certainly exacerbated by the temptation, as researchers, to highlight and focus on positive results.

3. Correct but useless results

    Certain phenomena, while analyzable, are not worthy of analysis, as they provide answers to questions that are not worth asking in the first place. Many examples of "low-hanging fruit" fall in this category. Although they are often attractive, because they are easy, they should be avoided just the same. In other words, if a paper "practically writes itself," let it be and move on to something else.

4. Correct but obvious results

    Certain phenomena may be worthy of analysis, but only if it is not already clear ahead of time what results the analysis will yield. Empirically confirming a hypothesis or a suspicion, even if they appear well founded and likely, is an important part of science. Answering questions that have already been answered, or that can be answered much more quickly and easily than through a given data analysis procedure, is wasteful.

5. Correct, somehow interesting, but not actionable results

    Analysis of certain phenomena may correctly yield conclusions that are somehow interesting (ie, they are not completely useless) but are "dead ends." In other words, those conclusions may prove to be neither usable to practicing engineers in solving the problems they face nor a reasonable foundation for further studies. In such cases, the analysis is little more than an intellectual exercise à la "we do it because we can"—the kind of work performed by researchers who live in the proverbial ivory tower.

6. Correct, nonobvious, modest steps

    Certain conclusions may enrich an engineer's palette of methods, techniques, and tools. Even a moderate improvement over the current state of the art is valuable, regardless of the complexity of the underlying analysis that yielded that improvement. The assumption is, of course, that the complex analysis was not undertaken in lieu of a simpler, much more straightforward approach that would have yielded the same answers (see the previous section).

7. Correct, Nonobvious game-changers

    This is the "holy grail" of software analytics research and practice—a result that can change how researchers think about and approach their field, as well as how developers think about and do their work. This type of result is often obtained through a combination of painstaking work, subtle insights, unique perspectives, and sometimes also luck. It is not necessarily repeatable, it cannot be forced, and at least some parts of it cannot be taught.

WHICH BIN IS MINE?

We believe that the principal risk faced by research on data science for software engineering is that its results, when clustered into the preceding seven areas, will form a bell curve such as the one shown in Fig. 1. Note that, in this hypothetical diagram, only a small fraction of research falls in Categories 6 and 7, which represent the most beneficial work. By contrast, the work in Categories 3, 4, and 5 is most abundant, but not particularly useful. The latter three categories are what we would refer to as "software analytics under the lamppost:" instead of asking important questions, one asks questions that are easy to answer.

EPILOGUE

There is a range of questions one can ask and a range of conclusions one can draw from the same data. Even when we pursue the right questions, the biggest problem we face as a community is that many of the questions about what, how, when, where, and why software engineers do what they do falls in the category of inadequately understood phenomena. This means that our suspicions and biases may, and often do, influence what specific questions we ask, how we go about trying to answer them, and the slant we put on the data we collect in the process. For this reason, as in Dr. Crusher's case, at least some of our findings are at risk of being not useful or even meaningless.

To avoid this situation, we believe that researchers in the area of data science for software engineering should carefully assess where their work falls in terms of usefulness and the actionability of their findings. We also believe that doing so, and acting accordingly (ie, by holding back the temptation to publish or considering more specialized venues in case of nonactionable or unsurprising results) could considerably improve both the quality and the longevity of this important area.

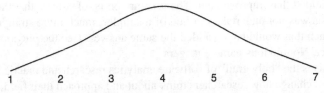

FIG. 1

A (not entirely) hypothetical bell curve for data analytics research.

What can go wrong in software engineering experiments?

S. Vegas, N. Juristo

Universidad Politécnica de Madrid, Madrid, Spain

CHAPTER OUTLINE

An astronomer wants to buy a telescope to observe a distant galaxy. While he is unsure about precisely what features the telescope he needs should have, he does know exactly how much he has to spend on equipment. So, without any further analysis of the required specifications, he goes ahead and orders the best telescope that he can afford and hopes for the best. But, viewed through the wrong telescope, the galaxy will be an indecipherable blur, and the equipment will be useless. Several factors regarding telescope design should to be taken into account (whether the objective should be a lens or a mirror, the diameter of the objective, the quality of the lens/mirrors, etc.). Apart from its price, they affect its magnification or power. In other words, what we will be able to observe through an instrument depends on the instrument's characteristics.

An experiment is an instrument that we use in software engineering (SE) to analyze software development. If our instrument is not properly aligned everything will be a blur, but we will mistakenly take it to be right. The reliability of the findings is critically dependent on the quality of the instrument, the alignment between the instrument and the phenomenon that we are studying.

As in any other discipline, conducting experiments in SE is a challenging error-prone activity. Other fields are tackling the issue of how much trust they can place in experiment results. Pashler and Wagenmakers report "a crisis of confidence in psychological science reflecting an unprecedented level of doubt among practitioners about the reliability of research findings in the field." The reliability of the results is highly dependent on design and protocol quality. Not everything goes right.

Experimentation is a fairly recent practice in SE compared with other much more mature experimental disciplines. Experimentalism is a paradigm that needs to be instantiated, translated, and adapted to the idiosyncrasy of each experimental discipline. Copy and paste, that is, copying from physics what an experiment is, copying from medicine the threats to the validity of experiments, or copying from psychology how to deal with experimental subjects, will not do at all. We can borrow from all these experiences, but our discipline needs to adopt its own form of experimentalism. We all need to learn more, and much more effort and research is needed to adapt the experimental paradigm to SE.

Based on our experiences of running experiments and reading the reports on other experiments, we have spotted some common mistakes in SE experiments. As a result, we have identified some good practices that may be helpful for avoiding common pitfalls.

OPERATIONALIZE CONSTRUCTS

Operationalization describes the act of translating a construct into its manifestation. In an SE experiment, we have cause and effect constructs, which are operationalized as treatments (methods, tools, and techniques to be studied) and dependent variables (software attributes under examination), respectively. For cause constructs, it is necessary to specify how the treatment will be applied, as SE's immaturity (which very often shows up as informality) might lead different people to interpret the treatment differently. Effect constructs should take into account not only the metrics used to measure the dependent variable, but also the measurement procedure. The measurement procedure in SE is context dependent and requires to be specified.

EVALUATE DIFFERENT DESIGN ALTERNATIVES

The simpler the design is, the better it will be. Experiments that study one only source of variability (one factor designs), and if run with subjects, where each subject applies one only treatment (between-subjects designs) are the most manageable. Because of SE's intrinsic properties, however, they are very often not the right choice in this field.

- Small sample sizes and a large variability in subject behavior make it almost impossible to use between-subjects designs in experiments run with subjects. The alternative is that each subject applies all treatments (within-subjects designs).
- The influence of the intrinsic properties of the experimental objects (programs/software systems/tasks) and subjects (if any) very often obliges researchers to

randomize according to them (stratified randomization) or use blocking variables.
- Software development process complexity makes it more or less impossible to rule out the influence of other sources of variability (typically experimental objects and subjects), and more than one factor needs to be added to the design.

Consequently, experimental design has to be approached iteratively, trying out different designs and then analyzing trade-offs.

MATCH DATA ANALYSIS AND EXPERIMENTAL DESIGN

Data analysis is driven by the experimental design. Issues such as the metric used to measure the treatments and dependent variables, the number of factors, whether the experiment has a between- or within-subjects design, and the use of blocking variables will all determine the particular data analysis technique to be applied. This data analysis technique maps the design to the statistical model in terms of the factors and interactions to be analyzed. However, the choice of data analysis technique and/or statistical model is not always as straightforward as all that:

- Parametric tests are the preferred option, as they are more powerful than non-parametric tests and are capable of analyzing several factors and their interactions. But the data do not always meet the data analysis technique requirements (normality of the data or residuals and/or homogeneity of variances depending on the technique in question). An alternative to non-parametric tests is transformation of the dependent variable. Additionally, some tests are robust to deviations from normality.
- Complex designs may require the addition of some extra factors to the statistical model. Take, for example, crossover designs, where each experimental subject applies all treatments, but different subjects apply treatments in a different order. The order in which subjects apply treatments (sequences) and the times at which each treatment is applied (periods) have to be added to the factor analysis, and a decision has to be made about how to deal with carryover.

DO NOT RELY ON STATISTICAL SIGNIFICANCE ALONE

All experiments report statistical significance. However, statistical significance is the probability of observing an effect given that the null hypothesis is true. In other words, it measures whether the observed effect really is caused by the population characteristics or is merely the result of sampling error. But it gives no indication of how big the difference in treatments is. For relatively large sample sizes, even very small differences may be statistically significant. On this ground, we need a measure of practical significance. The question is whether the differences between treatments are large enough to be really meaningful. This is generally assessed using a measure of effect size. There is a wide range of over 70 effect size measures, capable of reporting different types of effects.

DO A POWER ANALYSIS

Power analysis can be done before (a priori) or after (post-hoc). A priori power analysis tells experimenters what minimum sample size they need to have a reasonable chance of detecting an effect of a given size before they run the experiment. Of course, experimenters will require a bigger sample size if they are looking for small effects than to detect medium or big effects. Post-hoc power analysis determines the power of the study assuming that the sample effect size is equal to the population effect size. While the utility of a priori power analysis is universally accepted, the usefulness of post-hoc power analysis is controversial, as it is a one-to-one function of the statistical significance.

FIND EXPLANATIONS FOR RESULTS

The goal of the experiment is to answer the research questions. Experimenters should not, therefore, just stop when the null hypothesis is (not) rejected; they should question why they got the results that they got. They should hypothesize why one treatment is (or is not) better than the other and what might be causing differences in behavior.

FOLLOW GUIDELINES FOR REPORTING EXPERIMENTS

The way in which an experiment and its results are reported is just as important as the actual results.

IMPROVING THE RELIABILITY OF EXPERIMENTAL RESULTS

A key question after an experiment has been conducted is to what extent the conclusions are valid. Most of these good practices will help us to address the different types of validity threats that experiments suffer from:

- Constructs operationalization is related to *construct validity*.
- The evaluation of different design alternatives is related to *internal and external validity*.
- Matching data analysis and experimental design, not relying on statistical significance alone and doing power analysis is related to *statistical conclusion validity*.

Additionally, experimentation is part of a learning cycle. The outcomes of an experiment need to be properly interpreted to generate knowledge. The good practices *finding explanations for results* and *following reporting guidelines* will help us to generate this knowledge.

Running SE experiments is a multifaceted process. Many different issues must be taken into account so that the results of the experiment are valid and can be used for knowledge generation. Moreover, SE has some special features, leading to some issues concerning experimentation being conceived of differently than in other disciplines.

FURTHER READING

[1] Ellis PD. The essential guide to effect sizes: statistical power, meta-analysis and the interpretation of research results. Cambridge: Cambridge University Press; 2010.

[2] Jedlitschka A, Ciolkowski M, Pfahl D. Reporting controlled experiments in software engineering. In: Shull F, Singer J, Sjoberg DI, editors. Guide to advanced empirical software engineering. London: Springer; 2008.

[3] Juristo N, Moreno AM. Basics of software engineering experimentation. Boston, MA: Kluwer; 2001.

[4] Pashler H, Wagenmakers E-J. Editors' introduction to the special section on replicability in psychological science: a crisis of confidence? Perspect Psychol Sci 2012;7(6):528–30.

[5] Shadish WR, Cook TD, Campbell DT. Experimental and quasi-experimental designs for generalized causal inference. Boston, MA: Houghton Mifflin Company; 2002.

[6] Wohlin C, Runeson P, Höst M, Ohlsson MC, Regnell B, Wesslén A. Experimentation in software engineering. Berlin: Springer; 2012.

One size does not fit all

T. Zimmermann

Microsoft Research, Redmond, WA, United States

I've spent a large part of my career building defect prediction models. The goal of these models is to explain, and in some cases even predict, where defects will occur. Typically such models use a set of metrics, such as lines of codes, complexity, etc. and establish some relationship to the presence or the number of defects.

One day back in 2009, Nachi Nagappan, Brendan Murphy, Harald Gall, Emanuel Giger, and I ran a simple experiment [1]: Do defect models built for Internet Explorer predict defects in Firefox and vice versa? Our hypothesis was that the models predict defects well because both projects belonged to the same application domain (browsers) with similar features. The outcome was not what we expected: Firefox models could predict IE defects, but IE models could not predict Firefox defects.

To find out when models can be transferred from one project to another, we collected datasets for 12 more projects from multiple domains with multiple versions and ran a total of *622 cross-project prediction experiments*. The shocking number: only 21 times (3.4%!!!) was the experiment successful, that is, the defect model could predict with precision, recall, and accuracy of 75% or higher. Next, we identified *similarities* that mattered more for a successful cross-project defect prediction with a decision tree analysis. One of the results: to achieve high precision, it was beneficial to have about the same number of observations in the datasets, projects that do not use databases, and have about the same median churn.

The main lesson: *There is no one size fits all model*. Even if you find models that work for most, they will not work for everyone. There is much academic research into general models. In contrast, industrial practitioners are often fine with models that just work for their data if the model provides some insight or allows them to work more efficiently. In this context, I often bring up an analogy to the NFL. As a coach you want to figure out a technique that helps to improve your team by as much as possible. You're not interested if your technique also works for another team. If it doesn't, even better, because it could provide you with a competitive advantage. You want what's best for your team.

The good news is that while empirical findings often do not generalize to different contexts, the methods typically are applicable on different datasets. So, bad news for the NFL coaches among you. In most cases, I can follow the same steps that are used to build a prediction model on Internet Explorer data to learn a model from Firefox data. The Firefox model will then most likely work on Firefox data. From an academic perspective, it is important to document and share these steps; see also the essay by Barbara Russo on Data Analysis Patterns in this book.

But what if we don't have enough data from within a project in order to create a predictive model? Fortunately since our initial analysis in 2009, other researchers figured out how to build more effective cross-project prediction models [2–4], which can help projects with no or low-quality data to also benefit from predictive models.

REFERENCES

[1] Zimmermann T, Nagappan N, Gall HC, Giger E, Murphy B. Cross-project defect prediction: a large scale experiment on data vs. domain vs. process. In: ESEC/SIGSOFT FSE; 2009. p. 91–100.
[2] Turhan B, Menzies T, Bener AB, Di Stefano JS. On the relative value of cross-company and within-company data for defect prediction. Empir Softw Eng 2009;14(5):540–78.
[3] Nam J, Pan SJ, Kim S. Transfer defect learning. In: ICSE; 2013. p. 382–91.
[4] Minku LL, Yao X. How to make best use of cross-company data in software effort estimation? In: ICSE; 2014. p. 446–56.

While models are good, simple explanations are better

Venkatesh-Prasad Ranganath

Kansas State University, Manhattan, KS, United States

I am pretty sure you have heard the phrase *Keep It Simple, Stupid (KISS)*. Even so, I am certain that you have been reminded about it time and again because "simple" varies with contexts. Here is my encounter with an incarnation of KISS while using data mining for software engineering—*tell me what I need and not all that you know.*

HOW DO WE COMPARE A USB2 DRIVER TO A USB3 DRIVER?

During the development of Windows 8, the USB team responsible for the USB driver in Windows had the option of extending the USB driver in Windows 7 (which we will refer to as the USB2 driver) to support the USB3 protocol. Instead, they decided to implement a new USB driver (which we will refer to as the USB3 driver) that supported all three versions of the USB protocol. Since USB2 driver was time-tested on previous versions of Windows, the USB team decided to ship both USB2 and USB3 drivers with USB2 driver servicing devices on the USB2 port and USB3 driver servicing devices on the USB3 port.

The success of the USB3 driver depended on supporting the following use-case: *when a user plugs in a USB2 device into a USB3 port on Windows 8, the user experience should be similar to that of the device plugged into a USB2 port on Windows 8.* In other words, *when servicing a USB2 device, the behavior of the USB3 driver should be similar to that of the USB2 driver.* Since the USB3 driver did not share any code with the USB2 driver, this problem amounted to ensuring/checking behavioral similarity between programs at well-defined external interfaces.

349

Around this time, my team was working on *mining structural and temporal patterns* [1] and we were introduced to the preceding problem. After some discussions, the USB team suggested that it might suffice to compare USB2 and USB3 drivers in terms of the request-response (traffic) patterns observed at their external interfaces when servicing the same device. The rationale being that observable behavior of drivers is dictated by the requests and responses exchanged via their external interface. So, all we needed to do was to mine patterns from the request-response (traffic) logs and compare the mined patterns.

THE ISSUE WITH OUR INITIAL APPROACH

After configuring the pattern mining algorithms to process USB driver traffic logs, we used them to mine patterns that took one of the following forms:

1. A conjunctive propositional predicate that describes an event. For example, the predicate `method="fopen" && path="passwd.txt" && mode="r"` describes an event in the log where `fopen` was invoked to open `passwd.txt` file in *read* mode.

2. Two conjunctive propositional predicates linked by a simple temporal operator that describes relative temporal ordering of the events. For example, `(method="fopen" && path="passwd.txt" && return="0x1234")` followed by `(method="fclose" && file_handle="0x1234")` describes two events *e1* and *e2* in the log where `(method="fopen" && path="passwd.txt" && return="0x1234")` describes *e1*, `(method="fclose" && file_handle="0x1234")` describes *e2*, and *e1* is followed by *e2* in the log.

The algorithms associated the mined patterns with numeric measures of significance such as *support* and *confidence*.

To compare the patterns mined from a pair of traffic logs, we mulled over how to rank patterns present in both logs and patterns unique to each log. We experimented with various thresholds of the difference between measures of a pattern common to both logs. We pondered over the order in which to consider the measures when comparing common patterns. Finally, we settled on some thresholds and presented our findings to the USB team.

While *patterns-based comparison of logs* [2] helped the USB team to identify instances of different traffic patterns exhibited by USB2 and USB3 drivers, the instances did not make immediate sense as *the reasons for reporting the instances were not apparent* (due to the seemingly ad-hoc choice of various ranking orders and thresholds). Consequently, the developer could not easily identify the interesting instances that required further exploration; hence, the solution could not be used in its current state.

We had the required information but it wasn't readily accessible.

"JUST TELL US WHAT IS DIFFERENT AND NOTHING MORE"

At this point, we asked the USB team "How could we improve the results?" They said "just tell us what is the different and nothing more (no ranking, no statistics)." They suggested that we just identify:

1. *patterns common to the USB2 driver that are not exhibited by USB3 driver* and
2. *patterns uncommon to the USB2 driver but exhibited by USB3 driver.*

In other words, given a set of USB2 devices, (1) amounted to identifying patterns observed with every USB2 device and USB2 driver combination but not observed with a USB2 device and USB3 driver combination and (2) amounted to identifying patterns observed with a USB2 device and USB3 driver combination but not exhibited by any USB2 device and USB2 driver combination.

This suggestion led us to disregard information about measures of significance and focus on identifying differences. The differing patterns identified with this suggestion had a simple explanation—*absence of common patterns and presence of uncommon patterns*. Consequently, this result was easy to process and, consequently, identify the differences to explore further. In the end, the USB team was happy with resulting solution and used it to quickly identify behavioral differences between USB2 and USB3 drivers that needed triaging.

While trimming down to the essence was crucial, we also needed to simplify the textual representation of patterns, remove redundant information, incorporate domain/expert knowledge, and work with existing driver framework to collect data. All of this was necessary to make the results readily accessible to and actionable by the user.

LOOKING BACK

When we started our effort to help the USB team, we incorrectly assumed all information in the model of the system (ie, the set of mined patterns along with various measures of significance) generated by our approach was important. This might have been due to various reasons such as our lack of expertise in USB, our past success in using all information, or our lack of understanding of the problem. Independent of the reasons and the complexity of the underlying model, *we were excited by and interested in detailed models while our customers, the USB team members, were interested in simple explanations of observations that could help them with quick project planning decisions.*

Time and again, I have heard similar arguments in discussions about which machine learning or data mining technique to use—support vector machines provide highly accurate but hard to interpret/explain models while simple regression provides easy to interpret/explain but possibly less accurate models. In a way, the preceding experience provides better perspective for these arguments.

For example, consider a linear regression model that can explain both the polarity (ie, positive or negative) and magnitude of influence of independent variables (factors) on the dependent variable (outcome). All of the information in the model is not relevant to a user who is only interested in knowing if the effect of the factors on the outcome is linear. Similarly, the magnitude of influence is irrelevant to a user who is only interested in identifying the factors that negatively affect the outcome.

USERS PREFER SIMPLE EXPLANATIONS

To summarize, when using data science for software engineering (and possibly other purposes), we should keep in mind that *users are interested in simple explanations (of course, backed by robust and detailed models) of the observed phenomenon that can help them make good and quick decisions.*

This insight proved to be rather useful in my subsequent flings with data analysis. Now, I hope you too will consider this insight in your next data science excursion and either be more effective or challenge the insight.

ACKNOWLEDGMENTS

The USB compatibility testing effort was carried out at Microsoft by Pankaj Gupta, Venkatesh-Prasad Ranganath, and Pradip Vallathol with advice from Randy Aull, Robbie Harris, Jane Lawrence, and Eliyas Yakub.

REFERENCES

[1] Lo D, Ramalingam G, Ranganath V-P, Vaswani K. Mining quantified temporal rules: formalism, algorithms, and evaluation. Sci Comput Program 2012;77(6):743–59, http://www.sciencedirect.com/science/article/pii/S0167642310001875.

[2] Ranganath V-P, Vallathol P, Gupta P. Compatibility testing via patterns-based trace comparison. In: International conference on automated software engineering (ASE); 2014, http://dl.acm.org/citation.cfm?id=2642942.

The white-shirt effect: Learning from failed expectations

L. Prechelt

Freie Universität Berlin, Berlin, Germany

CHAPTER OUTLINE

A STORY
REVELATION

Shortly after waking up unusually peacefully on this mild, friendly, sunny, simply wonderful August morning, you have a revelation: Programmers will make *much* fewer mistakes if they are wearing a white shirt!

You are a software manager and oversee the work of more than 700 software engineers, so you straighten up, excited. This is it! This is what will turn your good software development organization into a top-class software organization! Higher productivity! Improved quality! Happier engineers *and* customers! (Remark: I should point out that this is a deliberately silly example to make it easier to focus on the principles in the story rather than getting distracted by certain details. But back to our story.)

Yet, you also know that sound management practices will require you to prove your insight at least correlationally. You get to work immediately and will end up having invested half of your capacity for the next 5 weeks to prepare your coup.

WORK, WORK, WORK

You convince half of the key people in your organization of the White Shirt Effect (WSE) and convince most of the other half that the WSE is at least worth checking out, so your organization backs you up in the subsequent steps.

Having followed the literature on the latest techniques for defect-correction-to-defect-insertion mapping (DCDIM) you know how to find out with good reliability (once a defect has been corrected) who has produced a defect. The data needed to do this is available in your bug trackers and version archives. Easy.

You decide you will find the daily white-shirt bit for each software engineer via photos. Much tougher. You enlist one of your best toolmakers. A few days later, a prototype software works that can determine who is wearing a white shirt and who is not, based on reusable face recognition technology and a custom white-shirt-bit plugin.

Over several days, you carefully calm down the privacy concerns by demonstrating that the single-purpose, in-house software solution will indeed only capture the white-shirt bit and nothing else. Your organization now allows you to install the 25 cameras required to capture nearly everybody often enough.

You have an assistant fill the face recognition database with clean portraits of each of your software engineers.

You let the solution run for a week, meanwhile two helpers capture manually as much of the white-shirt bits as they can to validate the reliability of the camera-based solution. The software proves to work very well.

Knowing that the more interesting defects will take some time to surface, you announce the beginning of a 6-month trial period: You explain the WSE to all of your software engineers and tell them to wear a white shirt at least 2 days and at most 4 days every week and to, please, randomize the weekdays.

You find that, in your initial enthusiasm, you had overlooked what comes now: A majority of your software engineers opposes the shirt rule (some nearly revolt against it), because they are not used to being told what to wear and many of them do not like shirts ("With a collar? Are you serious??"), let alone white ones.

It takes a stressful and dramatic plenary meeting, in which you remind them of the data-driven management principles of your organization and praise the wonderful consequences of the WSE, to get those people to agree, grumblingly. You estimate the white-shirt compliance rate will now be around 85%, which ought to be enough.

After this nice reminder that data science is by far not as straightforward (nor cheap) as its proponents claim, you turn back to your other duties, which have piled up a bit, and let your infrastructure accumulate data.

DISAPPOINTMENT

After 6 months, you evaluate your data. Comparing the white-shirt days to the non-white-shirt days, you find that the defect insertion rates per line-of-code added or modified is lower for only 6% of your engineers, is higher(!) for 9% of them (Ouch!

Maybe those programmers who claimed "I *cannot* work in a shirt" were at least partially right? You swear because you recognize you have not recorded who they were.), and is not significantly different for the rest.

The WSE does not appear to exist.

THE RIGHT REACTION

There are two possible reactions at this point:

1. Sigh, admit defeat, give away the cameras to the engineers, and hope everybody quickly forgets your silly WSE project. Or:
2. Think "Hey, what's going on here?" and follow up to understand *why* the WSE is not working as you expected.

It should be obvious that only option 2 respects the spirit of data science. Besides, with option 1 you would have wasted a lot of effort and money.

How might the follow-up work? Well, hopefully you did not pursue a WSE revelation without having any idea of how and why such an effect would arise. (If you did, option 1 may be preferable, really.) Rather, you will have some mental model of the causation mechanisms underlying the effect and can now investigate intermediate stages to understand why the end result is different from your expectation.

In the WSE case, the model might say

1. white shirts radiate an air of purity
2. therefore, engineers will be less likely to interrupt a colleague wearing a white shirt,
3. therefore, that colleague can work more undisturbedly,
4. which is known to reduce the frequency of mistakes.
5. To a lesser degree, the wearer of the shirt will also feel purer,
6. therefore, s/he will be less inclined to write unclean, disorderly code,
7. and unclean code is known to at least tend to increase the frequency of mistakes.

You could now go and check each of these items, for instance 1, 2, 3, 4, 5, 6 by means of surveys and 4, 7 by re-reading the literature. Thinking about the problem more closely, you might come up with interesting follow-up studies to be performed in your organization. For instance, you might be able to use the "local history" functionality of your engineers' IDEs to detect interruptions and then check whether they correlate with wearing white shirts or not (using the white-shirt bit or a smaller-scale manual data collection) and correlate with the insertion of defects or not (using DCDIM).

Following up in this manner has several positive effects:

• your understanding of your organization will increase, so that future improvement ideas are more likely to be helpful;

- your self-confidence and hence curiosity (an important resource!) will be restored;
- you will learn to find cheaper ways for validating new ideas incrementally;
- you may stumble over other problems worth addressing.

In the WSE case, learning to think more incrementally would probably be the most valuable outcome of following up: For instance, invalidating the connection from wearing white shirts to fewer interruptions would have invalidated the WSE expectation much more cheaply.

PRACTICAL ADVICE

Trying to generalize the preceding discussion, we come up with the following data science rules for the testing of expectations for which not all data is yet available.

ALWAYS THINK OF A CAUSATION MODEL

Learning from failed expectations is possible only when you can dissect your observations and derive intermediate insights. A causation model provides intermediate points of reference at which you can get those insights. Without a causation model, there is no chance to follow up in this manner and failing expectations will waste a lot of resources.

THINK OF A CAUSATION MODEL, *BEFORE* YOU CHECK THE EXPECTATION

The causation model usually provides opportunities for *partial* checks of your expectation that are so much cheaper that you should usually do them first.

BE WARY OF FAILING EXPECTATIONS

Being aware that hypotheses are often wrong provides the best motivation to come up with such partial checks. Try to do this, no matter how enthusiastic you may be about your hypothesis initially.

BE READY TO ACCEPT INFERIOR TYPES OF EVIDENCE

Even the partial checks may be shockingly expensive if you insist on data that is highly reliable and objective. Cheaper data sources, such as the surveys in the WSE example, are often preferable for initial validation, even if they are noisy, biased, or even (shudder!) subjective.

FOR RESEARCHERS: KNOW THE FNR

If you are an academic researcher who wants to publish, you know that studies about expectations that failed tend to be harder to publish, because they rarely provide immediate engineering progress. Be aware that the Forum for Negative Results (FNR), a permanent special section of the Journal of Universal Computer Science (J.UCS) specifically calls for such submissions: Stories of failed expectations that come with explanation.

Simpler questions can lead to better insights

B. Turhan, K. Kuutti

University of Oulu, Oulu, Finland

CHAPTER OUTLINE

INTRODUCTION

In this chapter we share our experiences in conducting a software analytics project on bug prediction. Though the project was a success in terms of *scholarly* outcomes and performance measures, we ran into difficulties in communicating the results to the practitioners. It turned out that our predictions on the likelihood of edited files to contain bugs were perceived as stating the obvious—even through many different modes of communication/representation; the most useful and insightful representation turned out to be a visualization of the existing issue reports that involved no predictions at all. The solution emerged when we changed our question from "where will bugs occur?" to "how are existing bugs processed?" In other words, a simpler analysis to answer a simpler question provided more actionable insights to the engineers than the more complex alternative.

CONTEXT OF THE SOFTWARE ANALYTICS PROJECT

The idea of bug prediction is to prioritize the test efforts to the parts of the system that are most probable to cause potential failures. This is expected to result in more cost-effective testing, especially when the resources needed for testing the project are

359

relatively expensive [1]. With this goal in mind, we started an analytics case project with an industrial partner. The data for the analysis presented here come from the software component of a mission-critical embedded system project implemented in C++ language with over 100,000 lines of code. The development activities were carried out in two distinct geographical locations by multiple development and testing teams, adding up to about 60 developers in total. Data collected from the issue management tool reflects the development history of the project spanning a period of 2 years. One development team volunteered to pilot the developed software analytics models and modes of information representation, providing feedback through personal communication with the R&D team during project meetings [1].

PROVIDING PREDICTIONS ON BUGGY CHANGES

The predictor model was selected among a multitude of machine learning algorithms [1]. Once the final predictor was created and its accuracy was fine-tuned, the results were presented to a team of practitioners. Fig. 1 basically says that 90% of all bugs can be detected by going through the top 30% of the predictions, which most scholars would think is a good result! However, the feedback from the practitioners was that the prediction performance graphs and measures were not that useful for them. They indicated that such performance figures do not provide insight to have an impact in their daily work, and pointing out error-prone sections within files was regarded as stating the obvious. Specifically, they mentioned that they had a pretty good idea of where the bugs will occur (confirming the accuracy of our predictions), but wanted to know how they can either avoid or fix them in a different and easier way.

Hence, we started working on finding different ways to help the development teams utilizing the results in practice. Consequently, we developed multiple ways of communicating our analysis to practitioners. After several attempts with no

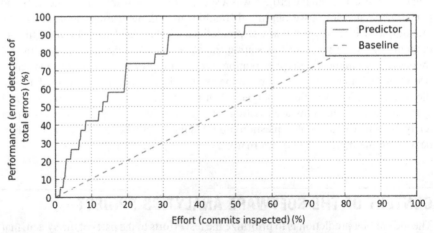

FIG. 1

Performance of the predictor model in terms of the percentage of total errors detected with respect to the percentage of commits that needs to be inspected.

acceptance [1] we have come up with an *error-handling graph*, which visualizes the interactions among teams based on the errors introduced and fixed. To our surprise, this turned out to be the most helpful representation as it helped in pinpointing communication-related issues within and across software development teams.

HOW TO READ THE GRAPH?

An error-handling graph, such as the example provided in Fig. 2, shows the *latent* interactions (ie, there, but not visible unless you specifically extract them) among software development teams in terms of errors that are reported and fixed. The errors are linked to the teams that have reported or fixed the error. There are two types of nodes in the error-handling graph. The nodes with text labels correspond to the teams involved in the project. Text labels start either with the prefix DevTeam or Test-Team, meaning that the corresponding team is a development or testing team, respectively. The nodes between the text labeled "nodes" represents bugs extracted from the issue management tool, and they are color coded by the level of testing at which they are detected. A green edge from a team node to an error node means that the

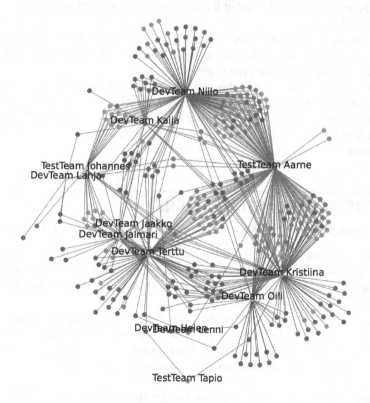

FIG. 2

An Example Error-handling Graph. For color version of the figure, the reader is requested to refer to the online version of the chapter.

corresponding team has fixed the reported error. On the other hand, a red edge means that the corresponding team has reported that error. Finally, blue lines represent the errors that are reported and fixed by the same team [1].

(ANTI-)PATTERNS IN THE ERROR-HANDLING GRAPH

In an ideal scenario, one would expect to see patterns in an error-handling graph, where all errors are either reported by a testing team and fixed by the responsible development team, or reported and fixed by the same development team. Moreover, an ideal scenario would assume that there would be no issues originating from the interactions among the teams, ie, an anti-pattern. Such errors are likely to have been missed in team level testing, propagated to higher levels causing re-work, and should have been detected earlier within the team.

Analysis of the example figure in terms of (anti-) patterns reveals the following insights:

- Pattern (a): It can be seen that the testing team named "Aarne" is reporting most of the errors, eg, the density of the red edges are very high around that team's node.
- Pattern (b): Development teams named "Oili" and "Niilo" are following the good practice of transparency by sharing the errors discovered and fixed within the team with the rest of the project teams.
- Anti-pattern: There exists a cluster of errors between the development teams "Terttu" and "Kristiina." This indicates that the development works of the teams are most likely to be dependent on each other and errors propagate out of either team's internal quality assurance process, impacting the work of the other.

HOW TO *ACT* ON (ANTI-)PATTERNS?

Based on the preceding findings, the following actionable insights can be considered:

- *Improve testing levels to identify errors earlier*: Depending on the amount of errors detected in each testing level (corresponding to color codes in the graph), an analysis on the nature of errors can be conducted to understand which level of testing needs to be improved.
- *Improve transparency*: Development teams can be encouraged to report the errors found within their internal processes to the global issue repository in order to improve the transparency of the development process. This will enable collaborating teams to share insights about the problems encountered in the shared code.
- *Improve inter/intra team communication*: Internal quality processes of the teams can be improved, especially when errors are propagating across development

teams. This would save time and effort spent on re-work activities. In addition, the communication and coordination practices between the teams can be improved in order to reduce the number of errors reported across teams.

To elaborate more on the last item: there are two potential reasons for the conflict between "Terttu" and "Kristiina" teams. One reason could be that the teams' way of working may be lacking quality gates for checking how their changes affect the work of others. Alternatively, there might dependencies between the parts of the code that the teams are concurrently working on. Such dependencies may have not been noticed and flagged when the division of labor between the teams is planned. So, the error-handling graph can point to problems in two levels: programming and testing practices/tools inside the teams, and in planning and dependency identification practices. Indeed, the nature of dependencies may not necessarily be code-based, but rather conflicting requirements from different stakeholders or changes in requirements that were not communicated to the both teams. In other words, code-based dependencies may just be a symptom of dependencies not detected at higher levels of abstraction. In any case, the root cause is a communication/coordination related issue that can be further investigated, yet can easily be identified by a visual inspection of the error-handling graph.

SUMMARY

The goal of software analytics is to propose actionable changes to the way the projects are run [2]. Practitioners need to be convinced about the benefits before even considering taking actions. Our experience revealed that asking the right questions that are deemed relevant by practitioners is a key factor to provide useful insights for them. As in our case, this might require simplifying complex questions and analyses to simpler ones that are more relevant to practitioners in terms of providing actionable insight.

Answers to relatively simpler questions sometimes lead to better insights for practitioners.

REFERENCES

[1] Taipale T, Turhan B, Qvist M. Constructing defect predictors and communicating the outcomes to practitioners. In: Proceedings of the 7th international symposium on empirical software engineering and measurement (ESEM 2013 Industry Track); 2013.
[2] Menzies T, Zimmermann T. Software analytics: so what? IEEE Softw 2013;30/4:31–7.

Continuously experiment to assess values early on

J. Münch

Reutlingen University, Reutlingen, Germany; University of Helsinki, Helsinki, Finland; Herman Hollerith Center, Böblingen, Germany

CHAPTER OUTLINE

The troubles began when Tom, the business analyst, asked the customer what he wants. The customer came up with good ideas for software features. Tom created a brilliant roadmap and defined the requirements for a new software product.

Mary, the development team leader, was already eager to start developing and happy when she got the requirements. She and her team went ahead and created the software right away. Afterward, Paul tested the software against the requirements. As soon as the software fulfilled the requirements, Linda, the product manager, deployed it to the customer. The customer did not like the software and ignored it. Ringo, the head of software development, was fired. How come?

MOST IDEAS FAIL TO SHOW VALUE

Nowadays, we have tremendous capabilities for creating nearly all kinds of software to fulfill the needs of customers. We can apply agile practices for reacting flexibly to changing requirements, we can use distributed development, open source, or other means for creating software at low cost, we can use cloud technologies for deploying software rapidly, and we can get enormous amounts of data showing us how customers actually use software products.

However, the sad reality is that around 90% of products fail, and more than 60% of the features of a typical software product are rarely or never used.

But there is a silver lining—an insight regarding successful features: Around 60% of the successes stem from a significant change of an initial idea. This gives us a hint on how to build the right software for users and customers.

Many software projects fail to deliver or only deliver little value due to the wrong assumptions made on requirements. A questionable assumption is, for instance, that customers or experts can come up with the right requirements. In consequence, projects usually have an upfront business analysis phase before the development starts. There are of course projects such as large-scale contract software projects in well-understood domains where upfront analysis is feasible and successful. But we should consider that these projects represent a very small percentage of all software projects.

If we're not solving the right problem, the project fails.

Woody Williams

Nowadays, nearly all software projects are conducted in complex environments where the relationship between cause and effect with respect to features and their success can only be understood in retrospect. Nobody "knows" upfront if and how features will create value for customers. Making decisions on what to develop based on opinions is highly risky in dynamic and non-predictable environments. Developing wrong features creates cost for development and maintenance as well as opportunity cost representing the missed opportunity to develop something of value instead.

A promising way to create software products in complex environments is to quickly and systematically iterate an initial product idea toward success before running out of time and other resources. Simply speaking, this means that you need to create a plan A that describes the scope of the software, identify the underlying assumptions of this plan, test the riskiest assumptions, and iterate until you have a plan B that works. The initial ideas we come up with are seldom successful. Identifying, testing, and refining multiple options helps to discover better ways to provide value for users or customers.

EVERY IDEA CAN BE TESTED WITH AN EXPERIMENT

A means for doing this is continuously conducting experiments to test assumptions and making being wrong cheaper. Insights from experiments directly influence what is given to the users. This process of continuous experimentation consists of three meta-steps:

1. Break down your product idea into a product roadmap that can be efficiently tested. Be aware that the roadmap changes over time and is basically a list of assumptions. Constantly reprioritize the assumptions.

2. Run frequent and additive experiments to test assumptions. This includes systematically observing users' behavioral responses to stimuli such as features. An example for a hypothesis is "The new posting feature will increase sign ups

of new users by 5% in 2 weeks." If an experiment does not deliver the expected result, do not test another option at random. Carefully choose what to test next.

3.   Use results from experiments to iteratively modify your product roadmap. This might lead to an improvement of a product or a significant change of the strategy. It might also mean that you need to stop the project.

Success cases from companies such as Etsy, Amazon, and Supercell show that a hypothesis-driven development approach helps companies to gain competitive advantage by reducing uncertainties and rapidly finding product roadmaps that work. However, experimentation is hard.

HOW DO WE FIND GOOD HYPOTHESES AND CONDUCT THE RIGHT EXPERIMENTS?

Customers and users are a questionable source for novel ideas. What they say often does not match what they will do. Consider the wish of users for privacy and the way they use Facebook. However, customers often have a good understanding of problems and asking the right questions can help reveal good hypotheses in the problem space.

Developers are usually good at coming up with solution proposals. They are familiar with technical options for solving a problem and can be a good source for revealing hypotheses in the solution space. Creating a "UserDevs" community by intensifying the communication between users and developers promises to be another good source for hypotheses.

A further source for identifying hypothesis is usage data. It can be used to gain insights and new ideas on what to develop if the right data is collected and appropriately analyzed. Further hypotheses to test, often hidden and not directly visible, can be found in the respective business models.

One test is worth one thousand expert opinions.

Wernher von Braun

What about the HiPPOs? HiPPOs are the highest paid person's opinions. HiPPOs currently dominate decisions about what to develop. However, there is no guarantee that their ideas are better or successful. Listen to HiPPOs and take their ideas into account when prioritizing what to test. But make development decisions based on validated assumptions.

It's not an experiment if you know it's going to work.

Jeff Bezos

The experimentation process follows the scientific method. It is important that you state upfront what you expect. Otherwise you just see what is going on. And many people are excellent at rationalizing what they see and would be surprised if they would have stated their expectations upfront.

There are many techniques available that support experimentation such as multivariate tests, prototyping, or customer interview techniques. But consider that choosing the right experiment technique requires that you know what you want to learn. Do you want to better understand the problem? Do you want to test the feasibility of a solution? Do you want to compare solution alternatives? Do you want to understand a behavior change? Do you want to test the efficiency of a distribution channel? All these questions lead to different experiments.

Overall, continuous experimentation requires a deep integration of testing critical assumptions in the overall development process. It emphasizes rapid and constant learning by empirical means in order to create software that provides value for users, customers, and the developing organization. Success with software is not luck. We all have the opportunity to deliver high-value software. What is your most critical assumption?

KEY TAKEAWAYS

- It's more important to do the right thing than to do things right.—Peter Drucker
- Success in highly dynamic application domains traces back to disciplined experimentation.
- Defining and running the right experiments is hard.
- Experimentation must be deeply integrated in the design and product development process.
- Platforms for experimentation can be seen as a core part of future development environments.
- Data Scientists can play a critical role by supporting the planning and execution of experiments as well as by ensuring their quality.

FURTHER READING

[1] Lindgren E, Münch J. Software development as an experiment system: a qualitative survey on the state of the practice. In: Proceedings of the 16th international conference on agile software development (XP 2015). Springer-Verlag; 2015. Sketchnotes.

[2] Fagerholm F, Guinea AS, Mäenpää H, Münch J. Building blocks for continuous experimentation. In: Proceedings of the 1st international workshop on rapid continuous software engineering (RCoSE 2014), Hyderabad, India; 2014. p. 26–35.

[3] Maurya A. Running lean. Sebastopol, California: O'Reilly; 2012.

[4] Olsson HH, Bosch J. From opinions to data-driven software R&D: a multi-case study on how to close the 'open loop' problem. In: 40th Euromicro conference on software engineering and advanced applications; 2014. p. 9–16.

[5] Ries E. The lean startup: how today's entrepreneurs use continuous innovation to create radically successful businesses. New York: Crown Publishing; 2011.

[6] Anthony S, Duncan D, Siren PMA. The 6 most common innovation mistakes companies make. Harvard Business Review 2015.

Lies, damned lies, and analytics: Why big data needs thick data

M.-A. Storey

University of Victoria, Victoria, BC, Canada

CHAPTER OUTLINE

HOW GREAT IT IS, TO HAVE DATA LIKE YOU

Software Analytics and the use of computational methods on "big" data in Software Engineering is transforming the way software is developed, used, improved and deployed [1].

We now have vast amounts of software data at our fingertips. Data on usage patterns, development methods, software quality, user opinions, and more. This is data at a scale that researchers and practitioners alike could only dream of in the past. But more than that, we also have sophisticated and "intelligent" methods for mining, cleaning, classifying, clustering, predicting, recommending, sharing, and visualizing this data. We can discover unproductive developers and teams, identify development processes and programming languages that lead to buggier software, spot unusable or insecure software features, and recommend how the software should be used in different contexts. There is still much to be done to improve the types and the scale of data that are collected and to improve tools for analyzing such data, but the path to our desired future is clearly illuminated, isn't it?

In this short chapter, I ask you, the reader, to consider the risks from following and pursuing this utopian Software Analytics Path and to ponder: are we asking the right questions, are we answering the questions correctly, are we anticipating the impact these answers may have, and more importantly, are we ready to handle the inevitable changes these potentially disruptive insights may bring.

LOOKING FOR ANSWERS IN ALL THE WRONG PLACES

As humans we often have a tendency to "look for the car keys where the light shines" or to chase after the "low hanging fruit." Indeed, some technologists may be particularly attracted by the "shininess" of data that are quantifiable and relatively easy to collect. But important insights that our stakeholders may care about will often lie in qualitative data that are unstructured, messy, and resistant to automatic collection and analysis methods.

Consider for example data from A/B testing, although this data may help a designer understand which feature is preferred, there may be "thick" qualitative data from blog posts and tweets that provide insights into why a particular feature is shunned by its users. Qualitative data require the application of sound and rigorous manual analysis methods to make sense of them [2]. But a warning, these manual qualitative methods are both time consuming and expensive, and such efforts to reveal rich and insightful stories are unfortunately often not valued by some stakeholders that have a tendency to only trust "numbers" and "statistics."

BEWARE THE REALITY DISTORTION FIELD

But no matter which data are analyzed (quantitative or qualitative), it is important for software analysts to do a reality check and to ask if the data under consideration are really bringing about an "epiphany" or an "apopheny" [3]. That is, it may be possible that when we have so much data, meaningless patterns and correlations may emerge. The New York Times mentioned this example when discussing limitations of big data: "The first thing to note is that although big data is very good at detecting correlations, especially subtle correlations that an analysis of smaller data sets might miss, it never tells us which correlations are meaningful. A big data analysis might reveal, for instance, that from 2006 to 2011 the United States murder rate was well correlated with the market share of Internet Explorer: Both went down sharply. But it's hard to imagine there is any causal relationship between the two" [4].

Furthermore, we may start our exploration of a phenomena with an awareness that the metrics or measurements defined may only be loosely connected to the concepts to be studied, but over time this connection becomes hardened and the risks in relying on the construct are long forgotten. The answers that emerge may be completely wrong (verging on lies) if the constructs that are used are poor representations of reality (eg, number of commits as a proxy for developer productivity). Or the data that can be collected may have biases that are hidden (eg, some developers may game the number of commits when they realize commits are being counted) or the insights gained may be completely wrong (eg, if layers of tool integrations result in multiple counts of certain commits).

Finally, software analysts need to remember that although "data" may be rational, the creators of much of this data (the humans), whether they passively or actively create it, may not be rational and may not do things in a way we anticipate [5]. All human stakeholders may have hidden motivations that even they do not wish to acknowledge or due to their own distorted view of reality.

BUILD IT AND THEY WILL COME, BUT SHOULD WE?

Even assuming we can find a reasonably fair way to represent and provide insights on some version of "reality," should we? We sometimes witness a "build it because we can" attitude with the tools and methods software analysts develop. But access to data—especially derived data—brings many potential opportunities for misuse, or worse, for abuse, especially when there are power imbalances or politics at play.

We have yet to consider the ethics behind the kinds of trace data—ie, from the direct or indirect actions of one or more humans—that can be collected, aggregated, analyzed, repurposed, and presented, in some cases, it is of course very hard, if not impossible, to predict the negative implications that may arise. But software analysts need to acquire skills in recognizing and anticipating some of these ethical issues, or to form alliances with those that do. The fallout from a "mood manipulation" study at Facebook led to data scientists across many domains calling for an ethical framework or set of policies they can use as guidance (http://www.informationweek.com/ big-data/big-data-analytics/data-scientists-want-big-data-ethics-standards/d/d-id/ 1315798). Some domains, notably health, do have such guidelines in place but this is not the case for many other domains, such as web-based businesses.

TO CLASSIFY IS HUMAN, BUT ANALYTICS RELIES ON ALGORITHMS

Even when we are armed with the best intentions and do pay attention to ethical issues, there may be other risks lurking in the shadows.

Human beings have an innate desire not just to count things, but also to classify. Bowker and Star in their landmark article [6] warn us about the drastic implications that some classification systems have had on the world we live in and on people. They describe how health classifications (such as those going back to the 1900s) are used to determine which diseases are "counted" and so are recognized as treatments that will be paid for by insurance companies. People suffering from rare diseases may be out of luck as such diseases do not occur frequently enough to be part of a classification scheme designed to support statistics.

Similarly, when we use software analytics, and choose to count some features, but not others, we make decisions about what is valued and what is not. Managers, for example, may implicitly make decisions about the value of certain activities their employees do and they may count the number of code reviews done in a week signaling those are valued, but they may not count (because they can't!) the number of times those same employees mentored newcomers to do more effective code reviews.

Furthermore, when humans make judgments, as humans ourselves we may have at least some insights into the biases they are likely to have. But when judgments are made or based on algorithms, many of the biases will be opaque to the consumers of those analytics [7].

LEAN IN: HOW ETHNOGRAPHY CAN IMPROVE SOFTWARE ANALYTICS AND VICE VERSA

Software analytics is an important field of research and practice, there is no doubt. But how can it be improved? It is too simplistic to quote the mythical quantitative-qualitative divide in software engineering. The more important difference to consider here is about **who** generates the data. Is it the participants of the phenomenon under study that create the trace data (or as McGrath refers to them "outcroppings of past behavior" [8]), or is the data generated by researchers (eg, through interviews, surveys, or observations in the field)?

This latter kind of "thick" data (much of which may qualitative, but not always), may be much harder to collect and analyze (http://www.gousios.gr/blog/Scaling-qualitative-research/), but such insights can be used to augment and enrich the big data that are harvested and analyzed with the purpose to form richer insights about a software scenario under study. Ethnographic methods [9], that involve observations or contextual interviews [10] of the stakeholders in their workplace, can be used to inform which questions we should spend time trying to answer, which data we should collect (and conversely which data we should **not** collect), what is the meaning of the data that is collected, and how those insights should be shared and used.

Moreover, data may tell us what is going on, but they won't necessarily tell us why a phenomenon is happening nor how we can fix a noted problem [11]. For example, we may be able tell which developers engage in code reviews, but we cannot tell why some do not do code reviews from the code reviewing data that can be captured.

On the other side, ethnography can likewise benefit from data science! Ethnographic methods can be subject to respondent and researcher biases as well as issues with ambiguity and lack of precision in the data collected. Furthermore, the findings from such methods can be dangerous to generalize to broader populations of actors. In light of these limitations, data science is being seen by many social scientists as the "new kid on the block" and many ethnographers are thus turning to "ethnomining" methods to enhance the work they do and to benefit from the big data they can gain access to (http://ethnographymatters.net/editions/ethnomining/). There is no doubt that this big data can increase the reliability of and speed up many kinds of insights,